Gender and Sexuality in *Star Trek*

Gender and Sexuality in *Star Trek*

Allegories of Desire in the Television Series and Films

DAVID GREVEN

McFarland & Company, Inc., Publishers
Jefferson, North Carolina, and London

Portions of this book previously appeared as "The Fantastic Powers of the Other Sex: Male Mothers in Fantastic Fiction" in *Journal of the Fantastic in the Arts* 14:3 (Fall 2003) and as "The Twilight of Identity: *Enterprise*, Neoconservatism, and the Death of *Star Trek*" in *Jump Cut* 50 (Spring 2008) at http://www.ejumpcut.org/.

LIBRARY OF CONGRESS CATALOGUING-IN-PUBLICATION DATA

Greven, David.
   Gender and sexuality in *Star Trek* : allegories of desire in the television series and films / David Greven.
     p.   cm.
   Includes bibliographical references and index.

   ISBN 978-0-7864-4413-7
   softcover : 50# alkaline paper ∞

   1. Star trek (Television program)   2. Sex role on television.
3. Homosexuality on television.   4. Sex on television.
5. Star Trek films — History and criticism.   6. Sex role in motion pictures.   7. Homosexuality in motion pictures.
8. Sex in motion pictures.   I. Title.
PN1992.77.S77   2009
791.45'72 — dc22   2009030776

British Library cataloguing data are available

©2009 David Greven. All rights reserved

No part of this book may be reproduced or transmitted in any form or by any means, electronic or mechanical, including photocopying or recording, or by any information storage and retrieval system, without permission in writing from the publisher.

Cover images ©2009 Shutterstock

Manufactured in the United States of America

McFarland & Company, Inc., Publishers
  Box 611, Jefferson, North Carolina 28640
    www.mcfarlandpub.com

Table of Contents

Introduction—Star Trek, *Gender, Race, Allegory, and Desire*   1

ONE—LONELY PLANETS
   Original Star Trek, *the Male Gaze, and the Allegorization of Desire*   9

TWO—FUTURES END
   Star Trek *Allegory and the Representation of Queer Characters*   34

THREE—PROJECTING DESIRE
   Holograms, Artists, and Gay Male Allegory   48

FOUR—QUEERING GENDER
   Voyager's *Neelix as the Male Mother*   74

FIVE—THE SEETHING SKIN
   Star Trek, *Masculinity, and Race*   97

SIX—THE TWILIGHT OF IDENTITY
   Enterprise, *Neoconservatism, and the Death of* Star Trek   118

SEVEN—WHITE WHALES
   Rage and Masculinity in Star Trek II: The Wrath of Khan *and* Star Trek: First Contact   135

EIGHT—AN EPIC FOR WOMEN
   Star Trek: Voyager's *"Dark Frontier"*   165

NINE—THE ECHO OVER THE VOICE
   Star Trek: Nemesis *and Patriarchal Narcissism*   187

Afterword—J. J. Abrams and the Fate of Trek   203
Chapter Notes   211
Bibliography   223
Index   229

For the great *Star Trek* lovers I have known —
Viki and the Zavales clan, Schreier, my brother Ozzy,
and the folks at the Coffee Nebula

INTRODUCTION
Star Trek, Gender, Race, Allegory, and Desire

To use terminology developed by Northrop Frye, *Star Trek* is a *monomyth*, a collection, at this point, of every genre and mode of narrative.[1] This book touches on the many versions of *Star Trek*, principally the original 1960s series, the later series *Star Trek: The Next Generation, Star Trek: Voyager,* and *Enterprise* and the films. But my effort here is not to provide anything like a definitive guide to or an overview of the monomyth (I freely admit that I'm not a follower of *Deep Space Nine*). *Star Trek* encompasses so many permutations of its premise and divergent, fan communities at this stage in its over forty year history — the original series debuted in 1966 — that any general attempt to account for it will be hopelessly inadequate. My focus, instead, is a very specific one. In this book, I explore the ways in which *Star Trek* has consistently provided a space in which difficult questions about gender and sexuality can be raised, sometimes providing disquieting answers, but more often just allowing the questions to hover in the air.

Star Trek chiefly accomplishes this salutary question-raising through allegory. Allegory emerges as a politically powerful mode in *Trek* for exploring the human experience of gendered identity and sexuality. In making this point, I am specifically challenging the contention that *Trek* has never "represented" homosexuality, a view of such sturdy provenance as to go unquestioned by most commentators. I argue in this book that *Trek* has indeed represented homosexuality throughout its history, albeit in allegorical terms, which can be discovered by interested viewers but can also be ignored or overlooked by those uninterested.

As Robert B. Ray has argued in his study of classical Hollywood film, popular representation plays to the ironic and the non-ironic audience at once, which is certainly true, I argue, in *Star Trek*'s case.[2] *Trek* plays both to the ironic and the non-ironic audience by representing queer sexuality through allegory. Queer allegory is the domain of the ironic audience, those looking for aspects of cinematic, television, and other kinds of narratives that either would not interest or would not occur to the non-ironic audience, who accepts what is literally presented on the screen (big or small) as the sum of the narrative's meaning.

The trouble with Ray's terms is the inherent class biases that undergird them: the phrase "non-ironic audience" smacks of elitism — who would want to be part of such a group? Moreover, who wouldn't want to be in the know? Nevertheless, Ray's terms come closest to articulating the kinds of readings of *Trek* this book attempts to make possible.

To those who love the monomyth but lament its failures to represent a significant chunk of its extraordinarily diverse global fanbase, namely its queer viewers, I propose that we add a little irony to our love. Reading *Trek* ironically, which is to say, allegorically, yields ample, if not entirely satisfying or always palatable, rewards. Of course, to read *Trek* allegorically is to take *Trek*'s own hyperallegorical sensibility to an almost delirious extreme. *Trek*'s queer allegories take allegory to the *nth* power; they are allegories of allegories.

None of this is to suggest that homophobia doesn't exist in *Trek*, or that *Trek* should be exculpated for its cowardice about representing same-sex desire. It is to say, however, that *Trek* is a maddeningly and exhilaratingly complex text. While there are deeply frustrating aspects of its treatment of queer desire, there are also powerful ways in which *Trek* speaks to precisely the issue of desiring differently. Indeed, *Trek*'s queer potentiality lies in its consistent interest in the *experience* of difference. Allegory on *Trek*, as I will show, provides same-sex desire with a powerful vent.

Allegory does not, however, work as well with race, which is deeply strange, given that Trekkian allegory is famous for its treatment of race. When it comes to race, *Trek* is consistently frustrating, often collapsing into the same racist practice that it also openly fights against. One of the questions this book explores is why allegory works so well for same-sex desire but not at all well for race.

Particularly in its post–September 11 incarnations, *Trek* has forfeited much of its liberal humanist urgency for a cold, cynical, opportunistic neoconservatism, as I argue in the chapter on the failed *Trek* series *Enterprise*. It is anyone's guess in which direction the 2009 reboot of the franchise will take *Trek*. But in this book, my primary goal is to *defamiliarize Trek* so that its odd achievements will be more apparent. I can think of few popular culture works that have more consistently and passionately provided viewers with an opportunity for what A. S. Byatt has called moral daydreaming, for imagining alternative possibilities but also for imagining what actually experiencing those moral possibilities might be like, for good or for ill. As Byatt writes of George Eliot's great novel *Middlemarch*,

Eliot ... demonstrates and argues the case for independent thought, in reader as in writer.... [We are granted the] freedom ... of the moral daydreamer who temporarily inhabits the world of *Middlemarch*, feeling out its spaces and limitations, knowing that daydreaming is indeed daydreaming and is also discovery.[3]

In my view, *Trek* allows us a similar license to roam created worlds and our own imaginative life.

The Uses of Allegory

Angus Fletcher describes allegory in deceptively simple terms as a mode of fiction that "says one thing and means another." But even when put in these "simplest terms," the essential volatility of allegory reveals itself. Allegory, writes Fletcher,

> destroys the normal expectation we have about language, that our words "mean what they say." When we predicate quality x of person Y, Y really is what our predication says he is (or we assume so); but allegory would turn Y into something other (*allos*) than what the open and direct statement tells the reader. Pushed to an extreme, this ironic usage would subvert language itself, turning everything into an Orwellian newspeak.[4]

What threatens about allegory is that, the more one contemplates it, the more pervasive a practice it seems. Fletcher invokes Northrop Frye's contention that *all* literature is "more or less allegorical."[5] Language itself is an allegory for whatever is being signified or communicated between people and even to oneself, a kind of approximation of description and communication that must do, for it is the only means of describing something and of communicating. But another dimension of Fletcher's point about irony is that, when allegory says "Y is x," we know it really *isn't* x, so it's not just that communication is an approximation of what we mean, but that we actually *say* things we know to be false. So if I say, "My love is like a red, red, rose," it's not that we know that she's only approximately a red, red, rose, but that we know she actually isn't a red, red, rose at all![6]

One can go batty trying to figure out — to stabilize — allegory. For our purposes, what I want to emphasize is that allegory is an inherently volatile form, one that has bedeviled theorists and philosophers for centuries. It is precisely this quality of volatility that makes allegory so wide-ranging and complex a vehicle for *Trek*: in allegorizing one thing, it often finds itself allegorizing something else as well, simultaneously. Race is most often taken to be the chief allegorical referent of most *Trek* narratives and characterizations.

Indeed, race is often made such an obvious referent for Trekkian allegory it almost ceases to be allegorical at all, collapsing into a mixture of the allegorical and direct, explicit reference. The queer themes of *Trek* are less visibly apparent in its allegorical framework. Queer themes do, I argue, manifest themselves within the larger racial allegory, but they do so in oblique ways. For example, the third-season episode of the Original series, "Let That Be Your Last Battlefield," guest-starring Frank Gorshin (who played The Riddler in the 1960s *Batman*), features two male characters, Bele and Lokai, who claim to be different races from one planet. At first glance, they both seem to be members of exactly the same race: each of their faces is black on one side and white on the other. Captain Kirk and his crew are befuddled by the racial conflict until one of the aliens points out that, while they *are* both black and white, they are black and white on *different* sides of their faces. That these aliens are black and white, in an episode made in the civil-rights movement decade, all but directly names race relations in the United States as the referent for the episode's allegorical narrative. But homosexuality emerges as an increasingly plausible allegorical possibility. Each of these males vehemently insists that their side is the right side, and they try to kill each other. They continue to engage in this murderous conflict even when they discover that their planet's entire population has been annihilated by civil war, leaving none but Bele and Lokai alive. Once off the *Enterprise* and on their devastated planet, Bele and Lokai continue their furious, apocalyptic wrestling as everything around them rages in flames, two men left on a world with only their homoerotic grappling to occupy their time. Race began as the most obvious allegorical agenda of the episode, but by its end, the episode seems to have moved into a different kind of allegorical territory altogether, as horrified and fascinated by the queer energies of the warring men as it is in what they war over.

Obviously, not everyone will read the episode in this way. "Perhaps naïve readers do not see the erotic allegory under the surface action of a Zane Grey romance," Fletcher writes, "but then in discussing allegory we are not much concerned with naïve readers. We are talking about sophisticated readers and what they read *into* literature."[7] If we can reformulate these paradigms a bit so that they are less laced with elitism, readers who simply are not interested in queer themes — a perfectly legitimate position — will probably not see the homoeroticism inherent in this episode because they aren't motivated to do so, either by their own tastes or by the series' own apparent ideological and commercial standards and dictates. But those who tend to read *into* texts (readers sophisticated and otherwise!) and specifically read into them for signs of queer life will find ample rewards (and, sometimes, disquieting discoveries) in *Trek*.

Very much in keeping with "Last Battlefield," the very origins of allegory have a homoerotic quality. Many of Plato's "dialogues include 'myths,' allegorical narratives or developed metaphors, which serve to image truths beyond the reach of the discursive intellect." Many of these dialogues consider what constitutes the human soul. "The *Phaedrus* provides an uncomplicated instance," writes John MacQueen, "when the soul is compared to a charioteer driving two steeds, one representing the spiritual, the other the sensual element in man, which the charioteer (reason) has to restrain. The *Symposium* contains a whole series of allegories, in different styles, on the subject of love."[8] "Last Battlefield" casts Captain Kirk in the role of the charioteer and two men in the roles of the steeds, but dispenses with the spiritual metaphor. Bele and Lokai both represent the sensual nature of man, the passions and the ire, and both careen out of control and the charioteer's grasp.

As a whole, the *Star Trek* monomyth is, like the *Symposium*, a series of different allegories on the subject of love; unlike Plato's dialogue, however, it does not name same-sex couples as one of those once fused creatures now dissevered, each forever looking for its missing other half, be it male or female. *Trek*'s allegorical treatises on love — the innumerable moments and the range of places in which love strangely springs throughout the universe — seem to bar queer desire from consideration. Again, it is only from an oblique angle that *Trek*'s queer presence can be seen.

Yet there are some occasions, as "Last Battlefield" demonstrates, in which this queer presence is very much in one's face. If we take into account the enduring interest in the Kirk-Spock relationship, we can consider another aspect of *Trek*'s queer life. K/S, as it is famously called in slash fiction, is a same-sex love story that is so visible and sustained for such duration that it threatens to explode its allegorical confines.

A Homoerotic Tradition: Kirk and Spock

The most famous example of a homoerotic tradition in *Trek* is the relationship between Captain James T. Kirk (William Shatner) and his colleague and friend, the human–Vulcan Spock (Leonard Nimoy). This relationship affectingly extends into popular culture what Leslie Fiedler described as a relationship central to nineteenth-century American literature, "the pure marriage of males, sexless and holy, a kind of counter-matrimony, in which the white refugee from society and the dark-skinned primitive are joined till death do them part."[9] The scholars Constance Penley and Henry Jenkins have both amply documented the gay fan appropriation of this relationship for the purposes of slash fiction: narratives, largely written by heterosexual women, that pair same-sex characters of popular film and television shows in erotic situations, sometimes loving, sometimes highly sexual, sometimes a combination of the two.[10] Numerous same-sex relationships involving *Star Trek* have been envisioned by slash fiction writers, but none more famously than Kirk/Spock. When watching the original series, one has little trouble understanding the basis from which slash writers derived their fixation on this male couple. The love between Kirk and Spock is quite palpable, lending their banter a depth and urgency that exceeds the boundaries of typical male friendships on television. What comes through most vividly in the Original Series is Spock's conflicted but insistent love for Kirk, a love that breaks through the boundaries of Vulcan propriety. In the Second Season episode "Bread and Circuses," Dr. McCoy (DeForest Kelley) characteristically chides the Vulcan for his lack of emotions, telling him that he feels nothing for the imprisoned, endangered Kirk. "Oh really, Doctor?" Spock responds. As Nimoy gravely but also ironically delivers the line, it conveys reserves of sad, unspoken feeling.

The feature films made from 1979 onward deepen the ardent nature of the relationship. Few scenes in film are as emotionally overwhelming as Spock's death scene in *Star Trek II: The Wrath of Khan* (1982). As a metaphor for closeted homosexuality it couldn't be more acute. As Spock dies, Kirk reaches out to him, but they are separated by a glass partition.

The public nature of this death and the expression of love between Kirk and Spock threatens to explode what D. A. Miller and Eve Kosofsky Sedgwick have theorized as the "open secret" of homosexuality in our culture.[11] Indeed, one could say that this is a queer relationship that hides in plain sight. Never shown to be married, Kirk and Spock (as well as McCoy) share their most intense emotional bond with each other. The subsequent films with the original cast only deepen this point. The 1984 *Star Trek III: The Search for Spock* begins with a replay of Spock's wrenching death scene from the previous film, treating it as a kind of exhibit of grief and longing. The entire film plays out as an elegy to the person that Kirk described as "the friend I leave behind." The fifth *Star Trek* film, the much maligned *Final Frontier* from 1989, directed by William Shatner, takes the Kirk-Spock relationship, as well as theirs with McCoy, to truly astonishing heights. Indeed, few films more affectingly express enduring same-sex ties.

What chiefly prevents the Kirk and Spock relationship from being broadly recognized as a preeminent example of same-sex love in popular culture is that *Trek* never acknowledges the relationship as such. Yet for many the relationship can be experienced as emotionally meaningful in ways that traverse the lines of friendship and romantic love. It is in this liminal space —

between explication and allegory, encompassing a range of audience identifications, desires, and experiences — that *Trek* lives on as a profound monomyth.

Psychoanalysis, Gender Studies, and Queer Theory

This study approaches *Trek* from the perspectives of Freudian psychoanalytic theory, gender studies, and queer theory. In drawing from these related but also distinct methodologies, I am making the case that the best approach is a fusion of these schools of thought. While both feminist gender studies and Foucauldian queer theory would appear to be quite opposed to classical psychoanalytic theory, especially in its Freudian cast, I believe that Freud still has much to teach us about the importance of sexuality in our culture and in our lives. Gender studies, with its focus on the construction of gendered and sexual identities, and queer theory, with its challenge to normative ideologies that constrict these identities, allow me to provide necessary correctives to the traditional and normalizing aspects of Freudian theory. Overall, this book is part of a larger project that I call *queer Freudian aesthetics*, a synthesis of Freud, gender studies, and queer theory that maintains a belief in the power of sexuality and its importance to culture, representation, and experiential life.

Gender and Sexuality in Star Trek, *Chapter by Chapter*

Chapter One challenges the common associations of the Original 1960s *Star Trek* with sexism, specifically in terms of the skirt-chasing sexual rapacity of Captain James T. Kirk. I argue instead that the series is most notable for its deconstruction of the male gaze and the traditional assumption about male visual mastery. I argue that *Trek* does not represent anything like a normative version of heterosexuality but, instead, an allegorical heterosexuality with defamiliarizing, uncanny qualities that lend themselves to queer interpretation. In Chapter Two, I explore the homoerotic/queer potentialities of allegory in the *Trek* monomyth, focusing especially on episodes such as *Star Trek: Voyager*'s "Course: Oblivion" and *Star Trek: The Next Generation*'s "The Outcast." In Chapters Three and Four, I treat specific *Trek* characters, the Doctor and Neelix, respectively, as queer allegorical narratives developed over the course of the series *Voyager*; Chapter Three includes a discussion of *Buffy the Vampire Slayer*. In Chapter Five, I shift gears and explore the allegorization of race on *Trek*, specifically its relationship to black masculinity; I also make a provisional case that it is in its decentering of white masculinity that *Trek* is most politically valuable. In Chapter Six, I examine the series *Star Trek: Enterprise*, arguing that the reason for its commercial as well as aesthetic failure was its adoption of a neoconservative politics, rather than, as commonly believed, a decline in fan ardor for *Trek*. In Chapter Seven, I return to the issue of a decentered white masculinity, both problematizing this view and demonstrating that powerful homoerotic themes can emerge from even very conservative *Trek* works, such as the films under discussion, *Star Trek II: The Wrath of Khan* and *Star Trek: First Contact*. In Chapter Eight, I examine the construction of femininity on the series *Star Trek: Voyager*, focusing on the relationship between Captain Janeway and Seven of Nine; and in Chapter Nine, I discuss the film *Nemesis*, which I vindicate as a profoundly important film that daringly explores the major themes that have informed this study as a whole. In the Afterword, I discuss J. J. Abrams' reboot-film *Star Trek* and the ambiguous fate of the franchise.

One

LONELY PLANETS
Original *Star Trek*, the Male Gaze, and the Allegorization of Desire*

In "Charlie X," an episode from the first season of the 1960s *Star Trek* series, teen-aged Charlie, gifted with overpowering psychic abilities he cannot control and plagued by even more overpowering and uncontrollable sexual urges, plaintively begs Captain Kirk for advice. This plea, Charlie's pained need for guidance, is treated as a bit of a joke between the principal characters; the ship's physician McCoy relishes Kirk's palpable discomfort with having to teach Charlie X about sex. (Charlie, a sympathetic but monstrous mutant, sexually harasses Yeoman Janice Rand, to the embarrassment of all involved. He also routinely, by angrily furrowing his brow, brain-zaps crew members who displease him into the cosmic void.) Kirk's near-inability to discuss sexual matters with Charlie seems out of keeping with the iconic image of Kirk as the Great Galaxy Lothario. The archetypal Kirk of the ongoing series and our imaginations is the invincible seducer, yet the authentic, private Kirk blushes at sex-talk. The private, abashed Kirk of this early episode prepares us for what the series will demonstrate is his character's endless capacity to be pierced by desire's arrows.

The original *Star Trek* series (1966–69) is commonly associated with the sexism of its era. The skirt-chasing of its infamously promiscuous hero, Captain James T. Kirk (William Shatner), embodies white male heterosexual privilege, and the procession of vapid, objectified women characters on the show evinces its misogynistic view. Or so goes the usual take on the series. The conventional association of Kirk with male sexual rapacity obscures the weirdness with which *Trek* depicts his desire—depicts desire itself. Far from being reducible to the common charges of sexism, Original *Trek* (as I will refer to the series) unsettles questions of desire and sexuality.[1] The argument I will be making here pushes against the obvious point of the surface sexism in *Trek* to

---

*My great thanks to the anonymous readers at *The Journal of American Cultures* for their invaluable feedback to an article version of this chapter, which was accepted for publication by the journal. Due to conflicting publishing schedules, the article will not be appearing in the journal, but I warmly acknowledge JAC's support of my work.

get at something else, something heretofore undiscussed: the manner in which *Trek*'s treatment of desire, even if it intersects with sexism, also *defamiliarizes* the presumably obvious nature of heterosexuality. The strangeness of heterosexual relations in Original *Trek* has a radical potentiality for the representation of queer desire and for queer audience responses to popular culture texts.

Loss, Desire, and Trek*'s Queer Themes*

The chief means whereby *Trek*'s has spoken to, as well as for, queer subjectivity from the Original series forward has been through its foregrounding of a profound sense of loss. This theme of loss speaks to the social experience of being a member of a subaltern population, which can be a sexual as well as a racial subaltern. It also speaks more generally to the condition of modern subjectivity, the lack that haunts cotemporary identity, not the gendered lack of classical psychoanalytic theory, but a kind of social lack that is felt in individual terms.

Loss —figured as loneliness — is one of *Trek* main themes, and one of the most consistent ways in which the monomyth thematizes this loneliness is by depicting the Captain of each series as essentially unmarriageable. Captains Kirk, Picard, Sisko, Janeway, and Archer have all been, for the most part, unmarried (Sisko's wife Jennifer dies, in a Borg attack, before the narrative proper of *Deep Space Nine* begins; he does marry again, but only at the end of the series). In one famous first-season episode of Original *Trek*, "The Naked Time," the crew, infected by a virus that forces them to reveal their innermost feelings, act upon their repressed urges. Nurse Chapel tells Spock that she loves him; in confessing her love, she tells him how much she empathizes with his unspoken but intensely palpable loneliness. Spock reveals to Nurse Chapel, ever-pining for him, that he desires her as well. But Kirk reveals, tearfully, that, married to the *Enterprise*, he is piercingly lonely. The loneliness of the Captain is suggestive for queer readings because it conveys the pangs of unsatisfiable, unrealizable desire, and suggests an identity that has no easy or predictable place in the world. The Captain's loneliness complements the Trekkian theme of exploration: so many planets and all so lonely, to riff on Whitman's *Leaves of Grass*. Though it has certainly repeatedly come under fire for its associations with colonization and imperialism, this theme directly relates to the program's radical treatment of desire. The series represents isolation, apartness, and loneliness as ineluctable aspects of exploration. These charged motifs contribute powerfully to the series' overall tone of estrangement and loss. In Original *Trek*, the universe that extends beyond the ship connotes the infinite plangency of loss, a loss shown to be the logic of desire.

Overall, the series amply conveys the sense of *desire* as loss, not fulfillment, desire as the relinquishment of power, not access to it, and the desirer as one left bereft. As I argue below, though ostensibly the subject of Original *Trek*'s construction of a male gaze, Captain Kirk is most often shown to be *bereft* of visual mastery, not the subject who dominates the visual sphere.

Joan Wallach Scott argues:

> Gender is a primary way of signifying relationships of power. It might be better to say, gender is a primary field within which or by means of which power is articulated. Gender is not the only field, but it seems to have been a persistent and recurrent way of enabling the signification of power in the West, in the Judeo-Christian as well as the Islamic tradition.[2]

If gender exposes and reveals power relationships, what is striking about Original *Trek*'s representation of gender is how perilously close it often comes to suggesting that the condition of masculinity is one of vulnerability to all manner of assault, no assault being more destabilizing and transformative than the sensory, emotional, and even physical impact of Woman on the male. As I will argue throughout this chapter, the encounter with the female guest-star leaves the male, usually Captain Kirk but sometimes Spock or McCoy, bewildered and often transformed by the experience; while efforts at dominance are made, the pervasive attitude on the part of the male in the encounter with Woman is one of awed, disoriented submission. My argument is that this odd, defamiliarizing representation of heterosexuality in the series has considerable potentiality for queer readings because (a) it is in part a refusal of heterosexual presumption (in that it occults heterosexuality, the ostensibly most natural of sexual registers), and (b) puts the male in a feminized, non-heteronormative position.

To make the case that it is precisely in Original *Trek*'s representation of heterosexuality that it most vividly conveys its queer sensibility, I first examine the series' idiosyncratic aesthetic, a discussion that will employ perspectives from psychoanalysis, queer theory, and film theory; I will then consider three episodes from the series in depth. Beyond the representation of heterosexuality, the series' foregrounding of loving same-sex ties is another important aspect of its queer potentiality, and I discuss these themes as well in one the final sections of the chapter.

Allegory and the Encounter with Femininity

With good reason, the *Star Trek* franchise has been criticized for failing to represent homosexuality in any explicit way. Are there no gays in the future? Reading the innumerable *Trek* websites, one is struck by the recurrent rebuttals to these queer challenges from the presumably non-queer *Trek* fanbase, which usually consist of dismissals such as, "In the 24th century homosexuality will have been cured, so they don't need to present it." These grim eugenics fantasies notwithstanding, the admittedly difficult argument I am making in this chapter will probably please neither the activist fans who demand that *Trek* represent genuine, explicitly named gay characters or the more conservative fans who find the entire question appalling. I argue that *Trek has* powerfully presented queer themes, not through explicit means, to be sure, but through the technique of allegory. That *Trek* has employed allegory with such resonant results does not exculpate it from its responsibility to the human population it casts into the shadows by refusing to represent homosexuality. Nevertheless, if we fail to acknowledge the importance of Trekkian allegory for the representation of homosexuality, we miss out on one of the most remarkable accomplishments of the series, and the *Star Trek* monomyth generally: its evocative treatment of the *experience* of queerness in a homophobic, difference-denying culture. There are many ways in which *Trek* has suggested this experience — through its tales, characters, and even its premise of the exploration of unknown worlds and areas of space.

Our culture and its fictional narratives are heterosexist and heterosexualizing.[3] Heterosexuality is compulsory and the key rubric by and through which standards of sexual normativity are maintained.[4] Heterosexuality, like whiteness and middle-classness, is the American standard. Heterosexuality, however, if (for just a moment) freed from its ironclad normative bearings, is also quite elegant as a thematic, allegorical, symbolic representational system.

To broaden Joan Wallach Scott's argument on gender, heterosexuality is an interesting and useful system through which to understand, interpret, register, and contemplate the dynamics of desire. Original *Trek* turns heterosexuality into an allegorical system through which the disruptive and destabilizing forces of desire can be represented, mediated, and registered. On *Star Trek*, "men" and "women" are broadly symbolic figures, not only men and women but also archetypes of gendered ideals, allegories of masculinity and femininity at the same time as they are gendered characters.[5]

In almost every episode, a female guest star appears. The series stages her first appearance with a stylization that becomes a convention of the series, a convention that is one of the most important aspects of the series' representation of heterosexuality. The woman's appearance brings the action of the episode to a halt as she is revealed both to Kirk and to us; but in being revealed she also reveals *Kirk*. The spectacle of her appearance makes Kirk as fully a spectacle as she, as we watch Kirk's reaction to her appearance.

Throughout the series as a whole, Kirk is presented as a sign of manhood in its archetypal form — a combination of strength, virility, and noble bravery, all of which work to connote phallic authority. In contrast, the weekly female guest star represents womanhood and femininity.[6] The meeting between Kirk and Woman is a ritual that is performed anew in each episode: a perpetual pageant of desires awakened and acted upon. We see the spectacle of womanhood, her corporeal embodiment of the abstract concept of beauty; then we watch as desire is stimulated in Kirk, and the effect this stimulation has on him. It is the destabilization of Kirk's masculine authority — the penetrability of the very borders of his body, his susceptibility to desire — through the stylized encounter with woman, an encounter that is built into every episode, that lends the series a provocative gender and sexual fluidity.

Kirk experiences the flush, the burn, the jolt of desire anew in each episode. Each episode treats desire like the New Thing, the unprecedented revolt of the senses, the flaring up of previously unknown sensations. Original *Trek*, then, does not present us with a realistic depiction of man-woman relations but, rather, with *a perpetually reenacted, allegorical ritual of desire*. (It should be noted that on occasion some of the other male characters experience this first encounter with femininity in an episode; it is Kirk who most consistently and, as the show's lead, most momentously experiences it.) This ritualized heterosexuality negates conventional heterosexuality, refusing any sense of heterosexuality as a commonplace phenomenon. I argue that because of the irrational quality of this stylization, queer audience members can experience it as something unrealistic, strange, as something allegorical, which is to say, in terms other than or beyond what is being explicitly represented.

The consistently irreal, stylized form of these heterosexual first contacts between Kirk and Woman defies the general televisual style of the series, which strives for a realism that makes its futuristic premise believable, as it also takes the modes of gendered representation in classical Hollywood to a stylized height that approaches the parodistic, a point to which I return below. This stylization figures desire as a formidable force that triumphs through an overpowering of the senses. As Kirk and the female guest star move towards the fulfillment of their freshly inspired fleshly feelings, they appear to have little choice in the matter. Yet the radicalism of this representational scheme is that, rather than primarily or exclusively reinforcing institutionalized, compulsory heterosexuality, it denatures the heterosexual, so that normative heterosexuality is made to resist its own sexual and social agendas, left provocatively estranged from itself.

When the woman guest star first appears, we always see her through

Kirk's eyes. Certainly, the unselfconscious sixties sexism at work — the naked objectification of the women under Kirk's gaze — is the first thing we should point out. But sexism isn't the full story here. Given that each meeting between Kirk and Woman is customarily treated in the same highly stylized, deliberately unrealistic way, this meeting becomes the central topos of the series, synthesizing all other concerns and themes. The new woman, seen in soft, misty close-up, is presented to us — through Kirk's eyes — as an idealized version of Woman. She has a kind of romantic nimbus around her, and her appearance and presence suffuse the narrative like a memory of beauty; lush, languorous music, usually filled with the unsettling cries of a female chorus, heightens both the drama and the irreal aspect of the woman's appearance. Like a beautiful damsel or princess from a romance or a fairy-tale, the new woman appears and brings the narrative to an abrupt halt, as a languorous atmosphere of sensual appreciation, on Kirk's and our part, replaces narrative. It's like the moment in Book Six of *The Odyssey* when Odysseus, covered in sand and sea-salt, appears before Nausicaa, a young bathing maiden, and Athena, helping Odysseus out, *sweetens his appearance*, making him look comelier and more handsome. The new woman's appearance is always sweetened in Original *Trek* representation, and Kirk, despite his leering reputation, approaches and regards her (at least initially) as a divine apparition of beauty.

As an example of this Trekkian staging of femininity's appearance within narrative, let us consider one example amongst an innumerable many. In "Return to Tomorrow," from the second season, the crew encounter three surviving entities of an ancient telepathic species who claim to have "seeded" our galaxy, a recurring Trekkian theme; Sargon, the leader, refers to the *Enterprise* crew Kirk leads as his "children." Summoned to the transporter room by the alien beings along with his crew, including Vulcan science officer and First Officer Spock (Leonard Nimoy) and the cantankerous physician McCoy (DeForest Kelley), Kirk wonders aloud what the aliens — "they or it" — plan to do with them. "They or it, Captain?" questions a voice. The voice belongs to Dr. Ann Mulhall (played by the superbly intelligent actress Diana Muldaur, who would later appear in the great third-season Original Series episode "Is There in Truth No Beauty?" and play the appealingly grumpy Dr. Pulaski in season two of *Star Trek: The Next Generation*). Confused by the voice and unsure as to its source — *even though he walked right by her* when he first came into the transporter room — Kirk makes his way to Ann. We see the two framed in a tight two-shot, Kirk slightly beneath her since she stands on the raised teleportation pad. But then we get the stylized shot of Ann's face and the swelling music. Ann reveals that she has no idea how she got to the transporter room, only that she was summoned there.

Though confused, Ann, as Muldaur plays her, does not appear particularly fazed by these magically dislocating events brought about by deities who may very well be gods. But Kirk, as Shatner plays him, appears dazed, as if some unseen hand had just punched him, as he stares at the spectacle of Ann. What's especially interesting about this woman-appearance is that Ann, while given the spectacularization common to Original *Trek* women, is not especially coded to connote to-be-looked-at-ness, to use Laura Mulvey's famous phrase from her essay "Visual Pleasure and Narrative Cinema." She is one of the small but significant group of Original *Trek* women whose scientific acumen supersedes their sexual-object function for the episode. Yet even cerebral Ann creates the disorientation in Kirk of his destabilizing encounter with the gaze.

Star Trek *and the Universal Queer Spectator*

How is it possible that a trope that magnifies and reifies its heterosexualizing and heterosexist content — Kirk's encounter with Woman — can *also* be the queerest kind of viewing experience? Thinking through the queer implications of Original *Trek*'s aesthetic and emotional schemes will be helpful to our formulation of an answer. Given the legions of gay fans of both Original *Trek* and classical Hollywood films, the pervasively maintained heterosexual Hollywood standard does not appear to have interfered with gay ardor for Hollywood or *Trek*. This aspect of queer spectatorship needs some consideration. As gay viewers, what do we experience when watching traditional and therefore always already heterosexual narrative?

As I have been suggesting, the special romantic representation of sexual difference in Original *Trek* helps us to understand heterosexuality not as "standard" but as overpoweringly *odd*, a disruption of rational life. I theorize that both straight and queer viewers of Original *Trek* experience Kirk's desire for the new woman in similar ways (responding to the idiosyncratic details of the representation, the special idealization, the sexual allegory). But why would queer viewers experience the same rush of desire — to the extent that they do — as heterosexual viewers? I am well aware that I seem to be speaking on behalf of all gay viewers. To theorize about gay viewers' relationships to Hollywood's heterosexual meta-narrative, I need to paint with broad strokes, even if I am quite aware of the risks in doing so. I write from the perspective of, in Steven Drukman's terms, the "universal gay male spectator" in order to generalize "a new position of interpretation, desire, meaning and subjectivity" that believes in the "ultimate undecidability" of positions of queer spectatorship.[7]

Here we return to the elegance of heterosexuality as a symbolic system. Even in our broadly reactionary cultural moment, traditional heterosexuality — in its institutionalized, compulsory form — seems increasingly quaint, as does, it should be added, homosexuality; "queer," encompassing a broader array of sexual affiliations, at least suggests the greater sexual diversity that is becoming increasingly undeniable. There are so many new, emergent, competing forms of gendered and sexual identities; of sexual practices; of approaches to dating, romance, and sex that, despite the crushing of gay-rights legislation that is concomitant with the movement's considerable gains in recent years, the momentum of queer sexual energies is most likely unstoppable.

Heterosexuality is useful as a gendered and textual system for its elegance, symmetry, concision, and formal and thematic beauty. In her general argument in *Female Masculinity*, Judith Halberstam encourages us to see masculinity as a quality independent of gender, as, in the cases she lays out, a quality that can occur in women completely independently of their male counterparts. Though the link is generally unacknowledged, the decoupling of gendered characteristics from biological gender stems from Freud's radical views of the subject. As Freud wrote in one of his most bracing essays, "Some Psychological Consequences of the Anatomical Differences between the Sexes" (1925), "pure masculinity and femininity remain theoretical constructions of uncertain content."[8] Heterosexuality allegorizes the play of masculinity and femininity, imagining theoretical constructions as living bodies that override the uncertainty of the very essences they are presumed to embody and manifest. Queer viewers learn how to desire by watching it play out through the myriad meta-narratives of culture, and these meta-narratives are always already heterosexual. We learn to desire by watching heterosexuality and heterosexual desire unfurl and expand and *become*, a process some decide to emulate or to reject, an acceptance or refusal *not* necessarily tethered, it should be added, to sexual orientation.

Original *Trek* makes this process of heterosexual fulfillment a magical, allegorical ritual that vividly exposes the process *as such*. It doesn't posit that heterosexuality is rote, ordinary, familiar, tacit, given, but rather that it's unusual, sudden, unexpected, eerie, galvanizing, strange. To follow Freud's famous theory of the uncanny, the uncanny is both the familiar and the unfamiliar at once (the *heimlich* and the *unheimlich*, or home-like and unhome-like). By making the most familiar sexual orientation, heterosexuality, seem deeply unfamiliar, or both familiar and unfamiliar at once, Original *Trek* gives us *the heterosexual as the uncanny*. In so doing, it makes heterosexuality deeply alien, strange and defamiliarized, the antithesis of the Natural, the normative, the familiar. Original *Trek* seems to revert to a nineteenth-century conception of sexual difference, in which the opposite sex was deeply Other; it returns to the view of the intensely foreign nature of man-woman relations that characterized Victorian views of heterosexuality. But it does something else as well. By allegorizing heterosexuality, Original *Trek* forces us to see it not as the texture of life itself but as disruption, a break within and *from* quotidian life. Precisely because heterosexuality seems so exotic, so magical, on Original *Trek*, a queer viewer can find him or herself falling for it along with the desire-struck characters. We can respond to the sweetened appearances, the romantic haze, the desire-lit eyes, the swooning scores, the sheer weirdness of it all.

Kirk's Masochism: Trek *and Gaze Theory*

The representation of femininity and sexual desire in relation to the male gaze has been a controversial subject since Laura Mulvey's famous 1975 essay "Visual Pleasure and Narrative Cinema." Several innovations in gaze theory have occurred in recent years, most notably for our purposes the queering of the gaze. As Judith Halberstam writes of Laura Mulvey's "excessively neat formula for the increasingly messy business of erotic identification" (which includes Mulvey's own recasting of her argument), "the most relevant reformulations of spectatorship take note of the multiple gendered positions afforded by the gaze and provide a more historically specific analysis of spectatorship." Halberstam suggests that a "less psychoanalytically inflected theory of spectatorship is far less sure of the gender of the gaze. Indeed," Halberstam continues, "recent discussions of gay and lesbian cinema assume that the gaze is queer or multidimensional."[9] Both in its inherent queering of the gaze and through the new conceptualizations of the gaze that facilitate queer viewing of myriad kinds, Original *Trek* comes to seem less like a sexist series and more like a text that actively solicits the queer eye.

I argue that both queer theory *and* psychoanalytically-inflected film theory can help us to understand the unusual workings of the gaze in Original *Trek*, despite the problems Halberstam points to and those inherent in the use of a critical methodology for the analysis of one medium to discuss a related but distinct one. "The potential for a psychoanalytical approach within television studies is debatable and perhaps limited," notes one of the leading works in the field.

> A major problem is in considering the social (and therefore psychic) conditions of viewing, since watching television, unlike cinema-going, is a frag-

mented experience, subject to interruption and distinctive for its "immediacy" and its impression of being "live." Thus ... television viewers "glance" rather than gaze in a sustained way. Moreover ... the largely domestic conditions of viewing mean that the "dreamlike" qualities of the cinema are not necessarily reproduced (even when watching televised films) and this clearly throws doubt on the logic of the text-spectator relationship in psychoanalytic film theory when applied to television. [Some aspects of the psychoanalytic approach, however] transfer more easily. The gendered, voyeuristic characteristics of the camera are evident in much television output.[10]

The gendered and voyeuristic qualities of the gaze certainly apply to the *Trek* monomyth, and especially to Original *Trek*. But further, Original *Trek*, more than any of the other *Trek* series, lends itself to dreamlike reverie because of the woozy, dreamlike atmosphere created by the series in terms of set-design, music, and, on occasion, camera-work, as the woman guest star's first appearance exemplifies, even as the series as a whole strives for realism in order to make its futuristic time period and settings plausible. Moreover, the heavily allegorical approach taken by the series, especially as it fused classical mythology, literary references, and other kinds of cultural signposting with sci-fi plots and motifs, itself created an aleatory atmosphere, a special realm of fantasy where anything can happen, a realm with dreamlike possibilities.

Classical Hollywood stars were photographed in a manner designed to produce a sense of wonder in the audience — how could a fellow human being be *that* beautiful? Invited to bask in their refulgent beauty, the audience gazed upon the beautiful star in a ritual of mass consuming that could be described as a psychic cannibalism: feasting on beauty. Original *Trek*'s depiction of femininity uses the same techniques employed by classical Hollywood — the soft-lens close-up, the heightened music, the artificial appearance of the female star.[11] The weekly spectacle of femininity on Original *Trek* both preserves the classical Hollywood spectacularization of Woman and takes that spectacularization to a parodistic height.

Richard Dyer's discussion of the visualization of Marilyn Monroe in the 1955 film *The Seven Year Itch* illuminates the linkages between classical Hollywood and Original *Trek* representations of femininity. Monroe's first appearance in the film

> is an original instance of woman as spectacle caught in a shot from the male protagonist's point of view.... He looks and there is a cut to the hall doorway, where the curvy shape of a woman is visible through frosted glass. The woman's shape is placed exactly within the frame of the door window.... The coloring of the screen is pinky-white and light emanates from behind the doorway where the woman is. All we see of her is her silhouette, defining her

proportions, but she also looks translucent. The film cuts back [to the male protagonist], his jaw open in awe, bathed in stellar light.... Such moments conflate unreal angel-glow with sexual aura.[12]

If classical Hollywood spectacularized even actresses with as fleshly an appeal as Monroe as icons of distance and divine light, abstracted them into a remote emblem of their own femininity, and rendered the male position one of awe, Original *Trek*'s depiction of Kirk's encounters with femininity reproduces classical Hollywood staging of male awe at the spectacle of iconic woman.

Given the valences between classical Hollywood and Original *Trek*'s representations of women, it makes sense to incorporate film theory within the general psychoanalytic methodology of our analysis. In terms now almost unbearably familiar, Laura Mulvey argued in her seminal 1975 *Screen* essay "Visual Pleasure and Narrative Cinema" that the dominant Hollywood cinema is organized around the patriarchal white heterosexual male gaze, which spectacularizes and objectifies women's sexuality.[13] In a sexually imbalanced world, writes Mulvey, "pleasure in looking has been split between active/male and passive/female." The male protagonist/spectator's scopophilic pleasure (a ravenous desire to look) arises from "using another person as an object of sexual stimulation through sight"; the woman is "coded for strong visual and erotic impact" so that she may "connote *to-be-looked-at-ness.*"[14] Mulvey argued that the male spectator-protagonist has two strategies for dealing with the castration anxieties provoked by the spectacularized woman: either "investigating the woman, demystifying her mystery" or "[completely disavowing] castration by the substitution of a fetish so that it becomes reassuring rather than dangerous."[15] The films of Alfred Hitchcock, especially *Vertigo* (1958), provide a synthesizing example, for Mulvey, of the first strategy, *voyeurism*. Mulvey expands on Freud throughout this essay; voyeurism, as Freud brilliantly theorized it, is sadism in the form of the look, a desire to dominate others through the eyes.[16] Mulvey uses the ornately hyperstylized Marlene Dietrich films of Josef von Sternberg as her examples for the second strategy, *fetishistic scopophilia*, which centers on overvaluation of woman, "the cult of the female star."

Despite the severe limitations of Mulvey's theory — the ways in which it fails to address the many instances in classical Hollywood in which the male is made the *object* of the gaze or the woman is granted the power to look, the feminist relevance of her argument makes her work enduringly valuable, and it is a testament to her essay that it continues to withstand ongoing critical challenges. (Mulvey herself has revised her positions several times throughout the years.)[17]

Certainly, to some extent, the aesthetic design of Original *Trek* does conform to Mulveyan paradigms. One of the avenues of escape for the male protagonist/spectator from the fear of castration is, Mulvey argues, fetishistic scopophilia, the "complete disavowal of castration by the substitution of a fetish object or turning the represented figure itself into a fetish so that it becomes reassuring rather than dangerous." In that the sweetened appearance of the woman of Original *Trek* relies upon a fetishistic focus on the woman's face (the famous Season 1 episode "Mudd's Women," about the titular group of magically physically enhanced mail-order prostitute-wives, is especially rampant in its use of the stylized, soft-focus close-up), the series does indeed appear to express castration anxiety. Yet, as many later critics have pointed out, the essential problem with Mulvey's theory is the narrow view she takes of what, exactly or possibly, constitutes male sexuality, and Original *Trek* allows us to see the ways in which such a narrow understanding of masculinity fails to encompass the kinds of alternative representational techniques that could have potentially radical effects.

Mulvey argued in "Visual Pleasure" that the film spectator, gendered male, identifies with the onscreen male protagonist and joins him in a project of shared narcissistic omnipotence, the psychic state of masculinist hegemony. Several critics have enlarged, in highly various ways, the paradigms of Mulvey's 1975 essay to include an economy of masochism within the theorization of both the spectator-protagonist relationship and the representation of gender. Given that Gaylyn Studlar wrote the most sustained such counterargument in her book *In the Realm of Pleasure*, I will take a moment to recapitulate her argument. Mulvey argued, as we have noted, that the male spectator-protagonist has two strategies for dealing with the castration anxieties provoked by the spectacularized woman: voyeuristically investigating or fetishizing the woman. In her study, Studlar revisits the von Sternberg–Dietrich films that embody fetishistic scopophilia, the second of the two Mulveyan avenues available to the male spectator-protagonist for the negotiation of the castration fears represented by the spectacularized female body. Studlar positively employs Deleuze's *Coldness and Cruelty,* a utopian study of masochism in the works of the nineteenth-century Austrian author Sacher-Masoch, from whose name the term masochism is derived, as a means of establishing an economy of masochism as a radical alternative to Mulvey's view of male sadistic, narcissistic visual reign over the spectacularized woman. Studlar argues that the pre–Oedipal relationship between the son and the mother provides a powerful alternative to the post–Oedipal, symbolic mode of male domination from which both Mulvey and Freud position male sexuality in relation to femininity. From a neo–Deleuzian position, Studlar champions masochism as a means of understanding the male relationship to femininity as a position of awe that recalls the infant male's subservience to the looming, powerful pre–Oedipal mother.[18]

Though I think that several difficulties exist in Studlar's argument, for our purposes it is very useful for thinking about Kirk's relationship to femininity. Rarely does Kirk, in his encounter with the spectacle of Woman, proceed in the manner that Mulvey's 1975 essay prepares us to expect: he does not proceed from a position of masculine aggressiveness and the physical might that would complement his visual domination. Rather, before the spectacle of femininity, Kirk stands wonderstruck, disoriented, *abashed*. When the woman appears, her appearance brings the episode — the action of the scene, the plot, the position of the actors in the frame — to a screeching halt, the screech of which remains audible only as the flare-up of Alexander Courage's languorous music. Kirk does not dominate the woman whose spectacular appearance reduces him to a state of gaping awe. Rather, he approaches her tentatively, almost awkwardly, in a state of supplication. It's almost as if her sweetened appearance provokes a sweetening of his masculine authority; it's almost as if her heightened femininity taps into and draws out Kirk's own femininity, just as her appearance, in its power to command his attention and to override the protocols of narrative, co-opts his masculine power as protagonist.

The third-season episode "Plato's Stepchildren" is famed for featuring the first interracial television kiss. This kiss is not fully seen (the way the actors are made to place their heads obscures the moment in which Kirk and Uhura's lips lock); moreover, it is a *forced* kiss. Kirk and crew are trapped on a planet with sadistic, classical-antiquity-model aliens that have telepathic abilities that allow them to control the away team's minds. What is fascinating about this episode is the vivid way it thematizes what is an ongoing aspect of the series, namely, male vulnerability, malleability, and powerlessness. Though Uhura and Nurse Chapel are tortured as well, the majority of the episode centers on the humiliation and manipulation of the male crew members. The scene in which Kirk is made to whip Uhura, in addition to having grim, obvious overtones of American slavery (imagery that was especially highly charged in the Original Series' 1960s era), provides Kirk with a sadistic overcompensation for his involuntarily masochistic yielding to the aliens' power; yet this sadism is itself a kind of masochism, since Kirk is made brutal against his will. Moreover, back to that kiss: while its major charge is the racial taboo it breaks, it is also a succinct, sharp image of heterosexual ambivalence, a scene of alienated, even horrified, conscription into compulsory heterosexuality, especially in that there are two, paired scenes of involuntary kissing, between Kirk and Uhura and Spock and Nurse Chapel.

In an essay collected in Stephen Greenblatt's *Allegory and Representation*, Leo Bersani, meditating on Freud, conjectures that all "sexuality originates in the masochistic excitement of fantasy," and one could plausibly say that the forever staged encounter between Kirk and Woman figures the birth of sexual desire as the result of Kirk's masochistic subservience to the power of femininity.[19] The woman's sweetened appearance makes her resemble the hazy apparition of private fantasy. Kirk's abashed reaction connotes an enfeeblement of the body as a result of the overpowering of the senses; one could argue that such depictions of male desire as a form of suffering render masculinity masochistic. In several ways, Kirk would appear to inhabit the place of masochistic acquiescence to feminine power rather than Mulvey's theory of male narcissistic omnipotence. This topos of desire, far from rendering male power tumescent, may be said to *dephallicize* masculinity — to make masculinity pliant, passive, waiting to receive stimulus rather than the agent that stimulates and penetrates a body — and thereby refuses both male authority and commonplaces about the meaning and role of male sexuality.[20]

Kirk's awestruck reaction to femininity suggests fetishistic scopophilia, a construction of Woman as a reassuring presence that defends against the profound male fear of castration. As Freud theorized, the primary male trauma is the infant male's discovery that the mother, this looming all-powerful being, has no penis. Fetishism assuages this psychic trauma by constantly replacing this penis with phallus-like parts of the woman's body — nose, feet — or things that adorn the body — boots, furs.[21] Kirk, far from being the sexually secure, great Galaxy Lothario of legend, perpetually revisits this original scene of sexual trauma, forever in need of reassurance, but a reassurance that can only momentarily quell the profound sexual anxieties that constitute his fraught subjectivity. Kirk's gaze transforms the woman into the phallic mother, the loss of whom inspires fetishistic fantasy.[22]

While Kirk within the female spectacle may be said to enact a masochistic response and to embody fetishistic scopophilia — providing a scenario that allows us to fuse both Mulvey's and Studlar's views of the male gaze — more deeply *the spectacle as a whole* reveals the limitations of the gaze itself, the paradoxical ways in which, in Lacanian terms, the gaze revolves around our *inability* to see. Kirk's subject position, if we view it in these terms, exists chiefly to mark the place where the subject cannot see and is seen by the blindness at the heart of the field of vision. As such, the spectacle of femininity in Original *Trek* shatters even the staging of sexual difference from the visual field, to say nothing of masculinist visual and sexual hegemony. Not the sight of woman but the act of *seeing the sight of woman* signals the evacuation of all sight, all identity, all power.[23]

As Todd McGowan puts it in a provocative re-reading of Lacan for film theory,

> Lacan's use of the term reverses our usual way of thinking about the gaze because we typically associate it with an active process. But as an object, the gaze acts to trigger our desire visually, and as such it is what Lacan calls an *objet petit a* or object-cause of desire. As he puts it in *Seminar XI*, "The objet a in the field of the visible is the gaze." This special term *objet petit a* indicates that this object is not a positive entity but a lacuna in the visual field. It is not the look of the subject at the object, but the gap within the subject's seemingly omnipotent look. This gap within our look marks the point at which our desire manifests itself in what we see. What is irreducible to our visual field is the way that our desire distorts that field, and this distortion makes itself felt through the gaze as object.[24]

To extend McGowan's reframing of Lacan to television, the incitement of the gaze in Original *Trek*—the depiction of the special appearance of woman in the narrative—constitutes neither the woman as object of desire nor the male as the subject of the gaze with access to the masculinist power to dominate the woman as object. Rather, the gaze is symptomatic of the blinding gap within the very heart of the visual, the traumatic wound of vision itself, a wounding concomitant with the rampant, unsatisfiable desire to see and experience pleasure through seeing that Freud referred to as scopophilia.[25] If Original *Trek* figures scopophilia as the logic of male desire, it does so in a manner that figures both masculinity and femininity as figments of this scopophilia, structuring points within the visual field that facilitates the gaze. Which is to say, concepts of masculinity and femininity are subservient to the gaze, which itself is a symptom of engulfing desire.

Feminism and the Third Season

If through its visual schemes Original *Trek* refuses its own right to the masculine authority that in other ways appears to undergird it, these are not the only means whereby the series troubles traditional understandings of gendered power. The series also disrupts normative categories of gendered identity through its allegorical narratives and its often unnoticed but sometimes daring depictions of its characters.

The third and final season is particularly rich with female characters who contradict the general view that the original series only took an interest in the sexual objectification of women. Though much maligned by fans, this season contains several episodes that feature female guest stars who resist the more conventional typing of the previous seasons, though, as I have been suggesting, this sexual typing could also lend itself to something much less conventional in aesthetic terms that were significant for the series' representation of the male gaze.

The intelligent, strikingly modern Romulan (savage relatives of the logical, peaceful Vulcans) woman commander of the third-season episode "The Enterprise Incident"—in which Spock woos the woman commander to distract her from Kirk's mission to steal the Romulan cloaking device—does not get her sweetened close-up until well into the episode, when she changes her appearance from military to evening wear, to appear more comely in Spock's brooding eyes. In this episode, Spock's sexuality seems as overpoweringly palpable as it is banked, a new understanding of the character that will inform the later episodes "The Cloud Minders" and "All Our Yesterdays" as well.

Rather than objectifying her, the idealized close-up serves to demonstrate that this woman captain can have it all—military might *and* erotic potentiality. Even though defeated, she remains a noble and respectable character—there is no elation over her defeat nor denigration towards her, and Spock confesses that he hopes she realizes that, despite the military deceptions, something genuine did occur between them. "It will be our secret," she says. Not all Original *Trek* women were vapid, as this and several other third-season episodes, such as "Is There in Truth No Beauty?" "The Empath," and "All Our Yesterdays," make vividly clear.

"Is There in Truth No Beauty?" is a particularly fascinating episode not only because it questions female spectacle and the male gaze but also because it is another episode that makes provocative use of the subversive intelligence and intensity of Diana Muldaur. (One can only imagine what directions the show might have taken had she been a regular on this series rather than its much-later sequel.) In this episode, she plays an especially intriguing character, Miranda (a nod to *The Tempest*), a highly, almost intimidatingly intelligent woman who escorts Kollos, the ambassador of an energy-based race called the Medusans. They are aptly named, apparently so hideous that one look at them will make any humanoid insane. The reason that Miranda can work with them is that she is blind; she wears, however, a "sensor web" in the form of a dress, keeping her blindness hidden from the crew for quite some time. Moreover, Miranda has telepathic abilities that may even exceed Spock's, being, as Spock himself notes, "quite formidable."

In a way that anticipates the final episode of the series, "Turnabout Intruder" (discussed below), Miranda openly chafes against male rule. In a manner that would be surprising in any series of this era, she vehemently competes with Spock, alternately challenging him about and chafing against his own ability to communicate with Kollos. Most interestingly of all, during the obligatory scene in which Kirk hits on her (in an arboretum this time!), Miranda, far from succumbing to his charms, exhibits no sexual interest in him whatsoever. If this episode is a version of *The Tempest* ("O brave new world," a character quotes), it is Shakespeare's valedictory play with Prospero — the white imperialist male ruler, who colonizes the planet of his abhorred slave Caliban — excised. This is *The Tempest* with Miranda, Prospero's daughter, and Caliban-Kollos as the protagonists: woman and the subaltern given center stage.

I consider this episode one of *Trek*'s finest, but it does get bogged down a bit in its attempt to make Miranda acknowledge her own "unwomanliness," in a scene in which Kirk shakes her into apparent submission. Yet despite this scene, one is chiefly left with the impression of a shockingly, intransigently modern woman bruising her heel against the enforced limitations of her sex — to lift from (and modify) Hawthorne's description of Zenobia, the new American feminist of his novel *The Blithedale Romance*. When Miranda departs, and she and Spock exchange compliments, this exchange has a philosophical character, Spock invoking the Vulcan credo IDIC: infinite diversity in infinite combinations. This episode allows a woman to join in the historically male tradition of rational discourse. A woman who rejects compulsory heterosexuality, ambitiously fights for her career, and participates in philosophical discourse, Miranda is a bracingly non-standard character.

"I Choose": "Requiem for Methuselah"

In "Requiem for Methuselah," Kirk, Spock, and McCoy, in need of elements for a medical defense against a fatal disease, beam down to a planet, which they discover to be the property of an aging, white-haired, but still vital man named Flint (James Daly). Flint, who once lived on Earth and left it for this isolated distant planet, is initially hostile, ordering the landing party back to the ship, but he relents, though an intimidating robot sentry continues to hover threateningly about. Flint introduces them to his pupil, Rayna Kapec (Louise Sorel), a stately blonde woman who looks like a princess from a fairy tale and speaks the language of Enlightenment rationalism (she sounds like a member of the Royal Academy of Science). Flint — who is immortal, having been at various points great men in human history (da Vinci, Brahms, et al.) — created Rayna, who is actually an android, to be his intellectual equal. He presents Rayna to the landing party to see what will happen — both to observe her experience of new emotions, such as love, and to test her feelings for him. *Trek* critic Jamahl Epsicokhan writes,

> The story asks how useful a person is once he has outlived his own sense of purpose — and for Flint, a life of hundreds of years has produced everything from music apparently written by Brahms to artwork apparently created by Da Vinci. Admittedly, I couldn't quite understand how Kirk was so taken with Rayna so quickly (perhaps I should remind myself that this is Kirk we're talking about), but the triangular relationship that develops and ends in a tragedy (Rayna's inability to cope with her feelings causes a fatal shutdown) is best utilized in the show's final scene, where Spock uses a mind meld to relieve Kirk of his burden of grief. These are characters who feel for one another more than the plots often let on.[26]

We will consider Spock's mind meld in the coda in a moment. But for now, Epsicokhan's point about the astonishing speed with which Kirk falls in love with Rayna is the most relevant. It is precisely the irrational, implausible instantaneousness of love in Original *Trek* that defines its treatment of desire.

Fans may complain about the rapidity with which Kirk falls in love here, but this episode makes only slightly more obvious the process whereby people generally fall in love on Original *Trek*. Interestingly, however, it is almost always the *women* who fall in *love*; usually, Kirk's fall is not into love but into desire. In the famous second-season episode "Space Seed," ship historian Lieutenant Marla McGivers (Madlyn Rhue), who has a pronounced taste for messianic leaders, falls irrationally, instantaneously in love with thawed-out twentieth-century despot Khan Noonien Singh (suitably magnificent Ricardo Montalban)[27]; in another second-season episode, "Who Mourns for Adonais?" Lieutenant Carolyn Palamas (Leslie Parrish) falls in love with the god Apollo. These notably intelligent and accomplished women plunge headlong into desire; it's an inversion of the screwball comedy, in which rational, intellectual men are unmanned by the presence of a singular, overpowering woman. In falling madly and instantaneously in love with Rayna, Kirk assumes a feminized role — a vulnerable, wracked submission to unmanning Love, the figure whom the Latin poet Petrarch in his "Laura" poems described as a masculine, martial figure who overpowers and dominates the male subject.

"Requiem for Methuselah" vividly demonstrates René Girard's and Eve Kosofsky Sedgwick's theories of triangulated desire, along with the concepts used in Gayle Rubin's famous chapter "The Traffic in Women." For Girard, woman is the battleground upon which two rivalrous men war; in Sedgwick, triangulation serves as a structuring schema for power relations in culture, in which male homosocial desire is negotiated and circulated through the contested figure of a woman. Flint uses Rayna to draw out Kirk's emotions, seeming as interested in Kirk's demonstration of experienced desire as he is in Rayna's. Like a carny huckster, but with a gravity that masks his sadism, Flint presents Rayna as spectacle, Woman as sideshow. The homosocial group of

Kirk-Spock-McCoy are the audience for Flint's spectacular presentation of femininity, put on display in the android Rayna; interestingly, only Kirk shows the ability to fall in love with the spectacle. McCoy is shown to be too busy with finding a cure for disease to bother with all the romantic fuss; but Spock intently observes and intervenes in Kirk's increasingly desperate immersion in this love-plot.

Throughout, Spock demonstrates a mysterious awareness of all of the future contours of the love-plot, especially interesting since, as a Vulcan (well, a Vulcan-human hybrid), he ostensibly views such antics from afar, never having experienced human love for himself. Seemingly dispassionate, Spock calmly observes the machinations of Flint, the desperation of Kirk, the tormented anguish of Rayna, the inexorable unfolding of this love-plot, which plays out with a rote, obvious, predictable pattern. Desire strikes like lightning, but the game of heterosexuality unfolds with archetypal, easily defined, predictable solemnity. By the climax, in which Kirk and Flint engage in physical battle over Rayna, then force her to choose which one she truly loves, Spock calmly cautions, "Stop — there is a danger." Complying with Spock's intuitive comprehension of the situation, Rayna the android short-circuits, a casualty of erotic warfare. Spock regards heterosexuality and rivalrous relationships between men as standard, surprise-free cultural tropes. Rayna is the trampled battleground for these inevitable, crushingly predictable forces.

"Requiem" plays out like a pastiche of Nathaniel Hawthorne's great short story "Rappaccini's Daughter." The experiments of sinister old scientist Rappaccini endow his daughter, Beatrice, with the same terrible power to kill through poison possessed by the beautiful, deadly plants she tends. Coldly, Rappaccini watches the love-plot unfold between her and a young man, Giovanni Guasconti, who observes her, falls in love with her, and shares in her doom — a plot Rappaccini has thoroughly orchestrated. Like Rappaccini, Flint coldly watches the unfolding of the love-plot he has engineered, the desire and despair and sorrow he instigates. Like Giovanni, Kirk falls for it all, engaging in predictable macho competitiveness with Flint. Like Beatrice, Rayna is beautiful and doomed. She short-circuits when presented with the terrible effects of the desires she stimulates. And like Beatrice, before she expires, she has a great moment. Beatrice tells Giovanni, who has cursed her for infecting him, "Thy words of hatred are like lead within my heart — but they, too, will fall away as I ascend. Oh, was there not, from the first, more poison in thy nature than in mine?" Beatrice exposes the hidden misogyny in Giovanni's condemnation of her. Similarly, Rayna exposes her status as pawn in this homosocial conflict. She defies her role as the battleground of triangulated desire: "I will not be the cause of this!" She declares, "*I* choose! *I* decide where I want to go, whom I want to be with!" As Rayna utters these defiant words, she seems to register the awesome changes coming over her, the power of newfound agency.

Then she dies. Rayna's death inchoately emblematizes what I call the theme of Tragic Feminism that will dominate media representations in the late sixties and 1970s. She anticipates Tyne Daly's novice female cop, partnered up with Clint Eastwood's implacable Dirty Harry, in *The Enforcer* (1976), who dies just as she's won Harry's grudging approval (her last words instruct Harry to avenge her death: "Get him..."); Gillian (Amy Irving) in Brian De Palma's poetic horror masterpiece *The Fury* (1978) who annihilates, in a bravura final sequence, patriarchy's symbol, the villainous Childress (John Cassavetes), destroying her own innocence in the process; Millie, Pinky Rose, and Willie in Robert Altman's hypnotic *3 Women* (1977), who destroy patriarchy (crudely embodied by silently seething artist Willie's philandering husband) but cannot escape their own gendered binds. Television shows of the 1970s like *Charlie's Angels, The Bionic Woman, Wonder Woman,* and *Alice* would explore the struggles of women to realize their own independence and wield their agency while tethered to masculine authority.

Spock, pontificatingly responding to Kirk's question, "What happened?" as the homosocial group hovers over the corpse of Rayna, explains that "the awful power and complications of her newfound emotions" were too much for Rayna to bear. But the episode makes the strong suggestion that Rayna's death is a "dying into freedom," to use Harold Bloom's phrase — an escape from the crushing gears of the social and desiring order.[28]

Kirk and Spock: Male-Male Love

A truly extraordinary moment occurs at the end of "Requiem," when Spock appears to take Kirk's pain away. Kirk, despondent after Rayna's death, says to Spock, "A very old and lonely man and a young and lonely man.... We put on a pretty poor show, didn't we?" Again, desire on Original *Trek* is always linked to loneliness. "I just wish I could forget," says Kirk. Then he rests his head on the table. McCoy walks in, saying he's glad to see Kirk sleeping off his pain. McCoy then turns to Spock and, in one of his least generous and, paradoxically, one of his gentlest anti–Vulcan tirades, tells Spock that he actually feels sorrier for the Vulcan than he does for Jim. You see, says McCoy to Spock, you'll never experience the joys and pains of love the way we humans can. Once McCoy leaves Jim's quarters, however, Spock demonstrates that he does indeed know about love. He walks over to Kirk — who cannot possibly actually be sleeping — and places Vulcan fingers on Kirk's face, saying, "Forget." But this alien ritual of forgetting is primarily a memorial, a marking of feelings, a testament from Spock — and to the viewers — of Spock's tender love for Kirk.

"You'll never know human love," McCoy tells Spock. But Spock does, clearly, love: he loves Kirk. Heterosexuality is the human, the story that decrees humanity upon us, from ancient times forward. If queer love is not heterosexual love, not *human* love, the non-human, and therefore, the queer, makes a pretty powerful showing here. This is another example of difference functioning as an allegory for queerness in *Trek*. Spock's non-human, queer love for Kirk, a profound display of which concludes the episode, is shown to be no less palpably powerful than any other love depicted. Moreover, by having Kirk fall truly, madly, deeply in love with a non-human woman in the first place, the episode seems to be problematizing these normative boundaries altogether.

Thus far I have been arguing that *Trek* denatures the conventional associations of heterosexual love by showing the male as, far from wielding mastery over the gaze, overwhelmed by the spectacle of the desirable object, largely powerless before it. Original *Trek*'s depiction of heterosexuality resists the normative structures it is commonly assumed to have upheld. Another way Original *Trek* defies normative structures of masculinity is in its depiction of ardent male love, which, as this last scene of "Requiem" evinces, is among the most consistent and passionate themes of the series. Little wonder that this theme has spawned the massive intertextual and diffuse writing project of slash fiction — narratives, largely written by heterosexual women, that pair same-sex characters of popular film and television shows in erotic situations, sometimes loving, sometimes highly sexual, sometimes a combination of the two.[29] This male love is highly suggestive when considered in relation to the *Trek* theme of the unmarriageability of the Captain; resisting or barred from the most normative and socially enforced form of institutionalized heterosexuality, the unmarried Captain leaves his or her desire a perpetually unanswered question, a trend especially notable given that, despite its considerable queer resonances, the Trekkian monomyth is also undeniably heterosexist.

Original *Trek*'s treatment of male love is fairly extraordinary: deeply felt, enduring, and profound. The intense love between principals Kirk, Spock, and McCoy, their depth of feeling for one another, remains an extraordinary statement of the capacities of love. The tender male-male love of the Kirk-Spock-McCoy triumvirate remains one of the most moving and unusual achievements of sixties television, especially noteworthy given Original *Trek*'s associations with masculine power and sexism. Most of the episodes end with the three bantering on the bridge, usually trying to get a rise out of Spock, whose ironic responses to them border on camp; suggestive of the *ménage-à-trois*, this is a kind of collective male marriage. What transcends camp is the knowingness of these exchanges — Spock is in on the joke, most of the time readably mock-offended, which only leads to more laughter on Kirk and McCoy's part — and the depth of feeling the three men palpably share for one another.

The depth of the friendship among Kirk-Spock-McCoy reimagines white male homosocial power as tenderness, humor, good-natured affectionate teasing, and lasting authentic bonds. The image of the homosocial in Original *Trek* is a world apart from the grim, inexorably despairing male world of the Wall Street law firm in Melville's great, harrowing story "Bartleby, the Scrivener." In Melville, the all-male world cannot take care of its own, leaving (despite the narrator's clumsy but also well-meaning efforts) Bartleby alone to die in the Tombs. In Original *Trek*, the one who "prefers not to," the potential Bartleby, Spock, has his conflicts with the crew, with McCoy, but the alien, exotic, cryptic, mysterious, non-joiner, intransigent, vulnerable Spock is not — is never — left out to die. Original *Trek* rewrites the homosocial as the homoaffectional, and in so doing resists one of the most problematic aspects of the patriarchal American social order. Spock's tender "Forget" is really an even tenderer "Remember," as he tells McCoy before he sacrifices himself for his crew and his friends in *Star Trek II: The Wrath of Khan* (1982). Ultimately reborn and restored, Spock, the alien Bartleby, gives his life for his friends, never leaving them out in the cold.

Red-Faced with Hysteria: "Turnabout Intruder"

In "Turnabout Intruder," the infamous last episode of Original *Trek*, a crazed, power-mad woman, Janice Lester, ingeniously switches bodies with Captain James T. Kirk, with whom she once had an unhappy love affair and whose masculine power she both craves and despises. "Janice," the woman in whose body Kirk resides, keeps trying to tell everyone what's happened to her; despite the aroused suspicions of the crew, she is kept sedated, treated like someone insane, but is then believed, while "Kirk," whose body power-mad Janice now inhabits, though initially successful, grows increasingly unstable, triggering a mutinous plot to bring "him" down. In the pivotal moment of the episode, Spock mind-melds with "Janice," and after doing so tells her, "I believe you," and then fights to free her — the Kirk inside her, at any rate — defying security guards, a court-martial, and the gyrating theatrics of "Kirk."

Finally, through the aid of Vulcan metaphysics, Real-Kirk once again takes possession of his own body, relegating Real-Janice back to her own.

Long hailed, due to William Shatner's extravagant hamminess, as one of Original *Trek*'s campiest episodes, "Turnabout Intruder" also wears a reputation as one of the most sexist, since it demonstrates female desire for power as a clear sign of insanity. Yet, in my view, "Turnabout," while perhaps not fair play, is less than foul when it comes to the representation of female sexuality — and queerness. Indeed, "Turnabout" is one of the most radical and moving of *Star Trek* episodes.

The sexism of the episode is certainly indisputable — power-hungry Janice exerts her maniacal female will on poor, rational Kirk, and, when she inhabits his body, acts in stereotypically histrionic, hysterical ways. Scotty, the dependably stalwart engineer, sides with Spock and McCoy, who also questions "Kirk's" authenticity, saying that the one thing he has never seen is his Captain "red-faced with hysteria."

But there is, in Bakhtinian terms, a strong dialectic at work here. While the main narrative of the episode propounds a sexist theme, a counter-narrative operates in a manner that, while not exactly woman-affirming, is strongly sympathetic to Janice and her subject position — and also lends itself to queer readings of the episode overall. For, though we know that Janice — the woman we see — is inhabited by Kirk, and though we know that Shatner's Kirk is inhabited by Janice ... we still watch the actors playing these roles; we still watch Spock interacting with a woman guest star whose cause he fights for, and see him siding *against* Shatner's Kirk. It may in the end be an inadvertent result, but, in my experience of the episode, I see military power — Spock in his capacity as second-in-command — joining forces with an institutionalized, hystericized woman, certainly an unusual maneuver. I watch this brave, measured, intelligent woman calmly and persuasively make her case, and watch Spock side with her after hearing her out. She may *be* Kirk, but I don't see Kirk; I see Janice. Janice emerges as the heroine of the episode, a strong, brave, resilient woman fighting for her rights — specifically, the right not to be deemed hysterical, the right not to be institutionalized for being an irrational woman, even if she ostensibly has Kirk inside of her the whole time.

Kirk emerges as a third-sex Kirk. He does not register as either "Kirk" or "Janice" but as the third space of possibility, a liminal, undecidable zone of fluctuating gendered identities. This may be largely the result of Shatner's courageously wild, flamboyant, theatrical performance. He comes across as a hyperemotional, theatrical male, emerging as a fascinating queer figure who disrupts codes of gendered identity, especially those governing the disciplined masculine performance of Starship Captain.

Janice has an accomplice: Dr. Coleman (Harry Landers). Coleman exudes sympathy for Janice, coming across, though a sexual relationship is implied, more as the Gay Best Friend then as her lover—Rupert Everett to her Julia Roberts in *My Best Friend's Wedding*. There is an extraordinary moment that demands a queer reading. Plotting "Janice's" death, "Kirk" attempts to seduce Coleman into murdering her. Coleman initially balks. But "Kirk," behind him, puts his hand on Coleman's shoulder and whispers insinuatingly in his ear. Whether or not this is the Real-Kirk, we still see the Kirk of William Shatner coming on to another man (though this queer reader wishes Harry Landers were less hard on the eyes! But I digress). "Kirk" or Kirk, the Captain Kirk of "Turnabout Intruder" is a radical embodiment of queer energy, a standout figure of queerness in sixties television.

This episode that appears so adamant a testament to anti-woman sentiment is also readable as a sophisticated critique of woman's position within patriarchy. "Kirk" and Coleman speak about Janice's motives: Dr. Coleman says, "You couldn't kill Kirk because you love him! You want *me* to be his murderer." To which statement "Kirk" responds: "Kirk: Love *Him*? I love the life he led, the power of a starship commander. It's my life now." What Janice craves is power, not Kirk himself. In this manner, she is pointedly *not* the virago Alex Forrest, played so memorably by Glenn Close, in *Fatal Attraction* (1987)—a succubus who wants to possess a man who has spurned her—but, instead, a woman thwarted by her culture (the advanced Federation of the twenty-third century, no less) who wants the same opportunities, the power, always already granted a man like Kirk. It should be remembered that Gene Roddenberry himself conceived the story for this episode, and that Roddenberry, in a protofeminist maneuver, attempted to make a woman the Captain's Number One, or First Officer, in the series: in the pilot episode "The Cage," he presented such a character (played by Majel Barrett, Roddenberry's wife, who went on to play the comparatively docile Nurse Chapel), but was not allowed to do so by NBC, the network that aired *Star Trek*, in the actual series. Perhaps Roddenberry had more sympathy for Janice than is immediately apparent.

When, in the end, Real-Janice is forced back into the shell of her own body, as Real-Kirk rightfully regains his, it is a truly piercing moment. She cries the heartbroken tears of recognition—of her inescapable status as woman, the ever–Second Sex. The restoration of proper gendered identities is not treated in celebratory fashion but as the grimly inevitable restoration of a necessary but inherently flawed social order. Kirk: "Her life could have been as rich as any woman's. If only ... if only...." This, the last dialog spoken on the original *Star Trek*, reveals a great deal about the gender politics of the episode, or at least the dialectical examination of gender roles. Kirk seems to be implicitly acknowledging that even in his futuristic, advanced, enlightened era, the role of women is delimited, constricted, curtailed, barren. The iterated phrase "if only" ostensibly refers to Janice's mental state — if only she had been a happier woman, none of this would have happened — but it could also be heard as Kirk's tacit admission of gendered disparity: If only my culture weren't so limiting in terms of gender roles, so misogynistic at its core, perhaps Janice would have had more opportunities and not been forced into so desperate a strategy. Despite all that he's endured, in the end, watching the pitiable wreck of the "restored" Janice, Kirk sadly states, "I don't want to destroy her." As the properly masculinist emblem of the futuristic but atavistic invincible, infinite patriarchal order he embodies, Kirk acknowledges that it is patriarchy, the very order he stands for, that has so wounded and vanquished deranged but understandably furious, driven Janice. Like *Paradise Lost*, an Original *Trek* touchstone (Khan refers to it in "Space Seed"), "Turnabout Intruder" shows us a woman negotiating a purloined patriarchal power she cannot properly access but intensely desires.

Original *Trek* often surprises in its depiction of femininity and desire. In the episode "Metamorphosis," Kirk, Spock, and McCoy meet the inventor of the warp drive, Zephram Cochrane, long thought dead, on a desolate planet. The Companion, a Calypso-like alien entity (Calypso was the goddess who kept Odysseus in amorous captivity, for several years, against his will), has kept Zephram alive and in her control for several years. The *Enterprise* crew also includes a frigid professional woman who, once possessed by the entity, experiences love for the first time; her frigidity melts away and she looks awakened by desire and longing. While the sexual frigidity of the woman professional aligns with negative stereotypes of the mannish, sex-hating modern woman, the episode's insistence on rendering desire uncanny and otherworldly makes it complexly affecting — by defamiliarizing normative heterosexual desire, it makes heterosexuality a new and unusual way to discuss and contemplate desire, in all its mysteriousness, itself. The same can be said of many Original *Trek* episodes, which is quite an achievement, even if always a partial and problematic one. There's no escaping Trekkian sexism; but it should be remembered that the show, when it comes to desire and sexuality, contains multitudes.

Two

FUTURES END
Star Trek Allegory and the Representation of Queer Characters

In Chapter One, we considered the ways in which Original *Trek* renders heterosexuality in such a stylized manner that it emerges as an allegorical version of itself. In this chapter, I make the case that queer desire is also represented in allegorical terms, though in very distinct ways. We constantly "see" heterosexuality in *Trek*; to say that heterosexuality is explicit in *Trek* is to say that water is wet. We never see queer life explicitly represented in *Trek*. Yet through allegorical means, *Trek* has a strong, stirring tradition of representing queer desire.

Trek has often been criticized, and rightly so, for its failure to represent homosexuality explicitly. Given that any representation of homosexuality on *Star Trek* is, at best and at most, allegorical; given the ban that exists to this day on any direct reference to queer life in *Trek*, it may seem strange to make a case for the value of queer Trekkian allegory. Clearly, the failure actually to represent queer life in *Trek* is an unsatisfactory situation not only for the legion of *Trek* fans but also for the liberal mythos of the franchise itself: how can a series whose philosophy is summarized by the famous acronym IDIC— "infinite diversity in infinite combinations"—continue to relegate a tenth of human life to the unspeakable sidelines? (It is telling that one of the major impetuses behind the current wave of fan-made films featuring characters from Original *Trek* is the representation of new homosexual characters.)

Without exculpating *Star Trek* for its failures in this regard, I will be suggesting throughout this chapter that the power of allegorical representation should not be dismissed: it can have an urgency and emotional resonance that make a significant contribution to the effort to challenge normative structures of identity and desire. Allegory, in other words, can be not only part of anti-homophobic representational efforts but also even more resonant and affecting than efforts that proceed from an explicit, "realistic" basis. Watching *Trek* with an eye on the queer potentialities of allegory enlarges the significance of many *Trek* episodes, many of which would appear to have no queer resonance at all.

Demon Eden

"Demon," from *Star Trek: Voyager*'s fourth season, is a perfect example of such an episode. *Voyager*, in desperate circumstances and in search of the deuterium the ship needs in order to function, investigates, as a last resort, a Class Y, or "Demon," planet — blood-red, volcanic, unpredictable, inhospitable to human life — for its promises of the grievously needed resosurce. Harry Kim (Garrett Wang), the earnest young ensign, and Tom Paris (Robert Duncan McNeil), the brash helmsman and pilot, first go down to the planet via shuttle.[1] Once on the surface, Tom and Harry discover a pool of lustrous silver liquid. When Tom has his back turned, Harry disappears. To Tom's horror, Harry has been submerged within the silver pool. Tom drags him out, but their spacesuits both malfunction as they lurch towards the shuttle and then fall inertly to the ground. When they are not heard from for an alarmingly long time, Captain Kathryn Janeway (Kate Mulgrew) makes the risky decision to land the ship on the Demon planet. Chakotay, the first officer, and Seven of Nine, a former Borg who is now a human woman, search the planet for the missing Tom and Harry. They discover them — without their spacesuits! Happily breathing in the noxious fumes of the Demon planet, Tom and Harry encourage Chakotay and Seven to discard their spacesuits.

Back on *Voyager*, Tom and Harry gasp for air. The Doctor, a sentient hologram, floods a force-fielded section of sickbay with fumes from the planet so that Tom and Harry can breathe. Later, the "real" Tom and Harry, still in their spacesuits and on the ground, are discovered on the planet. It turns out that the silver liquid is a silver blood, a biomimetic compound that copies DNA. The silver blood never experienced sentience until its contact with Harry and then Tom. And it wants more. The Demon-Harry says that they can't bear to be left alone. After some confused arguing with the Demon-Harry, Janeway decides to allow the silver blood to make copies of all of the crew members. In the last, haunting shot of the episode, *Voyager* takes off from the Demon planet, leaving behind a new, Demon crew.

"Demon" is emblematic of the queer potentiality in Trekkian allegory. For what "Demon" amounts to is nothing less than a rewriting of Genesis with two *males* as the first human pair of a new world. Tom and Harry are the first members of the new race of silver blood. They are given dominion over the planet; they seed it through their desire for replication. Bypassing normative heterosexual reproduction, they replicate themselves through the sampling of the crew members' DNA. A Demon Adam and Steve, this Tom and Harry are the parents of a new, alien, queer race.

As Judith Butler argued in her essay "Imitation and Gender Insubordination," gender is a copy for which there is no original.[2] To offer a variation on this theoretical proposition, we can argue the same for heterosexuality. That is, heterosexuality posits itself as the sexual originality from which homosexuality is a pathetic, derivative copy; but if we debunk heterosexuality's claim to originality, seeing it, as well, as a copy for which there is no original, the entire question of originals and copies becomes something altogether different, a queer phenomenon. These silver-blood beings are copies that contest the authenticity of their originals. Their uncanny, non-normative reproduction provides a queer alternative to heterosexual normativity.

Radical Otherness

The Season Five *Voyager* episode "Course: Oblivion" takes the "Demon" premise even further, in the process becoming one of the most provocative and moving of *Trek* episodes, with a tragic tone throughout. As *Trek* critic Jamahl Epsicokhan describes the plot:

> This *Voyager* crew is the copy of the real crew that was created in "Demon." Every individual on the ship used to be some sort of biomimetic silver fluid that obtained sentience when *Voyager* interacted with them in the previous episode. Somehow, the ship itself was also replicated. Now, enhancements to the warp engines, we learn, have caused this "sickness" ("Each and every one of you will disintegrate," Doc says helpfully)—leading to the crew's reversion to their original biological state where the only hope for survival might mean returning to their original environment.[3]

Epsicokhan goes on to denounce the episode for the ludicrousness of its plot, the same criticisms he (along with other *Trek* critics) leveled at "Demon," which generated even more critical opprobrium than its sequel.

The problem with a great deal of *Trek* criticism is that it is deeply literal-minded, almost entirely plot-based, focusing purely on plausibility. Epsicokhan is an intelligent critic. But if one reads *Trek* episodes either for plausibility or slavish devotion to continuity, one misses out almost entirely on the other aspects of *Trek*, namely the significance of its allegories, which have a value beyond the mechanics of plot.

"Course: Oblivion" seems to me precisely the kind of episode that raises profound questions that have little to do with its plot, although the plot provides the vehicle for these questions. There is a distinct chill in the air when the Vulcan security officer Tuvok (Tim Russ) announces the crew's real identity: "We are all duplicates." This entire episode is about beings that are not real, that have no originality or authenticity. Yet we watch them loving, laughing, suffering, dying. The episode ends with even their last desperate attempt to register their lives for posterity being squelched, as a memorial buoy, along with the disintegrating replica of the ship, explodes before the "real" *Voyager* can discover it. The silver-blood, biomimetic crew are *nothing*, and they go back to nothingness. They have no life, no future, no purpose. They seem emblematic of the death-drive-embracing, posterity-denying, queer subjectivity Lee Edelman describes in his study *No Future*, in which he urges queers to embrace the very marginal, anti-life, abnegated social positions to which they are consigned by a homophobic social order (a thesis with which, it should be added, I am very much in disagreement). Yet in inhabiting this episode and attempting to continue their existence, these nothing-beings, the copied *Voyager* crew, provide us with an extraordinary opportunity to contemplate what distinguishes the real from the fake, the original from the copy, and, I would argue, heterosexual love from queer love.

The episode begins with a wedding, but this wedding, full of laughter and friendship and love, is a harbinger of doom. As the mirthful crew shower the just married couple with rice, the visuals turn into slow motion, defamiliarizing the wedding scene and giving it an eerie effect. Ominously, those grains of rice, traditionally a symbol of fertility, fall on the floor and pour into the corridors of the floor beneath them; we watch as these corridors morph, bend, twist with decay (molecular decohesion). Immediately, the episode denatures everything we associate with the "normal": marriage, the chief ritual display of institutionalized heterosexuality, becomes a site not of joy, prosperity, and fertility but of imminent suffering, death, nullity.

Janeway's obsessive drive to get her crew back home to Earth becomes a fascinating problem here. What will their families and friends make of these silver-blood copies back on Earth? Would even the enlightened future-humans of *Voyager* embrace such radical difference? Even the real *Voyager* crew's ability to accept them is questioned. The biomimetic Doctor urges his Captain Janeway to find the real *Voyager* crew, whose DNA might be able to re-enhance the copy-crew's deteriorating bodies. "How do we know she'll help us?" copy–Janeway says of the real Janeway. "Because," urgently responds the Doctor, "she's *you*." Yes, but who is she? Who are *you*? "Course: Oblivion" puts forth the Trekkian proposition that you or I can be anyone and *anything*. But the copy–Janeway's worry that her human counterpart will not want to help her and her crew suggests that there are limits — embodiments of life — beyond the pale even for the freethinking futuristic individuals of *Trek*.

At its most politically bracing, *Trek* asks us to accept the notion of a *radical otherness*, the authenticity of life that may be remarkably distinct from our own. In this capacity, the brilliant Season One Original *Trek* episode "The Devil in the Dark" is exemplary. A molten/solid rock that possesses sentience demonstrates that it can mourn and kill for its dead and endangered young and can even write a message of (literally) searing poignancy: "No Kill I," the ungrammatical nature of the message making it shockingly, almost unbearably child-like. Spock mind-melds with this creature, which he discovers to be part of a dying race called the Horta. Spock, melding, howls with the anguish of this devastated rock-mother, sharing in her grief over her murdered children and her rage against the human murderers. (Perhaps this is a nod to the classical myth of Niobe: inconsolably grief-stricken when the gods kill all her children after she vainly boasts of their superiority to the gods, she is turned into a weeping rock.)

In the Season Five *Voyager* episode "Warhead," the Doctor discovers a missile stuck in a rock. The missile speaks, in an algorithmic language that the holographic Doctor can understand. In another defamiliarizing, surprising moment, the Doctor expresses the missile's feelings: "*It's terrified.*" That this shockingly human affect is associated with a missile, a weapon of mass destruction, makes the situation more disorientingly strange. *Trek* is full of such oddly poignant moments that center on the revelation that an object seemingly devoid of any conceivable life not only has life but also emotions, dare I say it, *a soul*.

Being made to feel the longing, anger, and anguish of the copy-crew of "Course: Oblivion," we are made to consider that those different from us have a legitimate claim to their experiences and emotional life. When we think of the general human indifference to suffering and, worse yet, compulsion to force others to suffer, the radicalism of this otherness, the demand that we recognize its validity and the depth of its experience, is truly astonishing. In queer terms (it should be noted that one of the co-writers of the episode was Bryan Fuller, a very talented and openly gay screenwriter), "Course: Oblivion," with its scenes of love and grief between members of a different but also the same, "inferior," race, asks the audience to accept the legitimacy of difference, the legitimacy of loving differently, of love among those who are different. In this manner, when we see Tom and his dying bride B'Elanna Torres (Roxann Dawson) having their last, exquisitely tender conversation before B'Elanna dies — the disfigurations on her face evoke the grim splotches of Kaposi's sarcoma on AIDS patients — we are not just seeing love between marital man and woman but love between other and other, between beings that represent social abjection, as well as physical decay and the inevitability of mortality. In other words, this scene of heterosexual love and grief functions allegorically as a scene of *queer* love and grief. In allegorical

Trekkian terms, heterosexuality symbolizes queer love, a radical otherness with an undeniable legitimacy.

Along similar lines, when the crew, some of whom begin to "remember" their former silver-blood lives on the Demon Planet (a detail one wishes the writers hadn't dropped in so casually, or had actually taken the time to explore), question copy–Janeway about the authenticity of their identities, Janeway's response is that all of their emotions — memories, experiences — have a validity. "I'm not about to tell you that they're not real," Janeway says. Given the history of denunciations of homosexual love as "counterfeit," Janeway's words have deep resonance. This is a point worth emphasizing because some powerful figures in queer theory — such as Lee Edelman and David Halperin — make quite an insistent point that any belief in queer "love" is a slavish imitation of heterosexuality and that queers should celebrate in precisely their abject, counterfeit status. "Course: Oblivion" makes a strong case for the counterfeit, but this case is not founded on an embrace of decay, suffering, and death. Instead, it is founded on the legitimacy of emotional experiences, shared bonds, kinship, family, friendship, and love not based on normative models. When the copy-crew all, finally, die, they achieve the most radical state of otherness possible. They become death, true nothingness, leaving behind no record. But the episode asks us to question the nothingness of nothingness; that they lived and loved has "a consecration of its own," to lift from *The Scarlet Letter*.

The Possibilities and the Limitations of Queer Allegory: "The Outcast"

The most famous example of a Trekkian queer allegory is the Season Five *Star Trek: The Next Generation (TNG)* episode "The Outcast," written by Jeri Taylor. A close runner-up would be another *TNG* episode, "The Host," from Season Four. "The Host" has been widely criticized for its apparent homophobia, while "The Outcast," though similarly criticized, has also been much more emphatically appreciated as a positive Trekkian statement about gay rights. Robin A. Roberts has offered an excellent assessment of the episode's strengths and failings as an anti-homophobic effort, so I will not rehearse her points, with which I am in general agreement, save for her overlooking of the importance of the performance by the guest star actor, Melinda Culea, in the role of Soren, the titular outcast. Without Culea's sensitive, quietly devastating performance, the episode would not work nearly as well as it does.

"The Outcast" remains an interesting example of the possibilities and limitations of Trekkian queer allegory. It represents the effort of Jeri Taylor, who would go on to create the feminist *Voyager*, to get a Trekkian gay-rights story on the small screen. As has been widely reported, Gene Roddenberry, the creator of *Star Trek*, wanted to have a gay character on *TNG*, a goal that he was unable to accomplish before his death in 1991. Taylor's script is in many ways a laudable effort to represent queer sexuality. But what is most interesting about the episode is that—while having many deeply moving moments—it fails precisely because it is *too* explicit about its effort as gay allegory. Exploring exactly the ways in which the episode fails in this regard reveals a great deal about *Trek*'s views of queer life as well how allegory functions on *Trek*.

As Picard tells us in the first sentence of the episode, the J'naii are an androgynous race who need the *Enterprise*'s help to retrieve a shuttle from "null space." Significantly, that they are androgynous is the first thing we learn about them, as if their androgyny were so notable that Picard must include it in his first mention of them in his log. The J'naii are not only androgynous, but have abolished gender altogether, just as the fastidiously logical Vulcans have abolished all emotions.

Soren, a member of the J'naii, works with First Officer Riker (Jonathan Frakes) to retrieve the shuttle. As they work together, Soren reveals her deep dark secret to Riker: *She is a woman!* This is a calamitous situation for an individual on a planet that has abolished gender. Falling in love with Riker and finally, when on trial, openly declaring her gendered identity, Soren is clearly an allegory for the oppressed homosexual coming out in homophobic society.

To his credit, as Robin Roberts reports, Jonathan Frakes complained about *TNG*'s failure of nerve to make Soren "obviously male."[4] I would point out something that Roberts elides a bit: in her description of the harrowing tale of abuse suffered by a J'naii who identifies as male and is beaten and ridiculed by his classmates, Soren not only points out that this J'naii identifies as male but that he is attracted to *other* males. Robert Scheerer brilliantly directs Soren's monologue in this scene. In the extremely close space of the shuttle, Soren recounts the tale to Riker with an almost piercingly palpable yet restrained empathy; Scheerer films Culea and Frakes in close-up, allowing Soren's sad, steady words to take effect but also putting us in extraordinarily intimate contact with the actors. To my mind, this scene is the most powerful in the episode. Soren's bravura speech to the J'naii is a great moment also, but it has a showier, more platform-statement impersonality inextricably linked to its eloquence.

The episode also is notable for eroticizing Riker, initially represented as another Galaxy Lothario on the series, someone pursuing alien babes. Here, we are put in the position of admiring *his* sex appeal, as well as his very masculinity, exotic to the presumably genderless but transgressively gender-oriented Soren. She even asks him to describe his genitals to her. Seeing Riker through Soren's transgressive gaze, we are asked to fall in love with Riker along with her. What is it that Riker sees in Soren, however? In one of the most interesting moments, Riker asks his old flame, empathic counselor Deanna Troi (Marina Sirtis), if it's okay for him to pursue Soren romantically. The entire conversation feels oddly like a late-stage coming-out scene, a sense reinforced by sentiments Troi expresses about always accepting Riker for who he is despite the "change" he is going through. Then they kiss, as if to honor the validity of their former bond but also to acknowledge that Riker is no longer the same man.

In a scene in which cast regulars play poker, the Klingon Worf (Michael Dorn) expresses discomfort bordering on genuine disgust towards the J'naii, which Troi, to her (and Jeri Taylor's) credit, calls him on. This discussion strongly codes both the J'naii and Riker's desire for Soren as queer, as Worf is reproved for his all-but-explicit homophobia.

There are certainly notable anti-homophobic elements in the episode. But ultimately the problem with "The Outcast" is that it leaves one wondering why *Trek* bothered at all to represent homosexual love if it was simply going to do so in the guise of a conventional heterosexual love story. Indeed, the episode, as Roberts astutely observes, ends up tilting the balance towards the very homophobia it fights against:

> The most glaring example of the episode's conservatism is the positioning of Soren as female. This defamiliarization may make viewers see that being discriminated against because of your sexual orientation is unfair. However, casting all the J'naii as women and Soren as feminine reifies heterosexuality. Our sympathy is directed toward Soren, whose happiness seems to depend on her rejection of homosexuality. Her gendered, feminine self is more appealing than the stern, unemotional rigidity of the other J'naii. Our sympathy is directed toward what Soren has lost — her feminine self— rather than with what she becomes, an ungendered, androgynous self.[5]

Indeed, the episode seems to be a negative *lesbian* parable: the hostile older butch dyke rejects the younger, fragile femme (echoes of Robert Aldrich's controversial 1968 film *The Killing of Sister George*). The best that can finally be said about the episode is that it is a mixed bag of homophilia and homophobia, of both tolerance and fear, if not outright repugnance. As such, it is a classic instance of *Trek*'s attitudes towards difference generally, homosexuality specifically.

An Allegorical Crisis

The episode, moving though it is, is a failure. But it's a failure of a peculiar kind, a failure that stems from what can be described as *an allegorical crisis*. In so obviously straining towards redressing previous lapses in terms of gay characters yet remaining resolutely in an allegorical mode, the episode schizophrenically attempts to name and to unname, to speak the language of queer desire *and* to keep this language stringently coded. Metaphor collapses into direct reference: this queer allegory *names* heterosexuality as the oppressed sexual minority, which is then to be taken as an allegory for an *unnamed* queerness. What is named, then, because it is so intimately related to what is left unnamed, ends up taking precedence over anything else. In other words, the episode cancels out its queer content and becomes most heavily pitched as a commentary about aggrieved heterosexual relations.

Absurdly, the episode becomes a kind of poignant paean to the kind of simple boy-meets-girl romance the hardworking *Enterprise* crew, these wearied workaholics of the future, no longer have time for; androgyny emerges as the fearful fate that awaits those who sublimate all of their sexual desires for the sake of their work, a metaphor not for homosexuality, ultimately, but for the desexualization of those who toil in the corporate workplace. The dogged drones of the *Enterprise* are deprived of sex, and Riker's love for Soren emerges as a desperate attempt to reclaim his own closeted *heterosexuality*.

Reclaiming his lost masculinity and erotic life, Riker beams down to the androgyne-planet, accompanied, surprisingly, by Worf, who has implicitly come around to accepting Riker's desire and Soren's difference. Yet Worf has never appeared more overpoweringly, massively hypermasculine than he does on the planet when juxtaposed against the J'naii security force. Played by masculine-looking women, the security forces that charge against Riker and Worf seem like a lesbian army, one shown to be easily decimated by these aggressive Federation males. The ludicrous, camp-classic image of mighty Riker and mightier Worf toppling these comparatively puny androgyne/lesbian security forces completely overturns the sensitive treatment of sexual otherness previously exhibited by the episode. While it is effectively harrowing to learn that Soren has been brainwashed into accepting her "normal" ungendered, androgynous nature — shades of the grotesque shock-therapy treatments gays were forced to undergo in the Cold War era of the 1950s and 1960s — the final statement made by the episode resonates not with anti-homophobic but with *anti-feminist* feeling. Soren appears to have joined in with some prohibitive, man-hating feminist cult, a viewpoint reflective of Reagan-era conservative attitudes.

I am not about to suggest that allegory that resists altogether any explicit reference to homosexuality is preferable to an explicit treatment of queer life. But insofar as what *Trek* has actually managed to achieve — the aching, desolate loneliness of Original *Trek*'s eerie, depopulated worlds; the sense of profound aloneness as *Voyager* roams through uncharted space; the enduring, increasingly passionate friendship of Kirk and Spock; the strangeness, the otherness, the deeply displaced quality of non-human characters like Spock, Data, Odo, the Doctor, Seven of Nine, T'Pol — all of these allegorical representations much more powerfully evoke the experience of otherness than the clumsy and ultimately incoherent quasi-explicit allegory of "The Outcast." This is ruptured allegory, allegory straining to remain true to its own metaphorical form *while* speaking the language of direct reference. "The Outcast," however, is far more successful than the more explicit queer allegory of *Enterprise*'s Second-Season episodes "Cogenitor" and "Stigma."

Frustrating Allegory: "Cogenitor"/"Stigma"

"Stigma," which aired February 5, 2003, was made at the behest of Viacom, which demanded that all UPN shows (the former network on which *Enterprise* aired for four years) make an episode that dealt with HIV/AIDS. Apparently, the allegorical was the only mode in which the episode could broach the subject, with AIDS apparently having been cured by the 22nd century. "Cogenitor" is a different kind of episode, however. Here, queerness is literally named, as the "third gender" — a term evocative of "the third sex," as nineteenth-century sexologists called homosexuals.

In "Cogenitor" the *Enterprise* crew come in contact with a race, the Vissians, whose males and females use third-gender beings, the titular cogenitors, to procreate. The actual process is left up to our own imaginations, but as Memory Alpha, the *Star Trek* Wiki, notes, "the cogenitor does not pass on genetic material to the offspring they help create; they supply an enzyme during the sex act which facilitates conception." The problem dealt with by the episode is not this third-gender reproduction, however — which one might imagine earlier incarnations of *Trek* would have made the central, disturbing issue — but the treatment of the third-gender beings by their society. Completely depersonalized, given no clear identity and no education, called only "it," the cogenitors are an oppressed race, with no purpose save the role they play in their society's reproduction.

It is precisely in turning what appears to be an issue of sexuality and gender into an issue of race and class that the episode forfeits the potentially profound impact of the issues with which it initially appears to grapple, opting instead for a safer and more predictable Trekkian narrative. This is not to suggest that racial and class oppression—the theme the episode ends up exploring—are not vitally important subjects. The problem is that the sexual-gender themes end up being entirely incidental to the later race-class one, which, on *Trek*, has historically been far easier to represent.

Charles "Trip" Tucker (Connor Trineer, a dead ringer for George W. Bush), the young Southern good ol' boy engineer, first meets the cogenitor of the episode at dinner with the solidly upper-middle-class Vissian couple. Sitting silently at the table, its head down, the cogenitor has obviously been made to feel inferior, to occupy a position of social abjection. When Trip asks it what its name is, the cogenitor responds that it doesn't have one. The bland, smug Vissian couple are utterly mystified by Trip's increasing concern for the cogenitor's well-being, though they do try to answer his questions with a smooth politeness. Eventually, Trip, completely against Starfleet protocols of non-interference, teaches the cogenitor to read, thereby instilling in it a rapidly enlarging sense of personal identity and desire to explore. The cogenitors, it is discovered, are absolutely identical to the other Vissians in terms of mental capacity; it is only their class status that makes them different, a subaltern race. But the Vissians, once they learn of Trip's intervention, are appalled. They have no interest in the cogenitor apart from its reproductive function. When the cogenitor, who decides to call itself Charles, in honor of Trip, rebels and asks for asylum, the whole conflict intensifies. Refusing to let the cogenitor go, the Vissians take their cogenitor back. Shortly thereafter, the cogenitor kills itself.

This is a decent *Enterprise* episode, well-directed by LeVar Burton, who played Geordi LaForge on *TNG*. As with "The Outcast," a superb performance by the main guest actor enhances the episode: Becky Wahlstrom, as the cogenitor, is a remarkable mixture of the masculine and the feminine, and when her eyes light up as she smiles, for the first time, when discovering that she can read, the episode really shines along with her. But what is frustrating about this series entry is that it dispenses with the queer dimensions of the cogenitor-as-metaphor and becomes, instead, yet another in the tedious line of Prime Directive/non-interference episodes, as well as a predictable race allegory.

The whole question of the sweatshop-like oppression of the cogenitors, while a vital issue, has the unfortunate effect of blanching out the particularities of the cogenitor metaphor; this could be *any* enslaved race, any enslaved class. The "third gender" angle, initially promisingly provocative, transforms into a rote oppressed-race plot. One gets the sense again that the more literal-minded Trekkian allegory becomes, the less effective it is in queer terms. Named, the third-gender loses specificity; the episode becomes something familiar and predictable, even if, admittedly, the entire question of non-interference is hardly a safe and stable one.

A device that links "Cogenitor" to "Stigma" is that of using a sexually forward woman's erotic designs on a male as camouflage — or compensation — for the queer issues it raises, a kind of heterosexual fail-safe. In "Cogenitor," Malcolm Reed (Dominic Keating) and a Vissian woman (Laura Interval) share erotic banter over a cheese plate. Vissian food is highly pungent and fragrant, and cheese is the most "fragrant" human food Reed could find. As they banter over the cheese, which they sensually sniff, these two enjoy an obvious erotic frisson. Burton, the director, takes great delight in later visualizing the physical disparity between the actors: the Vissian woman looms over the comparatively diminutive Reed, and her seduction of him is comical as well as sexually charged. One gets the sense that she could pick him up with the same ease she did a piece of Stilton.

In "Stigma," one of the wives of the Denobulan Dr. Phlox (John Billingsley) visits the ship. Denobulan woman are the sexual aggressors; moreover, Denobulan have open marriages. Comedically and erotically, this sexually predatory, lasciviously smiling Denobulan woman attempts to seduce Trip, who painfully, awkwardly rebuffs her advances. The episode ends with Phlox and his wife guffawing over Trip's discomfort, emblematic of his species' apparently still Victorian strictures over sexuality. "Humans!" the Denobulans giggle.

"Stigma," the mandated HIV/AIDS episode, is a sequel to an earlier episode, "Fusion," in which the *Enterprise* encounters rogue Vulcans who want to reclaim their emotional lives, denied them by the protocols of Vulcan logic. But these rogue Vulcans are shown to be treacherous and violent; one of them goes so far as to force emotions out of T'Pol, the Vulcan First Officer (Jolene Blalock), in a kind of rape scene. (Similar rape-like mind-meld moments occur in the 1991 *Star Trek VI: The Undiscovered Country* and in the *Voyager* episodes "Meld" and "Random Thoughts"; what in the 1960s was a radical joining of consciousnesses becomes in later *Trek* an unleashing of violent will.) In "Stigma," T'Pol is shown to be suffering from Pa'nar Syndrome, an incurable disease that she contracted from the "Fusion" Vulcans. Herein lies the AIDS metaphor, with T'Pol shown to be an innocent victim of disease, akin to those who received an HIV–tainted blood transfusion. As *Star Trek.Com* parses the plot:

> T'Pol explains that Pa'nar Syndrome carries a certain stigma on Vulcan. A small number of Vulcans are born with the ability to form a "mind-meld," and it is through this act that the disease is transmitted. Anyone can be on

the receiving end of a meld, however, and T'Pol found herself in that very position when she was attacked by the Vulcan Tolaris the previous year. Because this telepathic minority's behavior is considered "unnatural" on Vulcan, those who carry the disease face prejudice — T'Pol would most likely lose her commission if the High Command were to learn of her condition. Archer urges T'Pol to tell the High Command that she was forced to meld, but she refuses, not wanting to fuel their bigotry.[6]

The day is sort of saved when Yuris, one of the Vulcan doctors, reveals that he, too, is a mind-melder, which leads to T'Pol being allowed to remain on *Enterprise* but also to Yuris's suspension. As played by the dark-eyed, tremulous Jeffrey Hayenga, Yuris is obviously meant to be read as a queer character, a sense deepened by the meeting Yuris and T'Pol secretly have in a dark nighttime alley, a scene coded as a coming-out moment or as gay cruising.

T'Pol's refusal to "name" the mind-melders as such is clearly principled, and the episode makes an admirable effort to speak out against prejudice and stigma against those with AIDS, in metaphorical terms. Indeed, the episode works to the extent that it does precisely in its allegorical terms, the mind-meld a fascinating allegory for illicit sexual contact. As I argue in Chapter Five, the mind-meld on the previous series, *Voyager*, was mined for its considerable homoerotic potential as well as its potentiality as a rape metaphor. But the problem with "Stigma" is that its focus remains on T'Pol's "innocent" victimization by both disease and stigma. For a queer-allegory episode, the focus on a series regular rather than on a guest-star is unusual, and a very safe, predictable maneuver. (Yuris is an ancillary character.) As "Cogenitor" and "Stigma" suggest, this series seemed more willing to "name" the queer, but at the same time was much less willing to explore the strange, lonely experience of difference. For all of its flaws, "The Outcast" truly puts the viewer in the outcast position, makes us like Soren precisely on her terms, as who she is, and, in that great monologue scene on the shuttle, puts us in immensely intimate contact with her pathos. There is pathos in these *Enterprise* episodes, but there isn't really the same emotional intimacy. We see the cogenitor from Trip's do-gooder position; we see the stigmatized mind-melder's from T'Pol's; there is no attempt to see and feel through the *outcast's* perspective. And by this late stage in *Trek*'s history, the very question of allegorical representation becomes more strained, more vexed, especially when the allegories are cast in such clumsy terms.

Futures End: Or, You Gotta Love That Borg Queen

Seeing the strained efforts of these quasi-explicit queer *Trek* allegories, one wonders if *Trek* can really *do* queer allegory at all. I would argue that it can, but when it does, it does so only through indirect means. The Borg Queen of the 1996 *Star Trek* film *First Contact* is a prime example of successful queer allegory precisely because of the indirectness of the allegory. I discuss the Queen in much greater detail in Chapters Seven and Eight; for now, I want to note the Borg Queen's queer potentialities, especially evident at the climax of the film.

The Borg Queen has captured Captain Picard, strapping him to a gurney. It seems that she has seduced Data into league with her; Data appears to send torpedoes from the *Enterprise* to destroy Zephram Cochrane's warp-driven shuttle. The Borg, with the *Enterprise* on their trail, have traveled back to Earth to rewrite history. After Zephram Cochrane made this historic 22nd century flight, the first of its kind, the peaceful, logical Vulcans, noticing the human use of warp technology, make first contact with Earth. The Borg plan to stop first contact from happening at all, and to turn all humans retroactively from this point on into Borg drones. When the Borg Queen captures Picard, it is to show him that not only has he failed but he has also failed humanity. "Watch your futures end," she says, as the torpedoes careen towards Cochran's shuttle.

What makes this a queer moment, and the Borg Queen an allegorical queer character, is the Borg Queen's ecstatic position towards the annihilation of the human future. If we recall Lee Edelman's thesis in *No Future*, the Borg Queen seems its perfect fulfillment, a queer character who positions herself *against* futurity, reproductivity, progress. This sexual monster ravenously relishes the thought of human annihilation, the *end* of the human.

Her plot is foiled: Data betrays her, programming the torpedoes to miss the shuttle and freeing Picard. But what lingers in the mind is the Borg Queen's passionate villainy, her appetite for the dashing of all of our hopes. What is rousing, in a queer way, about her dastardly desires is that they are not focused on normative goals—human sexuality in an effort to reproduce the human line—but precisely on goals that are their opposite. Queer desire can be located in *Trek* in characters that elude, resist, or thwart the normative patterns, standards, and practices of the *Star Trek* monomyth.

In the next two chapters, I focus on two extremely provocative and affecting allegorical renderings of queer male sexuality on *Star Trek: Voyager*. These allegorical projects occur not in one episode but across the run of the series as a whole.

Three

PROJECTING DESIRE
Holograms, Artists, and Gay Male Allegory

Despite its reputation for failing ever to do so, *Star Trek* does represent queer sexuality, though it does so through allegorical means. One especially significant dimension of this allegorical practice is the creation of characters who metaphorically represent queer identity without explicit signifiers of that identity. In this chapter and the next, I examine two such characters: here, the pointedly unnamed holographic Doctor from the series *Star Trek: Voyager*, whom I read as an allegory of the gay male artist; and in the next chapter, *Voyager*'s cook-nurse-ambassador alien Neelix, whom I read as an allegory of the male mother.

As an allegorical figure of the gay male author, *Voyager*'s Doctor emerges as a liminal figure between the *Trek*-text proper and the explicit representation of gay men. The gay male author disrupts and endangers the coherence of the dominant text even as the text contains his subversive energies and delimits his agency, such as it is. *Voyager*, the first and only *Trek* series to feature a female Captain, provides in Captain Janeway the figure of the phallic mother upon whom these queer allegories pivot. Of particular interest here is the conflict between the female icon — the star, the diva, the action heroine — and the gay male, stereotypically positioned as her sidekick, adoring fan, or rival. As this chapter will demonstrate, the female star of the genre television show represents, in Freudian terms, *the mother to the emergent homosexual child*, represented by the gay male artist, who refuses to identify with the father and remains transgressively and problematically identified with the mother. Dramatically embodied in the forceful presence of Kate Mulgrew, Captain Janeway has attracted huge numbers of gay male fans; the Janeway-Doctor relationship, then, not only generally allegorizes the straight woman–gay male relationship but also that between the diva-icon and the gay male fan. Through an analysis of *Voyager*, I explore the dynamics of gay male fetishization of the female icon, figured not only as the mother but as *the phallic mother*. This chapter makes the argument that not only does *Voyager* allegorically represent the gay male artist but that its representation has a radical dimension. In order to demonstrate the radicalism of *Voyager*, this chapter compares its representations of the gay male author to that of another significant genre television series, *Buffy the Vampire Slayer*, significant not just in its aesthetic brilliance and cultural influence but in that it, too, showcases a powerful heroine. In considering gay male authorship here in a mainstream genre text that pivots around a strong female character, the action heroine show — a genre that, while having been for some time on the wane, seems to be revivifying with the emergence of new series such as *Fringe* and *Terminator: The Sarah Connor Chronicles* (though not, sadly, the revamped *Bionic Woman*) — this chapter explores the representation of the gay male artist within a dominant text that is itself marked, through its unusual focus on a female protagonist, as "alternative."

Of particular interest here is the *agon*, or conflict, between the female star and the gay male and how it does or does not get resolved. Because this chapter is oriented around the interconnected Freudian views of the homosexual male artist and the phallic mother, it will be helpful to take a moment to revisit Freud's formulations.

Gay Male Artists, Fetishism, and the Phallic Mother

In his famous and enduringly controversial study *Leonardo da Vinci and a Memory of His Childhood,* Freud offers a portrait of the gay male artist as "gentle and kindly to everyone."

> But this feminine delicacy of feeling did not deter him from accompanying condemned criminals on their way to execution in order to study their features distorted by fear and to sketch them in his notebook. Nor did it stop him from devising the cruellest offensive weapons and from entering the service of Cesare Borgia as chief military engineer. He often gave the appearance of being indifferent to good and evil.... Leonardo represented the cool repudiation of sexuality — a thing that would scarcely be expected of an artist and a portrayer of feminine beauty [15–16].[1]

A homosexual artist who surrounded himself with "handsome youths" with whom he most likely did not engage in sexual activity (20), Leonardo "succeeded in sublimating the greater part of his libido into an urge for research" (30) and in converting "his passion into a thirst for knowledge" (22).

Freud's view of the homosexual artist remains as fascinating as it is problematic. For our purposes, my chief interest in this work will be in Freud's treatment of Leonardo as a homosexual male artist who sublimates his desires and occupies a strange, anomalous position between love and hate, sexuality and asexuality, good and evil. However one feels about this Freudian formulation, the portrait of the moral and sexual ambivalence of the gay male artist and his thirst for knowledge, a sublimation of his dangerous homosexual desires, continues to resonate in our culture, as several recent representations of the gay male artist evince. The recent popularity of such films as *Infamous* (2006), *Capote* (2005) and *The Hours* (2003), all of which purport to be about the experience of the gay male artist, and the appearance of other notable and similarly themed independent films such as *The Dying Gaul* (2005) and *Tarnation* (2003), evinces an ongoing, disparate interest in the gay male artist in both films aimed at mass audiences and those targeted at more specialized, "art cinema" moviegoers.

In terms of the concerns of this chapter, Freud's description of the intertwined aspects of Leonardo's sexuality and his early relationship with his mother is crucial. His repressed love for his mother drove him "to take up a homosexual attitude and manifested itself in ideal love for boys" (94). Mother-fixated, morally and sexually ambivalent, his sexuality sublimated into aesthetic endeavor, the gay male artist, a heightened, more grandiose allegory of the gay male himself, emerges in Freud and in popular culture as a beautiful monster, a figure of profound ambivalence.

One highly controversial aspect of Freud's *Leonardo* is his discussion of a very early childhood memory the adult da Vinci wrote down in his notebook. "There is, so far as I know," writes Freud in Chapter Three, "only one place in his scientific notebooks where Leonardo inserts a piece of information about his childhood." Freud refers to a passage about one of the artist's earliest memories: "It seems that I was always destined to be so deeply concerned with vultures; for I recall ... that while I was in my cradle a vulture came down to me, and opened my mouth with its tail, and struck me many times with its tail against my lips" (32).[2] Freud theorizes that Leonardo's homosexuality emerges, in part, from this early episode, which placed Leonardo in a homosexual — i.e., passive — position and also represented a particularly vivid version of a universal early male trauma, the discovery that the mother does not have a penis.

Speaking of the experience of the male child, Freud writes in *Leonardo* that the "erotic attraction that comes from his mother soon culminates in a longing for her genital organ, which he takes to be a penis." "With the discovery, which is not made till later, that women do not have a penis, this longing often turns into its opposite and gives place to a feeling of disgust which in the years of puberty can become the cause of psychical impotence, misogyny and permanent homosexuality" (50). Freud refines this argument further in his 1927 essay "Fetishism": "Probably no male human being is spared the terrifying shock of threatened castration at the sight of the female genitals. We cannot explain why it is that some of them become homosexual in consequence of this experience, others ward it off by creating a fetish, and the great majority overcome it."[3]

The strange aspect of Freud's theory of fetishism in 1927 is that fetishism emerges as a perverse form of heterosexuality, its feverish doppelganger, leaving homosexuality intact as its own perversion and an ingenious coping strategy for the trauma of recognizing the castration of the mother. The fetishist emerges as the heterosexual who failed to overcome this trauma, spending his life reverentially replacing the mother's phantom phallus with the famous substitutes of velvet and fur. It is surprising that Freud didn't take the argument to its logical conclusion: that the phallic mother becomes, for the homosexual male, the fetish. Homosexuality could then be said to employ images of the phallic mother fetishistically, in much the same way that heterosexual fetishists employ velvet and fur, or women's feet and shoes, to replace or restore the mother's phallus.

However one feels about these Freudian formulations, representation and criticism and theory all seem to share in and expand on them in their treatment of gay men's relationship to the phallic mother, most notably in the form of the diva. In the guise of the female star of classical Hollywood or genre television, the diva is the phallic mother worshipped by deviant males. Most of the theorizations of this subject have focused on gay male identificatory practices and the female star of melodrama. Laura Mulvey's original and exhaustively overanalyzed essay "Visual Pleasure and Narrative Cinema" subtly pivots upon just such a reading.[4] The "woman as icon," writes Mulvey, "displayed for the gaze and enjoyment of men, the active controllers of the look, always threatens to evoke the anxiety it originally signified," "the threat of castration." There are two "avenues of escape" for the male spectatorial unconscious: the obsessive reenactment of the original trauma, involving the investigation, demystification, and derogation of the mysterious woman, which results in her being either punished or guiltily saved (voyeurism); or the "complete disavowal of castration by the substitution of a fetish object or turning the represented figure itself into a fetish so that it becomes reassuring rather than dangerous (hence, overvaluation, the cult of the female star" (fetishistic scopophilia). Mulvey uses the Marlene Dietrich of Josef von Sternberg films as the prime example of the cultic fetishization of the female star. It is not difficult to hear a subtle reference here to the gay male audience who worships the melodramatic diva — like Garbo, Dietrich, or Bette Davis — counterbalanced against straight male "investigators" of the enigma of woman.

Writing many years later, Brett Farmer focuses on the same kind of cultic gay male fascination with the melodramatic female star, albeit with markedly distinct emphases. Discussing the difficulties of melodrama's complication and destabilization of "phallic male identity and patriarchal authority," which, following Peter Matthews's argument, "may be symptomatic of an underlying libidinal scenario that correlates to regressive infantile fantasies of Imaginary, maternal jouissance" (192), Farmer admirably complicates the issue further by reminding us that gay readings of such films as Billy Wilder's *Sunset Boulevard* (1950) may open up the possibilities for the "articulation of a transgressive matrocentric fantasy" (195).[5] The final image of the film, the oneiric and sensually heightened shot of the face of Gloria Swanson's demented silent movie queen Norma Desmond, now "ready for her close-up," may be seen as "a final, triumphal assertion" of the "pre-oedipal mother filling the space of the screen, and, by extension, spectatorial desire with the absolute plenitude of her delirious jouissance."[6]

If we extend the paradigms of the critical inquiries of melodrama to genre television, we can begin to understand that the cultic fetishization of the female star and the gay male idolater has far greater implications than the genre of melodrama. Melodrama shares with genres like horror and science-fiction a preference for *anti-mimesis*, a willingness to embrace, evoke, and realize an "alternative" reality not dependent on the normative strictures of realism. As such, these genres may be said, in Lacanian terms, to constitute an Imaginary realm of representation, a place for fantasy unconstrained by the Symbolic codes of plausibility.[7] The alternative realms of melodrama, horror, and science-fiction are all sites of especially powerful unconscious associations, symbols, and resonances. They afford the spectator the opportunity for an unusually broad series of identifications, and the chance to re-experience stages of Imaginary development with greater confidence and agency — at least, this is their utopian hope.

The figure of the gay male artist is a particularly problematic one for such questions. In allegorizing, in his relation to the diva/star, the gay male relationship to the phallic mother, he threatens to explode the limits of allegory by directly, *explicitly* articulating what he symbolizes. Moreover, the gay male artist threatens to topple the reign of the diva, to challenge her dominion over him, to rival her magnetic power with his own. It must be said that the "supremacy" of the diva depends on an inescapably misogynistic cultural fantasy of women as goddess-like — untouchable, removed. The misogyny of the fantasy stems from the refusal to grant women a "human" subjectivity, ensuring that they will always be mythologized and abstracted, made a useful tool. While a pivotal aspect of popular culture, the gay male fascination with the diva — the Streisands and Madonnas of our age — always represents unseemly excessiveness, unlicensed and unregulated desires that do not conform to properly "useful" deployments of libidinal energies.[8] Yet the gay male artist is also endowed with a mysterious and maddening power that thwarts, though it can never altogether escape, the general homophobia of our culture. Considering the relationship between the gay male artist and the diva/star as it plays out in such unexplored terrain as genre television allows us to discuss the emotional complexities and costs of this fraught and familiar relation, opening up an entire host of new questions, concerns, and possibilities.

Gay Male Representation

Thomas Waugh theorizes the "third body" of the gay cinema as "the looking, representing" subject who stands in for "the authorial gay self as well as for the assumed gay spectator." In Victorian gay photography, "the third body, the gay subject, became visible only in the minor genre of the self-portrait." What we had instead was the male sexual object, who was usually either Hercules (the great muscleman hero) or Ganymede (the beautiful boy whom Zeus, in the form of an eagle, ravishes and who later becomes Zeus's cup-bearer). In gay narrative cinema, the artist comes out, becomes the gay subject that completes "the mythic triangle" with the Herculean he-man and the Ganymedean ephebe. Among the roles the gay subject takes on are those of the artist, the intellectual, and the teacher. "The gay subject looks at and desires the object within the narrative. As artist-intellectual he also bespeaks him, constructs him, projects him, fantasizes him, in short, *represents* him."[9]

If in the alternative text of gay male self-representation, as Waugh incisively points out, the gay artist creates a stand-in figure for himself that often takes on the character of an artist or intellectual who looks and desires, what does it mean for a *dominant text*, such as *Star Trek*, to represent the gay male in the same manner? In other words, when the construction of queer manhood in dominant culture intersects with that in *queer* representation, when dominant culture and minority self-representation may be said to be doing the same *kind* of cultural work or, at least, to be deploying the same techniques of signification, what are the overlaps and the distinctions between the dominant and the alternative text? Moreover, why are dominant texts no less drawn to the representation of a particularly prized gay male figure, the artist/intellectual, than gay artists themselves are? The recent spurt of gay artist-films such as *Infamous*, *Capote*, *The Hours*, *The Dying Gaul*, and *Tarnation* is especially striking considering how rarely artists of *any* kind get represented in mainstream texts, and therefore how rarely the gay male artist does. Representations of the gay male artist, then, are occasions for both critical excitement and careful critical scrutiny.

Trick of Light

Though it never received any of the critical accolades and attention that several other genre shows of the time, such as *Buffy the Vampire Slayer*, continue to enjoy, *Star Trek*: *Voyager*, whose 1995–2001 series run overlapped with *Buffy*'s, was a show that, like *Buffy*, revolved around a female hero. *Voyager*'s premise is *Trek* meets *The Odyssey*: it's all about *nostos*, or homecoming, from which we get *nostalgia*, the desire for home. The Federation starship *Voyager*, led by Captain Kathryn Janeway, gets pulled from the Alpha Quadrant (where all the other *Trek* series are set) into the Delta Quadrant, 70,000 light years away from home, and spends the entirety of its series-run attempting to return to Earth.

One of the many astonishments of *Voyager* is how many of its characters can be read as queer. As I argue in the next chapter, the figure of Neelix the cook can be read as a Male Mother[10]; the perpetually heterosexually frustrated Asian-American Harry Kim can be read as a closeted gay man; and both Harry's relationship with blond flyboy-helmsman Tom Paris and the Janeway-Seven of Nine relationship can be read as crypto-queer romances. Another characterization reads quite promisingly as queer allegory. I argue in this chapter that the Doctor (Robert Picardo), the holographic EMH (Emergency Medical Hologram), is one of the most striking gay characters in television history, even if his gayness is purely a suggested rather than an explicitly embraced identity.

One of the pervasive themes of gay author David Leavitt's recent biography of British mathematician Alan Turing, *The Man Who Knew Too Much: Alan Turing and the Invention of the Computer* (2005), is the idea that a computer who thinks like a human being—which Turing proposed was a likely and inevitable development—is an allegory for gay "passing," the closeted gay man passing as straight.[11] As a hologram, the Doctor can be similarly read.

The Doctor is nameless until the very last episode of the series, "Endgame" (2001). His namelessness is significant for a queer reading of his character, for he remains undefinable, the blur of identity. Homosexuality has long been the "love that dare not speak its name" of Oscar Wilde's well-known phrase. It is interesting that it is only in the coda to the series, "Endgame," that the Doctor, with his new bride—a thin blonde woman—on his arm, decides upon a name ("Joe"). The series appears to suggest that the Doctor's character arc has been a journey towards the achievement of normative heterosexuality, proper acquiescence to the Name and the Law of the Father. Yet it behooves us not to be end-directed in our appraisal of the Doctor. As "Endgame" evinces, the future is not set. The ongoing development of the character is far more important and suggestive than the conclusions of a coda.

Judith Butler asks that we consider the name as a "token of a symbolic order, an order of social law, that which legislates viable subjects through the institution of sexual difference and compulsory heterosexuality." As Butler writes, "the name as patronym does not only bear the law, but institutes the law ... producing a subject." Insofar as it has the power to do so, the patronymic name produces the subject "on the basis of a prohibition, a set of laws that differentiates subjects through the compulsory legislation of sexed social positionalities."[12] If a name confers patriarchal and heteronormative legitimacy on a subject, what is striking is the nearly series-long duration of the Doctor's namelessness.

Part of the allegorical framework of the Doctor is his status as hologram. The *Trek* shows always feature a character who represents otherness, is at a remove from the human. Like Vulcan Spock on Original *Trek*, android Data and Klingon Worf on *Next Generation*, Odo the shapeshifter on *DS9*, Vulcan T'Pol on *Enterprise*, ex–Borg Seven of Nine and half-human, half–Klingon B'Elanna Torres on *Voyager*, the Doctor is a metaphor for difference. But unlike all of the other characters, the Doctor is not "real." He is, as the villainess Seska says ("Basics, Part II," 1996), "a trick of light," comprised of "photons and forcefields." "I cannot be bent, spindled, or mutilated," the Doctor says at one point, echoing by inverting Shylock's famous phrase "If you prick us, do we not bleed?" Much like Shakespeare's ambiguous character, the Doctor is off-putting yet strangely sympathetic. Querulous, with the worst bedside manner imaginable, especially in the early seasons, easily agitated and often apoplectic, the Doctor transgressed against Trekkian niceness from the first flash of his character.

Making a hologram a character is one of *Voyager*'s most daring decisions. Devoid of actual substance, the Doctor truly is a copy, an imitation of the human (his equally conniption fit-prone, cantankerous creator Louis Zimmerman appears occasionally throughout the series, and in the episode "Life Line" [2000], the Doctor travels back to the Alpha Quadrant to meet him and attempt to cure a fatal illness). Much to the chagrin of *Trek* fans (insofar as I've been able to gather), *Voyager* pushed the limits of allegory by turning holograms and the issue of holographic rights into one of its major themes. Previously, holograms on *Trek* series were simply computer-generated images, phantasms of pain and pleasure, often used for strength-training exercises, battle simulations, or sexual pleasure. (They are also the characters in fictional narratives, "holonovels.") Routinely, holograms on *Trek* shows are brutalized (sliced in half or otherwise dismembered) or made to perform sexual services. On *Voyager*, for the first time, holograms received an empathetic reappraisal, which forced viewers to consider the ethics of the treatment of the non-human and the implications of the *post*-human.

The Doctor as hologram serves numerous allegorical purposes. In addition to being readable (as I am arguing) as a queer character, the hologram can also be read as the subaltern, the socially disenfranchised and disempowered. "Computer, activate EMH": When someone who enters sickbay utters this command, the Doctor flickers to life, saying dutifully, "Please state the nature of the medical emergency." The Doctor is on call all the time, a figure who represents the constant expectation of labor and service. He also represents the shunned, the socially untouchable, that which receives no human recognition or the legitimacy of the human. The early episodes depict the obliviousness to the increasingly sentient and self-aware Doctor's identity even on the part of Starfleet officers, the most enlightened human beings in human history (the premise of all *Trek*).

Even Janeway, as compassionate as she is unflinchingly tough, fails to recognize the Doctor's humanity. As a scientist, Janeway views the Doctor as, essentially, an ingenious appliance. She maintains this view, in fact, well into the series' run. In a fifth season episode — the tellingly titled "Latent Image" (1999) — the Doctor malfunctions when faced with a moral dilemma: forced to choose which critically ill patient to treat first, Ensign Harry Kim or a female ensign, he treats Kim first and the female ensign dies. After the Doctor malfunctions, Janeway is forced to reprogram him, a decision that raises ethical dilemmas of its own. Only the ex–Borg woman Seven of Nine's intervention forces Janeway to reappraise her view of the Doctor, whom she compares here to a hypospray and a replicator. It's certainly chilling that this far into the series, Janeway and B'Elanna Torres both continue to regard the Doctor as a piece of technology. Still, the episode culminates in an extraordinarily moving scene in which Janeway — having been convinced not to reprogram the Doctor and to allow him to go through a kind of grieving process — sits with the Doctor as he mourns the death of the woman he could not save. In the final scene, he reads from Janeway's copy of Dante's *La Vita Nuova (The New Life)*. On *Trek* shared love of literature is the ultimate marker of humanity, and this episode ultimately affirms a growing friendship between Janeway and the Doctor, now properly recognized as a living being.

Coming Out as a Hologram

The Doctor's queerness lies in several aspects of his character. His social disenfranchisement emerges as one of the major ones. In the Season Two episode "Projections" (1995), the Doctor falls into a delusional state and begins to experience alternative realities. In one, everyone *else* is a hologram, he the only "real" person. There is an amazing moment when, after the command to deactivate all holograms, Janeway sizzles off as the Doctor, still intact, watches. By presenting the idea of the Doctor's authenticity in this episode as such a freakish phenomenon, *Voyager* powerfully communicates the isolation of the Doctor's life.

Moreover, we watch the Doctor experience events that human beings in our own culture take for granted, see as routine. These quotidian events become occasions for astonishing new sensations for the Doctor. He falls in love ("Lifesigns," 1996), has a family ("Real Life," 1997), becomes a father figure in an alternative reality ("Blink of an Eye," 2000), confronts his own "father" in a very delayed Oedipal face-off in "Life Line." *Voyager* deroutinizes the normative — always already a heterosexist and heterosexualizing trajectory for the social individual — by presenting each new development in the Doctor's life as momentous, staggering, alien.

I would further argue that the Doctor — as terrifically if, by the end of the series, overzealously, played by Robert Picardo — allegorizes a specific life passage in gay male identity: delayed adolescence. The Doctor's deportment transforms from taciturn, held-in, brusque to exuberant, loping, almost anarchic. We could theorize that the first three seasons of *Voyager* constitute the Doctor's closeted phase, in which his innate personality, notwithstanding some notable manifestations, remains hidden, banked. Once the Doctor becomes more confident, more "human," he comes out of himself more. On *Voyager* this process is metaphorized by the Doctor's acquisition of a "mobile emitter" ("Future's End," 1996) in the Third Season. Previously, the Doctor was confined to sickbay (and the holodeck), places where he can be projected by hologram-emitters. But the futuristic technology of the mobile emitter allows him to leave sickbay — in other words, to come out of the closet. The Doctor's often arrogant and narcissistic behavior disquiets in its solipsism, but psychologically, if we read the Doctor as a gay male allegory, this behavior is very plausible.

As Stanley Siegel and Ed Lowe explain, when gay men come out in adulthood, they begin the process of self-validation. (It should be noted that many queer people are now coming out at much younger ages.)

> If the growth process was linear and chronological, the stage would be roughly the equivalent of adolescence and early adulthood, wherein the individual would have his first major social and sexual experiences.... It is comparable to adolescence only in terms of the mission, not the timing. There almost always is a discrepancy in timing for the gay man, because there are no sanctions or approvals for his exploring of his sexuality when everyone else is, during chronological adolescence.... Surviving this stage requires courage and enough emotional stamina to carry the individual from giddy to morose and back without making a wreck of him. It also boasts all of the elements of adolescent and only slightly post-adolescent sexuality, complete with excessiveness, self-destructiveness, and high risk, much of it intensified by the incongruity of the experience.[13]

The Doctor's often egregiously self-involved yet vulnerable and embattled behavior appositely reflects that of the older gay man who comes out later in life. With his middle-aged look (balding and slightly paunchy) and teen-tantrum demeanor, the Doctor teems as if with newly realized longstanding desires, needs, demands. He is an unwieldy and sympathetic mixture of embarrassingly unconstrained and bravely bold behaviors.

The Doctor also reflects another gay male life passage: a growing politicization of his subaltern sexuality. The Doctor spends most of his *Voyager* life, much like Data on *The Next Generation*, attempting to "pass" as human. But in Season Four he begins to chafe against the restrictions of the human identity that represents the dominant culture that he must always imitate. In the episode "Revulsion" (1997), he meets a (regrettably psychotic, homicidal) fellow hologram who attempts to enlist the Doctor into a war against "organics," their flesh and blood oppressors. This episode plays like an abortive same-sex romance, with the Doctor encouraging the increasingly unstable other hologram to travel with him through the stars. Played by the inimitably neurotic, panic-eyed Leland Orser, this deranged hologram, who loathes organics, is like a dark parody of the stereotype of the fussy, fastidious, point-perfect gay man.

By Season Six, the Doctor is clearly in rebellion against the limitations imposed upon him, deciding to become an opera diva (!) on a planet where singing and music are the latest, most exciting phenomenon ("Virtuoso"). Season Seven depicts the Doctor as fully radicalized. In the amazing but also deeply problematic and frustrating two-part episode "Flesh and Blood," from the seventh season, he meets a group of renegade holograms who mount a bold revolution against their humanoid oppressors. Like the assimilated, conformist minority individual who accepts the codes of dominant culture, the Doctor initially balks against the rogue holograms' demands that he join their cause. But he ends up abandoning *Voyager* and joining them, in one of the gutsiest moves on the part of a *Trek* character. In one haunting moment, the Doctor must treat the gash cheek-wound of a female hologram, who flinches as he touches her face. Startled by her emotional, instinctual response, the bewildered Doctor asks why and how a hologram could experience fear and pain. She explains that the alien species (a hunter race called the Hirogen) whom they are trying to escape programmed these responses to heighten the hunt for the holograms and the intensity of the carnage that ensues. In a terrifying sequence, the holograms make the Doctor experience their pain and panic in a simulation of a Hirogen hunting scene in which the Doctor is the prey, chased by the massive, hulking Hirogen through the forest; as the sequence plays, it evokes images of persecution of the unarmed by the brute, hypermasculine forces of militaristic power that inevitably recall Nazi Germany. If we read the Doctor as a queer character, and the holograms as a metaphor for queer desire, and if we recall the persecution of homosexuals as well as Jews and other perceived threats to the Nazi state, these images deepen in resonance. (This episode ultimately exasperates because it depicts the leader of the revolutionary holograms as a demented would-be messiah — a kind of hologram Nazi whose own eugenics philosophy leads him to wish to destroy organics in favor of freeing holograms, whom he describes as the "children of light" that he will "deliver into freedom." The cautionary and reactionary message is that revolution is the domain of fundamentalist megalomaniacs; the episode also makes the Doctor, an allegorical queer character, the annihilator of another, the messianic leader. This is hegemony at its height: minority identities are made to war with each other while the dominant power maintains the status quo.)

The later episodes of Season Seven (the series' last), however, bring the Doctor's growing radical queer consciousness to a stunning height. They give the Doctor the opportunity to become a gay male author of a great new holographic revolution — one that inspires his human community as well. In "Author, Author," the Doctor creates a holo-narrative, "Photons Be Free," for a publisher in the Alpha Quadrant, with which *Voyager* can now communicate. "Photons Be Free" rollickingly and disturbingly sends up *Voyager* as a series. Told entirely from the Doctor's perspective, it depicts the struggles of an oppressed, lonely hologram within a tyrannical human environment. In this narrative, Janeway is a martinet who actually phasers to death a wounded crewman so that the Doctor can attend to her preferred candidate for his treatment (this seems a pointed nod to "Latent Image"). Given that this narrative stems from his fantasies, the Doctor would appear to fantasize about the murderous might and potential of the phallic mother. Most of the other characters in the Doctor's hologram-novel act in equally shocking ways towards him. The Doctor darkly represents the *Voyager* crew as cruel, selfish, and depraved, the inverse of the tolerant, benevolent, generous beings they and *Trek* as a whole insist that we see them as.

The nifty thing about the Doctor's hologram-narrative is that it forces its human participants to play the role of the Doctor, seeing *Voyager* life through his eyes. From his perspective, the mobile emitter weighs heavily, and in "Photons Be Free" it transforms from the small gadget on the Doctor's arm to a laboriously heavy backpack beneath which the Doctor staggers. "But your mobile emitter liberates you, Doctor!" an incredulous Janeway counters him, inspiring the Doctor to explain the purpose of his metaphorical burden.

Though a *Voyager* viewer might find the Doctor's depictions of the *Voyager* crew shockingly violent and unappetizing, bespeaking the Doctor's lack of gratitude and loyalty, it is precisely the unremittingly harsh nature of his critique that attests to his now fully developed radicalization. As the queer outsider, he is in a position to critique the conformist, implicitly heterosexist conventions of Federation/Trekkian society, decisively assuming a nonconformist, nonassimilationist position in the face of their hegemonic power.

But the show goes beyond simply positioning the Doctor as the inassimilable queer outsider. Instead, it demonstrates — in a way that beautifully corresponds to *Trek* ideals — that the Doctor's radicalism can affect the *Voyager* crew, his queer radicalism a model for the *dominant* culture to emulate. The Doctor eventually decides to soften the tone of his hologram-narrative, which can be read as capitulation to the demands of the dominant ideology. Yet his efforts to do so are impeded by the corrupt avariciousness of the Alpha Quadrant publisher, who ruthlessly intends to sell the Doctor's juicier original work for monetary gain. As a legal defense against the Doctor's suit, the publisher relies upon the notion that the Doctor is not a person with rights and therefore not an "author." What ensues in this ambitious episode is a trial in which Tuvok, the Vulcan security officer (played by African American actor Tim Russ), defends the Doctor's legal right to control his work and, more crucially, does so by demonstrating that the Doctor is indeed a person (an homage to *The Next Generation*'s superb episode "The Measure of a Man," in which android Data, defended by Picard, undergoes the same kind of trial to avoid being dismantled for scientific study).

Many testify on behalf of the Doctor, and Janeway delivers one of the most moving testimonials. We have seen how skeptical Janeway's position towards the Doctor's humanity has been; in "Author, Author," we see that she has come to recognize his personhood. Janeway attests on the Doctor's behalf to the Federation judge:

> Centuries ago, in most places on Earth, only landowners of a particular gender and race had any rights at all. Over time, those rights were extended to all humans — and later, as we explored the galaxy, to thousands of other sentient species. Our definition of what constitutes a person has continued to evolve. Now we're asking that you expand that definition once more to include our Doctor. When I met him years ago, I would never have believed that an Emergency Medical Hologram could become a valued member of my crew, and my friend. The Doctor is a person, as real as any flesh and blood I've ever known. If you believe the testimony you've heard here, it's only fair to conclude that he has the same rights as any of us.

Delivered in Kate Mulgrew's most thrillingly precise and nuanced style, this speech resembles one of Lincoln's during the Civil War. It also attests to the radicalization of Janeway's own position as an authority in Starfleet — here, she takes on the implicitly masculinist, racist, sexist, classist codes that apparently still dominate Federation "morality." This is an example of the phallic mother as heroic savior. If, as gay male viewers identifying with the phallic mother, we miss out here on the delirium of Norma Desmond's ravenous star diva in *Sunset Boulevard*, we gain the moral and ethical weight of Janeway's authority.

In the terms of Judith Butler, whose work so provocatively forces us to rethink concepts of imitation, originality, and "realness" in gendered and sexual terms — one of her brilliant formulations (in her *Bodies That Matter*) being that heterosexuality itself is a copy for which there is no original, disputing utterly the concept that homosexuality is heterosexuality's inferior imitation — perhaps Janeway's rhetoric here isn't all that thrilling. What's so great about being a real human, a person? Perhaps Janeway's obsessive rhetoric about "humanity" is its own form of stifling oppression. Perhaps the Doctor shouldn't be fighting for recognition as a fellow "person" but as a separate entity or species or creation altogether. Is the Doctor even here still denying his difference, conforming, imitating, assimilating? Again: perhaps. But contextualizing this speech and this episode in Trekkian terms, in which a utopian vision of an enlightened, moral, peaceful humanity is the universal standard, the Doctor's fight and Janeway's testimony emerge as stirringly, resonantly powerful.

Voyager champions the queer storyteller. Janeway's fight for the Doctor simultaneously confers upon him humanity and the right of authorship. In fighting for the Doctor's right to write, to tell his story, Janeway sanctions his right to speak truth to power. "Author, Author" ends with the most radical image of revolution in *Trek*. Though the white-haired (old money) Federation judge passes on making the decision to grant the Doctor personhood, he does grant the Doctor the right to control his own work. He grants him authorship, then, if not personhood. We then see multiple EMHs — all made, like the Doctor, in Zimmerman's image, all now requisitioned to a mining colony — as a genuine subaltern population, enslaved and engaged in the brutalizing and incessant work of the kind that Marx called alienated labor. But now these other EMHs pass around bootleg copies of "Photons Be Free." The episode strongly suggests that the Doctor's work will generate a revolution. (Indeed, Christie Golden's post-series *Voyager* relaunch novels confirm this.) "Author, Author" is a revolutionary television text.

To be sure, *Voyager* did not consistently make good on its promise to champion the Doctor's alternative identity and sexuality; there are several spots throughout the series in which the show settled for depicting him as a buffoonish blowhard. Yet if Freud's gay male artist is a beautiful monster, *Voyager* never treats its gay male artist as monstrous in any way. In its depiction of the evolving relationship between Janeway and the Doctor, the series works to heal the rift between the phallic mother and her homosexual-rebel son, and in so doing to heal the damage caused by the homophobic misapplication, throughout the history of American psychiatry, of Freud's enduringly provocative — and strangely insightful — theory. In the series' penultimate episode, "Renaissance Man," the Doctor risks the entire ship to save Janeway's life. Forever the Boss Lady, she chastises him for doing so, but she also reaches out to him, asks him to socialize with her, a privilege rarely granted to any of the crewmembers. The final episode, "Endgame," depicts an AU future in which an elderly (but ever-resilient) Janeway and an ageless Doctor enjoy a warm, bantering friendship. This evolving friendship is one of *Voyager*'s greatest achievements — the diva-mother emerges as a human woman (rather than a forbidding archetype), the holographic Doctor as a feeling person, and the viewer as an enlightened inquirer into the nature of the varieties of love.

Buffy *versus* Voyager

Buffy the Vampire Slayer, the Joss Whedon TV series that ran from 1997 to 2003, is in the enviable position of being both a cult hit and a prime example, for innumerable critics, of progressive, even radical, popular culture.[14] *Buffy* is indeed a brilliant television text that deserves, demands, and rewards critical engagement. But one aspect of the show remains disquieting: *Buffy*'s depiction of gay characters, which reveals a great deal about the dynamics and difficulties of gay representation even in a genre — the action heroine show — that one might imagine would be especially amenable to it. I argue that, while *Buffy* admirably depicts its gay characters with great visibility, this visibility is primarily what is admirable about the depiction. The show's depiction of its lesbian characters — Willow (Alyson Hannigan), the geeky girl turned "most powerful Wicca of the northern hemisphere"; her girlfriend Tara (Amber Benson); her later girlfriend Kennedy (Iyari Limon) — is troubled and troubling; but its depiction of its gay male characters is deeply disturbing. In terms of queer representation, *Buffy* can be provocatively compared to *Star Trek: Voyager*, for in its quasi-allegorical gay male character Andrew, the series portrays a character that is remarkably similar to the Doctor yet represented in ways that are just as remarkably distinct.

Death and the Maiden

Walter Benjamin's famous essay "The Storyteller" appositely provides a framing question for this essay: "Death is the sanction of everything that the storyteller can tell. In other words, it is natural history to which his stories refer back."[15] Intriguingly, the First Slayer — an African warrior woman with whom Buffy telepathically communicates — tells her at one dire point during the fifth season, "Death is your gift." (Buffy will later sacrifice herself to save the world.) That episode and this essay raise the question: What is the *queer* storyteller's gift? Is death also the sanction of the queer storyteller?

A close reading of the Season Seven *Buffy* episode "Storyteller" (2003), written by Jane Espenson and directed by Marita Grabiak, reveals the deeply odd ways in which *Buffy* both gave queer characters visibility and circulated homophobic fantasies. "Storyteller" constructs an exemplary gay male author. It gives Andrew (the talented Tom Lenk) the spotlight, as he attempts to film his own version of Buffy's story during a particularly apocalyptic point in the final season of the series. Andrew is a quasi-allegorical gay male figure (meaning that he is all but named as such), in contrast to the pointedly unnamed Doctor as an allegorical gay male figure (he is a metaphor for gay male identity without any explicit signification as such).

As Anne Billson describes, this "very funny Andrew-centric episode" is "simultaneously an examination of his nerdy mythomania and a send-up of the series itself."[16] Introduced in Season Six as the only previously unseen member of the Trio — vengeful nerds who will themselves into being the Big Bads (villains) of the sixth season by attempting to become Buffy's archnemeses — Andrew is pale, blond, neurotic, and highly stylized physically and verbally, oscillating between a childlike state of bewilderment and a high-strung whininess. The other members of the Trio — Warren (Adam Busch), a geek inventor turned dangerous misogynist (he ends up killing his girlfriend, attempting to kill Buffy, and inadvertently killing Tara instead) and diminutive Jonathan (Danny Strong), who previously hypnotized all of Sunnydale into believing that he was the center of their lives — are laughably bumbling villains (painting the half-finished Death Star on their secret van) until their efforts produce increasingly tragic results. But pallid Andrew stands out even within this inept group. Billson writes, "Andrew is the only one of the Trio who will survive to the end of Season Seven.... Andrew is the flakiest and most cowardly of the Trio, and also the funniest, though all three are played for laughs until 'Dead Things,' [in which Warren kills his girlfriend]."[17]

One of the major qualities associated with Andrew is repressed homosexuality. Billson notes that he is "almost certainly a virgin, may well be a closet homosexual, though he's so unworldly that he probably wouldn't be aware of it if he were."[18] Yet in the Buffyverse Andrew would be the only one without a clue about his queer leanings. Even increasingly psychotic, woman-hating Warren calls him on it. Andrew appears to be madly in love with Warren; he also calls Jonathan "the cutest thing." Though it is played for laughs throughout, Andrew's repressed homosexuality, in a manner analogous to Warren's sexism, emerges as more and more problematic, finally resulting in his murder of Jonathan, just as Warren's issues with women lead him to kill them.

The entire premise of the Trio (or Troika) — geeks who turn evil — is questionable, especially given Buffy's embrace of the socially disenfranchised, which goes back to the first episode of the series, in which she befriends social pariahs. But while Warren, who builds women-robots and mind-zaps his ex-girlfriend into believing she is his sex-slave-drone before he murders her, is clearly the unredeemable member of the Trio, Andrew is only somewhat less morally questionable. Only Jonathan seems truly penitent over their actions when Tara is killed, causing Willow, in an apocalyptic, grief-fueled rage, to transform into dark-haired, dark-veined, and delicious "Dark Willow" at the end of Season Six, hell-bent on annihilating the Trio, and then the world itself. (Through the efforts of the Scoobies, Willow stops at killing Warren, whose flesh she flays.)

Why include Andrew in Season Seven as a semi-regular character, then? Andrew serves multiple purposes. He is a male even more laughable than Xander (Nicholas Brendon), the affable white straight guy with a big heart and no superpowers (Xander mocks Andrew during one of the Dark Willow episodes, "You haven't even had a tiny bit of sex, have you?"; normally the butt of jokes, Xander now has someone he can deride), and Spike (James Marsters), the bleached-blond Cockney vampire who falls in love with Buffy and gets a soul. Beyond his usefulness as comic relief, Andrew serves an extremely important function — he exists as a scapegoat. He must suffer for the sins of the *Buffy* community and atone for them.

René Girard explains Oedipus's function as "human scapegoat" this way:

> In the myth, the fearful transgression of a single individual is substituted for the universal onslaught of reciprocal violence. Oedipus is responsible for the ills that have befallen his people. He has become a prime example of the human scapegoat.[19]

It should be remembered that Andrew makes his reappearance during the seventh season, in which the characters investigate the plague of a new Hellmouth, or a gateway to hell. "Storyteller" is an *Oedipus Rex*–like detective tale in which the protagonist investigating Buffy's secret world discovers that he is the source of contagion that must be purged, his myopic videographer-vision an apt analogy for Oedipus's initially blinkered, then literally blinded, vision. Castrated and forced to acknowledge his secret sin, Andrew weeps at the climax of the episode, and his tears stave off the universal onslaught of the new Hellmouth, if only momentarily. Moreover, he suffers for the sins of the principal characters, most of whom, by that point, have committed grievous sins — Willow, who killed Warren; Giles, who killed the human "brother," Ben, of Season Five's Big Bad, Glory; Anya, for her relapse as a vengeance demon (she annihilates a group of gang-raping fraternity boys); Spike, for his past vampire crimes; and Buffy herself, who kills as a calling and whose greatest sin perhaps lies in her belief in her own sinlessness.

The Ethics of Gay Male Voyeurism

"Storyteller" opens with Andrew in the guise of a faux *Masterpiece Theater*-cum-*Mr. Rogers* host, sitting in a plush chair and wearing a plusher velvet robe, "surprised" by the appearance of the viewer. "Hellooo, Gentle Viewer," he gently greets us, looking up from the tome he reads, and proceeds to extol the joys of reading. Comically stilted language marks Andrew-as-narrator's ruminations on "adventure and heroics and daring." Even in the guise of the PBS–style narrator, vulnerable, hapless Andrew telegraphs his discomfort with himself, being in his own body; as Lenk is directed, he conveys primarily a sense of funny fearfulness. This introduction begins by panning across the shelves of this unsure narrator's library, Nietzsche being one of the prominently displayed books. Will this episode be about Andrew's Will to Power? He seems more interested in Buffy's will and power, recounting thrilling tales of "Buffy, Killer of the Vam-*pi*-res," as he humorously and absurdly pronounces the series' signature term, continuing on in his stilted way, "Buffy didn't see the second vam*pir*e concealed under cover of darkness...."

We then watch Buffy through Andrew's video camera. She slays vamps in the cemetery as he films her, much to her loudly broadcast chagrin. Freud, noting the child's "intense desire to look" (50), theorizes that the "scopophilic instinct" precociously awakened in Leonardo's childhood may have sparked his career as a visual artist. If scopophilic desire drives childlike Andrew, his desire to see fixates on Buffy, the narrative of whose life he obsessively attempts to insert and inscribe himself within. Andrew will proceed to film Buffy and the other Scoobies at Buffy's sunlit house, sometimes narcissistically filming himself speaking directly to the camera — sometimes about the other characters, often about himself and his own experiences. We also get false flashbacks of Andrew's idealized versions of his own past, in which his ego-ideal self is the debonair leader of the more accomplished Trio of his private fantasies. Later, Willow will summon up Andrew's memories of lying in bed with Jonathan in Mexico ("Meh-hi-coh"). While in Mexico, the "First" — short for the First Evil, Season Seven's Big Bad — in the guise of Warren (the First impersonates various characters, most memorably, and tellingly, Buffy herself) tempts and taunts him into murdering Jonathan. Andrew must bring Jonathan to the basement of the new high school over the Hellmouth in Sunnydale, California. Deep within the basement lies the Seal of Danzalthar, a vast silver lid that bears the image of a goat with its tongue out. The First makes Andrew kill Jonathan over the Seal, Jonathan's blood activating the Seal's evil energies and releasing the First's minions, Uber-vamps, especially grotesque, ancient, and powerful vampires. The First plans to devour the entire world, and Andrew, by killing Jonathan and spilling his blood, facilitates the whole plan.

One of the central thematic questions raised by "Storyteller" is the ethics of gay male voyeurism, here a form of textual appropriation, as Andrew both intrudes upon a special, private world (which he does simply by becoming an unwieldy recurring member of the cast; his videography only reifies his intrusiveness) and reinvents and reimagines it in his own terms, for his own ends. So we must wonder how far Andrew is able to get — how far the *Buffy*-text lets him get.

In his published notes on the filmmaking process for his film *Ecce Homo*, gay filmmaker Jerry Tartaglia writes: "Challenge the audience to cross the boundary between the viewing of a sexual (queer) icon and *experiencing* the voyeuristic process. Make them do the thing itself!"[20] For Tartaglia, voyeurism becomes empowering, a form of radical desire that subverts the constraints on gay male looking. The complicating factor in "Storyteller" is that, while

Andrew voyeuristically fixates on Xander and Spike as potential queer icons, the *real* queer icon here is Buffy, the diva-star-princess–action chick–heroine Andrew ostensibly worships. Interestingly, the episode ultimately makes us wonder whether Andrew wants to worship her or to *be* her, which may amount to the same thing, or simply wants to displace her, be the center around which the *Buffy* narrative revolves. Does "Storyteller" make us do the thing itself—desire what Andrew desires? Does it allow Andrew to do so?

Andrew's relentless videography annoys the Scoobies, though some of the Potential Slayers, young women in Slayer-training against the apocalyptic designs of the First, say it "might be nice to have a record of what we're doing." (Perhaps not incidentally, this line is spoken by Rhona, an African American Potential.) It isn't initially clear exactly what motivates Andrew to transmute Buffy's world into his own narrative, but it becomes increasingly apparent that Andrew's drive to narrativize is figured as both conventionally narcissistic and a desire to insert himself into Buffy's major narrative. This idea has its humorous side in the relentlessly self-referential and parodistic *Buffy* realm, the sidekick wanting the spotlight. But more resonantly, Andrew does make the queer intervention of rewriting heterosexualized conventional narrative as his *own* plot. Dismayingly, however, the episode demonstrates that Andrew's desire is not only unrealizable but also morally reprehensible. The entire episode is designed to *silence* the queer storyteller.

Andrew appropriates *Buffy*'s dominant narrative. As a queer reader of the *Buffy*-text, Andrew is, in the language of Michel de Certeau, a textual poacher: "[The reader] insinuates into another person's text the ruses of pleasure and appropriation: he poaches on it, is transported into it, pluralizes himself in it like the internal rumblings of one's body."[21] If Andrew is a queer textual poacher, the protagonist and other characters of the dominant narrative vociferously object to his unseemly insinuations into their narrative. Buffy is far from the only one who chastises Andrew for his storytelling; "Why can't you just masturbate like the rest of us?" challenges ex-demon Anya, a fellow pariah who one might imagine would have more sympathy for Andrew. Spike also hollers at him, though he works hard to make sure he is captured just right on film as he protests. (Apparently, you can capture a vampire on film in the Buffyverse.)

In one of several instances of self-portraiture, Andrew recaps the season's high points plot-wise using his own drawings of several figures whose identities he explains, including the Seal, the First, and the Bringers (fiendish blind monk-like assassins who aid the First, namely by killing Potentials). The drawings of these figures resemble those done by a very young child, and Andrew's shy, childlike explanations, joined to hesitant, slightly scatterbrained, Pee Wee Herman–ish body language, appositely complement them.

This episode deploys Andrew's effeminacy in complex ways. It makes him an appealing, because funny and "sweet," character. But it also marks him as sinister—it is precisely his childlike, feminine softness that makes his murder of Jonathan specifically and murderous potentiality generally so terrifying. (Think Norman Bates.) Alan Sinfield writes that the "root idea" of effeminacy

> is a male falling away from the purposeful reasonableness that is supposed to constitute manliness, into the laxity and weakness conventionally attributed to women.... The function of effeminacy, as a concept, is to police sexual categories, keeping them pure. [Crucially, for our discussion of Andrew and his symbolic significance,] the effects of such policing extend vastly beyond lesbians and gay men.... The whole order of sexuality and gender is pinioned by the fears and excitements that gather around the allegedly inappropriate distribution of gender categories.[22]

Overall, Andrew is presented by the show and presents himself as an overgrown child—simultaneously sexless and assigned an onanistic sexuality (hence the "masturbation" reference and Pee Wee Herman affect) that perfectly complements his homosexuality. If his storytelling is a form of narcissistic onanism, his desires chiefly extend, in homophobic terms, to useless, socially and reproductively meaningless sexual objects, himself and other men. Astonishingly, "Storyteller" can be said to circulate the rhetoric and imagery of early nineteenth-century sex-phobic sex-reformers such as the American health and temperance activist Sylvester Graham (inventor of the graham cracker), who linked the onanist to the sodomite (the term homosexual was not coined until later on in the century). To his horror, Graham discovered that public school boys who masturbated even engaged in "criminal," "unnatural commerce with each other!"[23] Like the homosexual, the onanist is linked to useless, socially threatening non-reproductive sex. As a queer onanist, Andrew diddles as Sunnydale burns. Moreover, his narcissism also evokes the homophobic history of psychiatric pathologizations of homosexuals as stunted, self-seeking narcissists with mother-fixations. The Buffy-obsessed, self-filming Andrew embodies this stereotype.

"Storyteller" thematizes the politics of textual poaching by presenting Andrew as an example of the morally questionable, ruthless queer storyteller, much as the bewilderingly overpraised film *Capote* does, drawing on cultural fantasies of the cruelly derisive nature of gay men and of the perceived uselessness of queer desire. The episode also mashes together and offers up a queer version of Michael Powell's famous film *Peeping Tom* (1960), whose lethal videographer kills women with his phallic, protuberant camera; Hitchcock's equally famous film of the same year, *Psycho*, whose mother-obsessed murderer Norman Bates (indelible Anthony Perkins) seems like a fidgety, awkwardly sensitive, ultimately murderous precursor to Andrew, whose combination of vulnerability and villainy he prefigures; and Martin Scorsese's *Taxi Driver* (1976), another work in which a psychopath tries to impress a blonde (Jodie Foster's teen prostitute, Iris) and becomes consumed by his own narcissism. One can almost hear Andrew's version of Travis's legendary lines, "You talkin' to me? Well, I'm the only one here." And Andrew's combined obsessions with camera, self, and Woman seem to extend the character of Jame Gumb from *The Silence of the Lambs* into the realm of pastiche. With his avid desire to look, his sexuality sublimated into art-making that is a quest for knowledge, and his obsession with den-mother Buffy, Andrew is a postmodern Leonardo for a new-style Freudian study.

Andrew's skills as a documentarian, such as they are, never emerge. Instead, he chooses to film rapturously idealized versions of the principal Scoobies, demonstrating stereotypical gay snobbiness by shooing away a mere Potential, Amanda, who wishes to be filmed. Filming Buffy and Spike in a romantic situation, Andrew rivals Douglas Sirk in his melodramatically lush depiction of heterosexuality, though one could say that his shirtless fantasy Spike is a homoerotic wish-fulfillment. In a humorous but also pointed and loaded moment, Andrew announces, "Here's something you're going to be interested in"— Willow and her seventh season girlfriend Kennedy making out on the sofa — as he pans upward from the kissing women to focus on the wonderful window sashes Xander has put in. Obviously, the silly, murderous gay man erases lesbian desire, focuses on interior decorating and masculine expertise at once.

Andrew films Xander and Anya, whom he goads into an argument, as they discuss their current feelings for each other. (In the previous season, Xander had experienced last-minute doubts and left Anya at the altar.) Anya asks: "Do you still love me?" Xander responds: "I don't know if that means anything for us anymore." As Andrew endlessly rewatches this footage, he mouths Anya's words and keeps rewinding Xander's line, "I hope that you know that you never left my heart."

Andrew has already inserted himself into another's narrative. Looking into the camera, he says, "I am a man with a burden ... a supervillain." We then cut to a revised version of the scenes from the sixth season in which Dark Willow attempts to kill Andrew and Jonathan. The footage of Dark Willow remains the same, but now it is intercut with new scenes of Andrew triumphantly, and solemnly, countering Dark Willow's spells with his own. As blue currents of electric energy course from Willow's fingers towards Andrew, he waves them away in his fantasy, saying, "I deflect thy power!"

Joining his idealized (and perhaps satirical) versions of heterosexual love, Andrew's ventriloquizing of Anya's voice and rewriting of the scenes of his confrontation with Dark Willow add up to fantasies of gay male envy for woman's place and woman's power. By repeating Anya's words, Andrew effectively denies her the power of her own voice, which he usurps. By triumphing over Dark Willow, Andrew appropriates her demonic, queer energy for himself. This last appropriation is rendered more disturbing by Andrew's previous deflection of lesbian power—his shooting of the sashes above them rather than Willow and Kennedy kissing. And as is revealed later, Andrew has a clear alternative fantasy vision of what an all-male paradise would look like: a pastoral realm, with Jonathan, Warren, and Andrew in mock-classical clothing, flowers in their hair, strumming harps as they exclaim, "We live as gods!" His male paradise thematically resembles that in Herman Melville's story "The Paradise of Bachelors and the Tartarus of Maids," except that Andrew's is pointedly feminized, not a hint of phallic sexuality in sight. The episode represents phallic mother Buffy as the only properly phallic power, as if any demonstration of alternative accesses to phallic power would irreparably devalue her own.

Silencing the Storyteller

Throughout this richly complex and disturbingly homophobic episode, Andrew's interest in stories is treated as pathological, even sociopathic. Though Andrew's response can be summed up by his line, "I'm the detached journalist with an objective eye," his detachment from the gravity of the situations he records is viewed not as objective but as parasitic and, worse, morally vacant. When Robin Wood (tellingly named, an homage to the great film critic), the principal, announces, "We just spent the day keeping a lid on war," which he means literally, Andrew's response is, "That will be very exciting on tape." Buffy informs him, "I don't want a biographer, especially a murderer." Though it contains lushly idealized moments, Andrew's documentary does not appear to be a full-on hagiography of the Slayer. Is it possible that Buffy fears exposure—could Andrew's be a *moral* vision, a genuinely probing analysis of Slayerdom? We are never allowed to find out. Instead, he becomes *her* vision—the image of moral redemption.

When Buffy takes Andrew to the high school ostensibly so he can decipher the Seal's codes, he films her fighting the Seal-possessed high school students. When Buffy confronts Andrew about his murder of Jonathan, he first offers the version that it was Warren as the First who tricked him into killing

Jonathan. Then, after Buffy explains the way in which the Seal possessed Principal Wood, making him murderous, turning his eyes white, Andrew then offers another version of his killing Jonathan, possessed by the Seal, his eyes now seethingly blank white orbs. "You just completely changed your story!" yells Buffy.

When Buffy has Andrew near the Seal, she brandishes the same dagger with which Andrew killed Jonathan (he then placed it in the cutlery drawer), taunting him by saying that perhaps what the Seal really wants is blood. Andrew responds, "So this is my redemption at last. I buy back my bruised soul with the blood of my heart." Then this exchange follows:

> BUFFY: Stop! Stop telling stories! Life isn't a story.
> ANDREW: Sorry.
> BUFFY: Shut up. You always do this. You make everything into a story, so no one's responsible for anything because they're just following a script.... You didn't lose your friend. You killed him. [Buffy then reveals that she made up the story that they would all get through this new Hellmouth ordeal alive.] When your blood pours out, it might save the world. Are you redeemed?

At this point, Buffy holds Andrew over the Seal, the dagger at his throat. He begins to weep. Finally, he speaks the truth the entire episode has labored so hard to speak through him:

> ANDREW: I listened to Warren and pretended it was him. But I knew it wasn't. And I killed Jonathan. And now you're going to kill me and I'm scared. And this is how Jonathan felt. I killed my best friend.... There's a big fight coming and I probably won't live through it. I guess that's as it should be.

As Andrew blubbers these confessional words, rivulets of tears stream down his anguished face, and one of these tears plunks down to the Seal. Suddenly, its demonic, whirring energy subsides, then ceases. As Buffy explains, the Seal didn't want blood. It wanted tears, Andrew's tears, to be exact.

Buffy wields the power of duplicitous narrative, which works well for her, since she gets Andrew to cry out his redemption. Andrew, however, is not afforded a similar license. His constant manipulations of story and narrative — which could be read as the textual strategies for the undermining of traditional narrative, subversive responses to the crushing conformity and heterosexism of dominant culture — are not affirmed by the *Buffy*-text. Rather, his Trickster narrative art is demeaned, depicted as indicative of his moral bankruptcy and inability to take responsibility for his many crimes.

If, like all *Buffy* episodes, "Storyteller" allegorizes some social, cultural, or psychic problem of human life, what's this episode's problem? I argue that this episode is an allegory of postgay male identity. Andrew's repressed homosexuality analogously corresponds to his bent relationship to narrative, to its Truth. His inability to own up to his crime — to who he "really" is — can be read as his inability to speak the truly revealing words of his own claimed, affirmed sexuality. As Foucault would say, he refuses properly to turn his sex into discourse. Moreover, in enabling, accepting, and manifesting Buffy's campaign to out him and, even more crucially, to get him to out himself, Andrew assumes the role of proper spokesperson for his own reprehensibility. By affirming that his death at her hands is "as it should be," Andrew speaks the desire Buffy cannot, her desire to slay him. She settles for silencing the storyteller.

What this episode constructs through its meticulous yoking of disparate elements is the figure of the pernicious queer storyteller, the gay man as amoral observer. As *Buffy* represents the figure, the queer narrator is morally questionable, emotionally and psychically hollow, parasitic. In a television series that so persistently questions traditional narrative practices, facilitates textual poaching, and enables viewer engagement, "Storyteller" notably impedes the progress of queer interventions in dominant narrative forms. Most tellingly, it is precisely Andrew's attempts to gain entry into discourse, to make his own narrative, tell his own story, that leads to his moral reckoning at Buffy's hands — he speaks the words that classify him as killer, names himself as such. The Storyteller silences himself.

As actor Tom Lenk himself says in an interview, this episode is a very self-aware attempt to allegorize the fan relationship to the female icon-diva–action heroine.

> I think it's an interesting thing [his role in "Storyteller"] to play. I like it. It's nice because he's sort of gotten his ultimate wish, to hang out with Buffy, be part of the gang and possibly hang out at Buffy's house.[24]

Obsessed with Buffy, Andrew attempts to lose himself—to forget his awful "hidden" nature — in his idolatrous fantasies for Buffy. Buffy, like a great diva movie queen exasperated by the adoring adulation of a mincing fan, *educates* Andrew, forces him to acknowledge both his depravity and his inability to acknowledge it. She forces him to get Real.

Death is Buffy's gift, not the queer storyteller's gift. Andrew's chief function is to enable and facilitate the heroine's access to authentic narrative, as he penitently acquiesces to her power over narrative. The *Buffy*-text knows it is powerful because it can squash and subsume his own; his insignificance confirms his dominance. He is denied the big finish his own narrative destines him for — he is not permitted to buy back his bruised soul. He cannot die in the grand, dramatic, satisfying way he wants to; he cannot follow his own script. He can only tearfully accommodate his own self-abnegation. This episode climaxes with redemption as rape — Buffy forces Andrew to redeem himself. The queer man cannot tell his story. The last two lines of Emily Dickinson's poem "My Life Had Stood — A Loaded Gun" could be Andrew's *cri du coeur*:

> For I have but the power to kill,
> Without — the power to die —

Why *Trek* Matters

One of the most striking discoveries of comparing a series like *Buffy* to *Voyager* is the extent to which received opinion can distort the complexities of representation, leading viewers to expect certain rewards or frustrations not present in the text. *Buffy*'s hipster status as "radical" entertainment and *Voyager*'s status as "bad television" may lead many viewers to believe that enlightened representation would match the public profiles of each series. As I have attempted to demonstrate, the critically drubbed, "square" *Voyager* was, at least in terms of representing the queer male relation to the powerful female icon, the much more radical vision.

As two great television works with numerous strengths and flaws, *Buffy* and *Voyager* performed the extremely useful cultural work of allegorizing subaltern sexual identity, among other subaltern identities. What action heroine programs like *Buffy* and *Voyager* appear to suggest is that, far from outmoded, Freudian formulations of the phallic mother and male fantasy continue to resonate for our culture. The gay male artist represents both the height of this fantasy and the potential for its revision and even explosion. At the very least, *Buffy* and *Voyager* remind us of the emotional implications of all such formulations.

Four

QUEERING GENDER
Voyager's Neelix as the Male Mother

Another male character of *Star Trek: Voyager* lends himself to queer interpretation. I argue that *Voyager* develops one of its regular characters, Neelix, into a modern version of an important cultural figure: the Male Mother. A former ex-con who becomes the chef, amateur counselor, morale officer, security officer, shipboard journalist (he even has a morning TV talk show), and ambassador to other races, Neelix plays several roles on the series, but what unites all of them is Neelix's pervasive function as a nurturer (he is a security officer only in an alternate universe storyline). Though rarely afforded a sustained critical discussion, the trope of the Male Mother has been a recurring figure throughout Western cultural history, and *Voyager*'s development of Neelix as a version of this figure is one of the many surprising fascinations of a series whose representation of gender and sexuality remains underappreciated.

The theories of Bruno Bettelheim, whose 1954 study *Symbolic Wounds* questions the gendered nature of nurture, as well as feminist analyses of Bettelheim's work, provide a starting point for an investigation of the Male Mother. I will first examine Bettelheim's assumptions, delineate some of the figure's early embodiments, and then explicate *Star Trek*'s representation of the sexual and cultural politics of the Male Mother through Neelix and the evolution of his character. The Male Mother is a more complex and unstable queer allegory than the holographic Doctor as gay male artist; though it is a potentially liberating genderbending figure, numerous problems in the construction of gender and sexuality inhere in the Male Mother. One central question for us is why the depiction of Male Mothers has most often occurred in works that defy the constraints of realism, such as science fiction and horror. Is the Male Mother a figure too radical to be found anywhere else, or do speculative genres themselves dictate the investigations of non-normative gender and sex roles?

Competing Wounds

In his study *Symbolic Wounds: Puberty Rites and the Envious Male*, Bruno Bettelheim examines pubertal initiation rites of some "primitive cultures"— in a way meant to critique Freud's oversimplifying views in *Totem and Taboo*— and the schizophrenic children at the Sonia Shankman Orthogenic School at the University of Chicago. He pays particular attention to circumcision and sub-incision rituals to explore the idea of "male envy": the male envy for certain (essentialist) qualities of womanhood, namely, its magical reproductive power. This is Bettelheim's challenge:

> If we could give greater recognition to boys' desires to bear children ... our boys and men might feel less envy and anxious hostility towards girls and women.... The freer men are to acknowledge their positive wish to create life, and to emphasize their contribution to it, the less will they have to assert power through destructive inventions [151].[1]

In his 1962 revision, Bettelheim incorporates the views of his one of his critics, D. Riesman, who finds that some men want to avoid "the labor burden and the menstrual 'curse' imposed on women" while still being able to "enjoy the ... indisputable potentialities of being a woman" (Riesman refers to the Plains Indians and the *berdache*). Bettelheim adds, in affirmation, that "it is exactly because that wish is so deeply repressed in modern man ... that so many men escape into overt or unconscious homosexuality" (10–11). In these terms, the Male Mother can be seen as a man who retains his gendered identity and also (potentially) his heterosexuality while enjoying the benefits of womanhood. The figure of the Male Mother is, then, in Bettelheimian terms, a brilliant new strategy for men to avoid not just the labor and menstrual burdens and "curses" of women but also the arrested development of homosexuality (to use loaded and outdated terminology all around). Male Motherhood, then, allows men to correct the treacheries of sexual difference while reveling in the potentialities *of* difference.

By emphasizing the gendered dissatisfaction in both sexes, Bettelheim anticipates the work of Judith Butler, who has so arduously striven for an understanding of both sex and gender as cultural constructions. If both boys and girls chafe at their gendered assignments, the envious desire each feels for the other sex could be sublimated rage at being trapped within a defining and defined sex in the first place.

What Bettelheim leaves out of his work, in the words of Eva Feder Kittay in a sympathetic but not uncritical revaluation of *Symbolic Wounds*, are "the full importance of the fact of the woman's mothering in creating man's envy of women's procreative powers, and, finally, the persistent fact of woman's subordination."[2] He also, I would add (while noting that he is writing in a pre–Stonewall period), condemns homosexuality as a paranoid escape from the pressures of conventional manhood. Bettelheim's saddening homophobia aside, his treatment marks one of the few analyses of male envy for women's powers in criticism and theory, psychoanalytic or otherwise.

Boys, Bettelheim notes, often convincingly dress up as girls during Halloween rituals. The Halloween disguise represents the boys' "desire to be, and to find out how it feels to be, women. But it is also an anxious and hostile caricature of women" (35–6). As if addressing Kittay's crucial concerns, Bettelheim acknowledges that a certain hostility exists in boys' appropriations of femininity. This sense of hostility ties in with one of Bettelheim's most progressive statements, which links castration anxiety to inter-sex hostilities. He justifies his interpretation of initiation rites because it

> emphasizes in individual psychology and in certain social institutions the importance of pre–Oedipal experiences, particularly insecurity about and dissatisfaction of *both* boys and girls with their own sex, and their envy of the other sex. Were we to recognize the importance of such tendencies, and of the effect of maternal figures in creating a desire for female sex functions, and also castration anxiety in the male, it might lead us to reinterpret certain of our social institutions and clinical observations [57].

Giving this asseveration the most sympathetic reading possible, we might view Bettelheim as a psychoanalytic iconoclast, hoping to shake up the biases of society and psychoanalysis both. Bettelheim also productively figures the "mother" as generative not only of castration anxiety but also of male envy for her capacities and gendered "talents." This is a corrective to the Freudian-Lacanian view of the pre-oedipal realm of the mother, which we must reject in order to join the masculinist rational, orderly realm of the Symbolic, the entry into language that transforms us into social subjects. Rather than renouncing the maternal, boys and men may be powerfully attracted to and envious of it.

At its most progressive, *Symbolic Wounds* does away with the misogynistic adherence to classical psychoanalysis's phallogocentric ideology of penis envy, thereby displacing masculinity as the *sine qua non* of gendered life. As Bettelheim writes, he became more and more convinced as he worked on this study that "*one sex* [always] *feels envy in regard to the sexual organs and functions of the other*" (19, his emphasis). He goes on: parsing what Freud referred to as the "great antithesis of the sexes," "the great enigma of the biological fact of the duality of the sexes," Bettelheim comes to believe that initiation rites "might have originated in this antithesis, might even have been attempts to resolve the sexual anxiety and envy that flow from it" (20). By making the phallus only *one* site of envy, and women's reproductive organs (and nurturing breasts) another, Bettelheim at least begins to allow us the opportunity to view envy as a longing to break free of the binding logic, the imprisoning confines, of sex and gender.

In this regard, the sheer liminality of the Male Mother would appear to satisfy the demands Bettelheim placed on his discipline and on culture. Male Mothers represent the opportunity for access to certain powerful, profound traits in femininity and womanhood. But what happens when such access is granted? For a considered analysis of representation's response, as it were, to Bettelheim's urgent desires, we may turn to literature, film, and narrative television's amazingly persistent interest in the figure of the Male Mother and in granting male characters access, however fleetingly or vexingly, to the fantastic powers of the other sex. This overview will inform our analysis of the character of Neelix.

Within the Folds of History (and Jabba the Hutt's Stomach): Representations of the Male Mother in Western Culture

The Male Mother is a tradition that can be traced throughout representation, in myth, folklore, medieval religious writings, and other earlier sources. To offer only the briefest overview: Zeus, perhaps the first Male Mother, delivers Athena from his forehead and Dionysius from his thigh — perverse parodies of female birth or male appropriations of the birth-process. The Judeo-Christian-Islamic God is a parthenogenic Male Mother. Milton's *Paradise Lost* poetically describes the God of Genesis as hermaphroditic: God "Dove-like sat'st brooding on the vast Abyss / And mad'st it pregnant" (I. 21). Milton's God both broods and penetrates, bears and impregnates the Earth. The Christ-as-Mother of medieval English lyric is an important Male Mother figure. A passage such as this one, from a speech delivered by Christ about his relationship to man's soul, gendered female in a way that anticipates Jung's theory of *anima*, is exemplary:

> In my side I have made hir neste.
> Loke in, how wide a wound is heere:
> This is hir chambre, heere shall she reste,
> That she and I mowen slepe in fere.
> Heer may she wasshe if any filth were;
> Heer is socour for al hir wo.
> Come if she wyl, she shal have chere.
> *Quia amore langueo.*[3]

This beautiful passage reverses the expectations of gendered order, making Christ the mother, man the female child. The wound in Christ's side becomes, in a grotesque/beautiful image, a capacious womb. A place man's female soul can be washed of its "filth" and find succor to heal all of her woe, it promises the reverse of being born into original sin — an emergence into purity and cleanliness. Being born of woman plunges man into Original Sin; crawling into Christ's womb-wound removes the skin of human evil.

The Male Mother is part of a gender-bending continuum that includes the homosexual (especially when figured as the Third Sex of nineteenth century sexologists) and the hermaphrodite. As Thomas L. Long notes of the famous medieval woman poet Julian of Norwich's meditations on the theme of Christ-as-Mother, there were many such medieval meditations on gender-bending figures: the Ovidian Hermaphrodite was another "transgendered deity," and the hermaphrodite may also be seen as Christ, who combines God's male nature with humanity's feminine one. It is also important to note that only the thinnest of boundaries separates the figure of the hermaphrodite from that of the homosexual. Long's essay is helpful for our purposes here, for he both foregrounds the messy overlap between homosexuality and hermaphroditism in relation to the Male Mother — which I would argue is a compensatory compromise between the two — and establishes a connection between classical antiquity's and Christianity's figuring of the Male Mother.

Predating Ovid's Hermaphrodite and the medieval Christ, of course, is Teiresias. Prowling throughout Greek tragedy and T.S. Eliot's "The Waste Land," Teiresias is not exactly hermaphroditic; he is alternately male and female rather than both at once. What defines the continuum that exists between figures like Teiresias (his/her own category), the hermaphrodite, the homosexual, and the Male Mother figures a transgressive, transgendered opposition to fixed gender identity and practices. The Male Mother, a feminized male who actively nurtures or broods, is still irreducibly male — therein lies the potential for transgression. But there is also a potential for homophobic reaction against effeminacy to be inscribed within a depiction of a Male Mother — a revulsion against a realization of manhood that stretches out beyond the defined boundaries of gender.

One genderbending figure, the Male Medusa, a powerful image in iconography throughout English history, represents the terrifying force of Nature–dominated Man, a fusion of the brutal power of masculinity and the fertile, flowering power of a feminized Nature. As Marjorie Garber writes on the gender indeterminacy of *Macbeth*, the Male Medusa, "the foliate head or leaf mask which gained enormous popularity in England and throughout western Europe during the Romanesque and medieval periods ... with leaves sprouting from [its face] ... [is] often sinister and frightening.... [This] Green Man ... embodies a warning against the dark side of man's nature, the devil within."[4] It is interesting that this sinister figure represents the union between brutal masculinist power and generative female nature: it can be seen, then, as a demonization of the Male Mother, its doppelganger.

A modern instance of the male who resists definition — while seeming like a modern version of a myth figure Pan — is the gay bear. (Camille Paglia has made a similar argument.) Were Neelix assigned an explicitly queer sexuality, he would most likely resemble this contemporary symbol of feminized butchness. The gay bear, a hirsute and often immense man, represents a subaltern pop culture version of the mythic Male Mother. Hairy and abundant, macho yet soft, the gay bear — not to be confused with the equally hirsute but most often disciplinarian Leather Daddy (there are, of course, hybrid forms of sexual role-playing, e.g., bearish Leather Daddies) — is a blur of surface macho and loving kindliness. (I am not attempting to offer anything like a definitive reading of the gay bear, merely an evaluation of the gay bear's media representation.)

One pop classic, *The Return of the Jedi* (1983), third film in the *Star Wars* trilogy, fascinatingly toys with tropes of the Male Mother. Robin Wood has written that the evil Emperor, mightier even than Darth Vader (depicted as a fading, frailer monster on the way to redemption in this film), is an occluded mother: "the unredeemably evil Emperor ... seems modeled on the witch in Snow White (the heroine's stepmother). Her male disguise makes it permissible to subject her to [a] violent expulsion."[5] What Wood points to here is the original *Star Wars* trilogy's astonishing erasure of the Mother and its Restoration of the Father. Though Luke's aunt appears briefly in *Star Wars*, there are no female figures in the first three films who might be said to be mothers. Leia, revealed as Luke's sister (to multivalent controversy), shares with Luke a mother whom we never see — except, perhaps, in the ultimately annihilated, drag figure of the Emperor. But the Emperor may also be read not as the disguised mother but as a *Male* Mother. His cloak and its folds enclose and feminize him; his physical weakness — he needs Vader to battle Luke physically — compensated for by his manipulative control over the plots he devises make him a demonic mother, a parody of motherhood, what happens when a Male is Mother, a depiction that encapsulates male fears and envy over the power of the Mother.

The most recent *Star Wars* film, *Revenge of the Sith* (2005), only confirms the Emperor's role as Male Mother. Played with campy relish by Ian McDiarmid, the Emperor in this film darkly nurtures the young Anakin Skywalker (Hayden Christiansen), who will eventually become Darth Vader. McDiarmid's Emperor emerges as the anti–Mother who feeds her young bile, hate, evil. Hovering above the smoldering remains of Anakin — nearly dead from a volcano-planet battle with Obi-Wan Kenobi (Ewan McGregor) — the Emperor resembles a dark bird brooding over her young. The Emperor rescues Anakin only to transform him into a legendary metal-man menace. In the most interesting sequence of the film, the birth of future saviors Luke and Leia is intercut with the "birth" of Darth Vader, as Anakin's ruined remains are sutured to black metal, the man reborn as machine. The sobs of wife and mother Padmé (Natalie Portman) are counterbalanced by the anguished cries of Anakin-Vader as the metal melds with his flesh. The droids who help to deliver Padmé's babies resemble children's toys while those assisting the rebirth of Anakin darkly loom like sentinels of death. If the Emperor is a Male Mother birthing a new offspring, the new offspring represents a deformed, distorted version of life, an anti-life of pain and metal. As Darth Vader comes to tormented new, machine life, bursting with sorrowful rage as he learns that his beloved Padmé has died, the Emperor seethes with diabolical pleasure.

Padmé devolves from a tough, no-nonsense action chick in the first two films to a simpering, pathetic non-entity in *Revenge*. She is certainly no Juliet to Anakin's Romeo. Lacking the strong will and courage of Shakespeare's heroine, Padmé dies in childbirth of unspecified causes beyond "she lost the will to live." In Lucas's realm of male will-to-power, it is notable that the only significant female character has none. As the study of popular culture reveals, pop can become more reactionary, more limited, the older — or newer — it gets. Not only is Padmé a pale reflection of herself from her previous *Star Wars* films, she is also a pallid version of the tough, sarcastic, driven Princess Leia of the first *Star Wars* trilogy. Whereas *Return of the Jedi* ends with a queer, interspecies New Family comprised of friends — the Ewoks jabbering in song, the queer apparitional male group of Obi-Wan, the restored Anakin, and Yoda — *Revenge* ends with a John Ford–like frontier shot on Tatooine of Luke's aunt and uncle holding their new charge as they gaze out, in Adam and Eve fashion, on their vast, now properly reproductive world. The film erases the biological mother — Padmé — but restores proper reproductivity (we have also seen baby Leia being placed in the arms of her adoptive parents). The Emperor's Male Mother is fully counterbalanced with two pairs of adoptive heterosexual parents. So what appears to be a dark, despairing film of the triumph of evil — as *Star Wars* continuity would apparently necessitate — becomes instead a healing film about normative heterosexual continuity.

Other *Star Wars* figures are suggestive in this regard, especially Jabba the Hutt. Like the Green Man, he is a feminized male whose monstrosity lies in his blurring of gendered definitions. Like a vast fertility goddess, he spreads out on his stage-throne, expanding in abundance as his sloppy phallic tongue leaps out. And Salacious Crumb, the shrieky-giggly imp creature that is Jabba's familiar, resides within the kangaroo-mother-folds of Jabba's girth. The Emperor and Jabba are Male Mother representations of the Monstrous-Feminine discussed by Barbara Creed, embodying "the dread of the generative mother seen only in the abyss, the monstrous vagina, the origin of all life threatening to reabsorb what it once birthed."[6]

The climax of *The Return of the Jedi* presents a trio of spectral, phantom Fathers: Obi-Wan Kenobi, the redeemed Anakin Skywalker, and Yoda, all appearing to Luke from beyond the grave. Are these fathers or Male Mothers? Yoda, with his indeterminate but still male identity, and alien form, most readily appears to be a Male Mother, but Obi-Wan and Anakin, phosphorescently flickering, come close to Male Motherhood not only by beneficently standing in for the absent Mother but also by appearing to proclaim the utter lack of a need for her presence. *The Return of the Jedi* suggests that only a Jedi-trinity of Male Mothers can vanquish the power of the Monstrous-Feminine. And *The Phantom Menace* (1999), with its nakedly tender male-male love scene between the young Obi-Wan and the dying Jedi Master Qui-Gon, deepens the cult of male mothering by excluding the mother *onscreen* rather than leaving her out altogether. (Anakin's mother, Schmi Skywalker, whom we "meet" in the film, is left behind when Qui-Gon takes the boy away as his pupil.)

Other Male Mothers might include the Khan of *Star Trek II: The Wrath of Khan* (1982), whose broad powerful prosthetic male chest is offset by his feathery feminized 'do and who presides over a mixed-sexed brood of Kewpie Doll groupies. (We will examine Khan in greater depth in Chapter Seven.) Recently, the big, hairy figure of Hagrid (Robbie Coltrane) in the film versions of the Harry Potter novels is made *explicitly* a Male Mother, especially in the first film in the series (based on the first novel), *Harry Potter and the Sorcerer's Stone* (2001). After his baby Norwegian dragon hatches and instinctively crawls towards him, a beaming Hagrid, whose hairy head and hairy beard link him to the Male Medusa icon, exclaims, "Ah, he knows his Mummy!"

The most unsettling representation of the male mothering theme is without question Freddy Krueger's retooling as a demonic Male Mother. *The Nightmare on Elm Street* series, created by former English professor Wes Craven (was ever director more aptly named?), turns its archvillain Freddy Krueger, the hysterically horrifying burn-victim child-molester demon who haunts the dreams of suburban teens, into a parodistically demonic Male Mother in *A*

Nightmare on Elm Street 4: The Dream Master (1988). Freddy Krueger lifts up his striped hobo's sweater to reveal a stomach-collage of miniaturized victims' heads, all of whom, like freakish figures from a Francis Bacon painting, moan piteously, in one of cinema's greatest Surrealist effects. Freddy self-identifies as Male Mother. "They are all my children!" he howls in triumph as pulsating baby heads bubble and squeak within his cauldron-stomach. The subversive power of this image lies in its allocation of mothering to a creature who defies and resists all social norms, codes, strictures. But there is a suggestion even more chilling than any *Nightmarish* tableau: that the graphic depiction of male mothering can only be construed as a horrific orgy of pain and suffering. When the teen girl-heroine vanquishes Freddy, she relegates his gendered hubris to the status of nonexistence, sends his genderbending maternity to the Hell where it seemingly belongs, and pointedly frees all those damned children from Freddy's perverse male womb.

With his odd, unwieldy status as both monstrous pedophile and 1980s teen icon (Freddy became more and more an antic cut-up, a jokester–Id relentlessly satirizing suburbia), Freddy circulates multivalent anxieties about queer perversity. The pedophile as Male Mother is the embodiment of calumniating mass-culture fears about homosexuality and transgendered identities. With this understanding of the fascinating range of Male Mothers in representation, we can return now to a consideration of Neelix as a remarkably sustained and developed version of the figure.

Godmothers, Caretakers, and Hair Pasta: Neelix's Seasonal Changes

Of the myriad qualms passionately expressed in multiple online forums about *Voyager*, always a controversial series among *Trek* fans, the most aggressive complaints often revolve around the figure of Captain Kathryn Janeway (Kate Mulgrew), who, despite her legions of fervent fans, has been likened by some to a martinet and even a murderer. A strain in the ongoing critique of Janeway, the first female Captain to lead a *Star Trek* series, has been her role as "Mommy" to the crew, sublimating her erotic energies by aggressively, even stiflingly, mothering the crew she "stranded" in the Delta Quadrant (an event depicted in the premiere episode, "Caretaker"; all of the other *Trek* series are set in the Federation-dominated Alpha Quadrant). The Mommyism of Janeway, according to those who hold the character in contempt, has been Janeway's chief failing. There is a complementary critique of Janeway as a custodian of patriarchal values, an Alpha Male devoid of "femininity," a tyrannical upholder of the Law of the Father, who snarls out orders and controls every facet of life onboard *Voyager* in her guilt-ridden obsession to return the crew home.

To my mind, all of the relentless Janeway-as-shrewlike-Mother and Janeway-as-Ahab fault-finding has been thoroughly unfair, indicative of disappointing fan-base sexism. It has also obscured one of the more interesting and radical elements of a series often accused of being a reactionary reinscription of that "crucial social institution," the ideologically suspect nuclear family-structure[7]: the development of the character of Neelix as a Male Mother, a nurturing male figure who dispenses love, food, advice, and maternal warmth. A midwife of feeling on *Voyager*, Neelix dispenses love and advice to his brood (e.g., in the Season Seven episode "Drive," Neelix persuades the feisty half-human, half–Klingon engineer B'Elanna to break off her relationship with her boyfriend, Tom Paris). With his associations with cooking, exotic foods, alienness, and advice, Neelix becomes a relatively modern instance of the ancient female archetype of the sibyl: the mystic crone, wise woman, or witch, predating the rabbi, the priest, or the psychiatrist as guide and seer. His particular realization as a Male Mother is one of the most detailed in representation, and deserves a sustained treatment.

Voyager endured sweeping changes throughout its run in producers, writers, and cast; season by season, the show's look, feel, and intent changed. In Season Four, original creators Jeri Taylor and Michael Piller began to cede the reins to Brannon Braga; by Season Five, Braga was fully in control; in Season Seven, staff writer Kenneth Biller took over. Played by Ethan Phillips, the character of Neelix is an exemplum of the fluctuations from season to season, the decisive shifts from the Taylor-Piller era to the Braga to the Biller one, but also of *Voyager*'s remarkable interest in exploring gender and sexuality. Neelix goes through permutations that are a curious index of anxieties surrounding the depiction of alien — i.e., alternative, possibly queer — male sexuality.

The two-part episode that commences the series, "Caretaker," establishes Neelix, a trader from the planet Talax, as a bestial and pleasantly rank fellow. Deprived of water, he noticeably stinks, as the offended nostrils of Tuvok (Tim Russ), the Vulcan security officer, suggest. Tuvok is visibly miffed that Neelix gives him a childlike hug when they first beam Neelix to *Voyager* from his ship. With a golden hedge of hair that seems like an overabundant mohawk, a vast, protuberant forehead covered with dark spots, golden yellow patches of skin, tufted eyebrows, complementary rows of lower-face whiskers, and a rotund, compact medium-sized body, Neelix seems to be man crossed with psychedelic hedgehog. Given an opportunity to take a bath, he luxuriates in soapy water, and, happily, randily soaping himself before the visibly perturbed Tuvok, suggests nothing less than an alien Pan, with apposite sexual threat and bravado. The homoeroticism between Tuvok and Neelix — alien men — is one of the most consistent elements of the series, from first to penultimate episode, and will demand consideration in our analysis of Neelix's ultimate realization as Male Mother.

Voyager makes a deal with Neelix for information about a hostile race, the Kazon. Unbeknownst to *Voyager*, the Kazon tribe they are contending with holds a young woman, Kes, prisoner. (Kes is a member of a race, the Ocampa, who only live for nine years; she is also Neelix's mate.) Neelix helps *Voyager*, but secretly plots to free Kes. Ultimately, Neelix and Kes volunteer to stay onboard *Voyager* for its lonely and perilous *Trek* back home to the Alpha Quadrant, she as medic, he as cook. As Kes's lover, Neelix is initially developed, in Season One, as the jealous protector of this innocent lass. The resident flyboy, Tom Paris, the cocksure, arrogant blond pilot, seems to have a sexual interest in Kes, which drives Neelix into a fury. Many Season One episodes depict Neelix as an irate, violently angry, jealous lover.

In the Season Two episode "Parturition," written by Tom Szollosi, Neelix and Paris finally come to blows, with Neelix shrieking, in the mess hall over which he presides, at Paris to stay away from Kes, or else. This comic-cuckold scene, a stock tradition from Roman comedy and medieval texts such as "The Miller's Tale," culminates in Neelix dumping a vast quantity of an alien delicacy, "hair pasta," all over Paris — certainly one of the weirdest and most suggestive moments in a *Trek* series. Later, Paris and Neelix are forced to beam down to a planet in a hunt for supplies and end up having to nurse a reptilian humanoid baby until its foul-tempered saurian mother arrives. While nursing the child together, Neelix and Paris vent their frustrations and come to a new reconciliation. In an earlier Season Two episode, "Elogium," Neelix had been shown to be resistant to the thought of fathering a child with Kes (at the end of this episode about her Ocampan fertility cycle, she decides not to have a baby, after all). "Parturition" seems compensatory, then — an episode that clearly depicts Neelix as parent, correcting his previously exhibited cowardice in this regard — except that now he is co-parent to a child with another male character. In fact, the one who insists, over Paris's initial protests, that this child must be taken care of, Neelix is depicted as the maternal nurturer, a stand-in mother. "Parturition" signals a transition from Neelix's role as jealous heterosexual lover to that of healer and nurturer with no clearly defined sexuality. In fact, there is a shot in "Parturition" of Neelix secretly observing Paris and Kes as they giggle like sweethearts, decisively placing Neelix *out* of the scene of heterosexual love. In a later scene in which Neelix tries to hide his jealousy, he aggressively serves Kes abundant amounts of food, in a parody of maternal nurturing that suggests he is a Talaxian mother hen, force-feeding her brood.

In the Mark S. Waters film version of Wendy MacLeod's play *The House of Yes* (1997), the Jacqueline Onassis wannabe, Jackie-O (Parker Posey), simulates being drenched in JFK's blood and viscera by wearing macaroni and ketchup on her pink pillbox outfit. In much the same way, the tomato sauced hair pasta spread on Tom and Neelix's outfits — which adorns them when they are briefed by Janeway for their Away Mission — signify viscera. The image of the outfits drenched with red sauce and pasta cry out for interpretation as birth imagery — blood, flesh, the signs of birth. The hairiness of the pasta, with its immediate connections to disgust, metonymically suggests the terror of adult sexuality, but also specifically "the terrifying genitals of the Mother" that Freud located in the iconography of the Medusa — the writhing snakes being representations of pubic hair and also compensatory substitutions for the castrated penis.[8]

Because the hair pasta imagery associates them with birth, and the fact that this Planet Hell to which they are beaming down is described as a primitive, primordial place, both men are prefigured as maternal figures: a new style Adam and Steve, a male reimagining of Adam and Eve with their ready-made progeny, a child even more alien than Neelix. (This scene of a male-male couple as the first parents of a demonic race anticipates the fourth season episode "Demon," which we discussed in the second chapter.)

The hair-pasta fight ingeniously foregrounds one crucial trope that binds disparate Male Mothers throughout history: hair. From the Green Man to the gay bear to Hagrid to Qui-Gon to whiskered Neelix and his hair pasta, hair — springing and sprouting and swarming — serves as a sign of gendered anxiety. Hair links Male Mothers to the Medusa and her writhing hair-serpents suggestive of sexual terror, and to the Male Medusa suggestive of the terror of generative man. Hair — Freud's symbol, in its Medusan form, for adult sexuality generally and the simultaneous revulsion and excitement it inspires in the spectator — links Male Mothers to a wide range of sexual identities, desires, and the depictions of those desires. Bettelheim accounts for the power of hair this way:

> The growth of hair is [significant] ... because pubic hair signifies adult sexuality in both sexes, and, in women, is coincident with the onset of menstruation ... female pubic hair is of great interest. Disturbed children express their envy and anxiety about the adult woman's vagina in angry remarks about the "hairy vagina"; in some severely disturbed boys, it often seems an obsession. Perhaps the pubic hair, which is visible in boys but only an incidental sign of sexual maturity, is indirectly emphasized and ritualized to compensate for women's much more obvious signs [127].

The hair-pasta fight scene, in which both Tom and Neelix fling the offending, symbolically wounded and wounding nourishment at each other, suggests that neither of them wants full possession of hair's symbolic attributes. What each seems to struggle for is gendered supremacy, and what each seems to fear is effeminization, alternately represented as the cuckoldry of Neelix and the quashing of the swaggering libido and seducer's bravado in Tom.

"Parturition" plays around with these obvious gendered "signs." Once on the planet, the gender division between the two is clearly articulated. The Paris of Robert Duncan McNeill, lanky and blond and still, at this point, a *Voyager* sex symbol, is called the "uncle"—but Paris decisively refers to Neelix as the "godmother" of their temporarily adopted child. This episode makes the collapse between roles such as nearly cuckolded husband and Male Mother quite effortless. "Parturition," from the Latin, means the process or act of giving birth; since no actual birth takes place, the title must refer to a metaphorical act of birthing. This episode gives birth to a new Neelix squarely placed in the (god)mother role.

In a standout Season Two episode, "Deadlock," in which *Voyager* is split into two distinct but similar versions of itself, an ensign, Samantha Wildman, gives birth under great duress, given the attacks on the ship by the organ-stealing race, the Vidiians. On one of the *Voyagers*, Samantha's child, Naomi, dies; on the other, Naomi lives. On the ship on which Naomi dies, Neelix is there to guide Samantha through the pregnancy and, when the baby dies, to comfort and soothe her. Never a character the producers seemed especially certain about, Neelix in "Deadlock" now begins more clearly to assume his role as Male Mother, passing from the bestial, reeking, randy lover to the warm, compassionate, soft nurturer. Brannon Braga, co-creator of the series *Enterprise*, the sixth *Trek* series, wrote "Deadlock," and he must have liked Szollosi's reimagining of Neelix as the maternal soother. From "Deadlock" on, Neelix's character coheres into the role of maternal nurturer; "Deadlock" into reinforces the idea by having him be *two simultaneous* versions of his new Male Mother persona.

Tied to his role as maternal comforter is Neelix's ongoing role as chef. Forever whipping up delicacies culled from planets being explored, Neelix prepares foods that are widely regarded, in the first two seasons, as inedible, ghastly—all of which he offers with almost maniacal cheer. Neelix's favorite item recurs throughout the series: Leeola Root, a priapic vegetable that generates stews, soups, casseroles. Medicinal and bitter (Lieutenant Joe Carey retches after tasting it in the Season One episode "State of Flux"), this root comes to symbolize Neelix himself—once you get used to his flavor, you appreciate how good he is for you. Yet Leeola Root, over the course of the series, loses pungency, its association with strong, bitter, even disgusting, but salutary, properties. It remains as a marker for Neelix's character — nearly every episode that mentions Neelix mentions Leeola Root — but it loses its specificity as a strong taste to be reckoned with. In much the same way, Neelix does, too. Transforming from a bad chef to a great one, from a cook whose food is the butt of shipboard jokes to a warm, beneficent dispenser of healing, homey, tasty foods, Neelix trades in his distinctive flavor and becomes blandly palatable.

In Season Two, he is also developed as a voice of tolerance and compassion. In another episode, "Investigations," it appears that Paris, widely regarded as a traitor, troublemaker, and con-man, is leaving *Voyager*. Neelix openly mourns the departure of his former rival, again giving him that Neelix-hug that transcends male boundaries.

Neelix's alienness allows his sexuality and gendered identity a fluidity that would be denied a "human" character. Before Kes's departure from *Voyager* at the start of Season Four, to make room for the eye-popping spectacle of womanhood Seven of Nine, Neelix is still depicted as a liminal figure, moving towards his role as Male Mother while maintaining ties to his older jealous-lover self and also his "past" as an ex-con. (At the climax of "Investigations," Neelix goes *mano a mano* with a traitor, a conflict that ends with this enemy's rather violent death, but we never see Neelix in such a physical conflict again, even in his security officer guise; the Season Three episode "Fair Trade," about the reappearance of his criminal past, depicts Neelix as a man with dark secrets — which never come up again.) But once Kes leaves, Neelix spends the rest of the series (up until the episode that culminates his arc, the Season Seven "Homestead") developing and enhancing his role as Male Mother. His role as the nurturer is solidified by his ongoing relationship with Naomi Wildman, *Voyager*'s resident child. He also becomes the morale officer, the ambassador to other worlds, the public relations chief (he shows One, the Frankenstein's monster–like 29th century Borg, around the ship in the Season Six "Drone"), the midnight-snack father confessor who makes banana pancakes for B'Elanna, serves nocturnal black coffee to Janeway, prods fussy eater Tuvok into imbibing homemade Vulcan stew, counsels Seven of Nine when she is troubled, coaxes Harry (the perpetually green ensign) to be more manfully captain-like (in the Season Seven episode "Nightingale"), and, as we have noted, even becomes an accomplished cook — an alien gourmet. Tom sums up his character in the Season Seven episode "Repentance": "You're the softest touch in the Delta Quadrant." Neelix also becomes the character, from Season Four on, with the least amount of screen-time, a strongly sweet spice to be sprinkled only sparingly over the proceedings.

After his never clearly defined relationship with Kes ends in the middle of Season Three (in "Warlord"), Neelix is never shown in a romantic relationship of any kind until the last Neelix episode. True, he does fantasize about a blonde telepathic moppet stroking his whiskers in the Season Four "Random Thoughts," but this young woman is an eerie facsimile of Kes, another *child*-woman with psychic powers, and this moment is an anomaly. His relationship with Kes is never depicted in explicitly erotic terms; more than anything else, despite his comedically jealous rage, his relationship to her, a character from a race with an nine-year life span, seems more avuncular than anything else; Kes seems more child than woman in a way that anticipates the child objects of Neelix's attentions throughout the bulk of the series. Whenever Neelix is at the center of an episode from Season Four on, he is almost exclusively in the position of the nurturer to children (Naomi Wildman, Borg children rehabilitated by *Voyager*) or the impaired (Tuvok in the Season Six episode "Riddles"). Nearly all of the Neelix episodes from Season Four deal with his role as Male Mother: in Season Five's "Once Upon a Time," Neelix must nurture Naomi during a terrible time in which it is very likely that her mother has been killed on an Away Mission (she hasn't been, it turns out); in Season Six's "Riddles," Tuvok, zapped by an alien weapon, becomes a space-child whom Neelix nurtures until the Vulcan's mind is restored; later that season, Neelix tells the children a story for an entire episode, keeping them occupied with the tale of "The Haunting of Deck Twelve"; in the final season, Neelix has no special character episode save the one in which his character exits ("Homestead"), which, incidentally, provides an explicitly heterosexual resolution of his character that corrects the indeterminacy both sexual and gendered that defines, by not defining, the character for the last four seasons.

Anticipating this heteroerotic coda to his character arc, that season's Klingon episode "Prophecy"— in which *Voyager* accommodates a huge bunch of Klingons, and Neelix and Tuvok must be bunkmates — has Neelix presumably making passionate, violent love to a ferocious Klingon woman, a scene that might be seen as spellbinding in its total distinction from the previous four seasons' depictions of Neelix as wholly sexless. Yet even this depiction of carnal explosiveness is handled with pointed ambiguity. The Klingon woman with the voracious sexual appetite has been hounding Harry Kim; Neelix relieves Kim (who is wholly uninterested in her) of the burden of her attentions. When Tuvok, in the comic resolution to the scene, discovers Neelix and the Klingon woman supposedly *in flagrante delicto*, Neelix is fully clothed, albeit disheveled. We have no way of knowing if any kind of sexual experience occurred between them, or if merely a violent bout of Klingon wrestling had taken place. This scene is comic, a sexual burlesque. As the Amazonian, feral Klingon woman looms above his relatively puny frame, Neelix is presented not as the phallic pursuer but as the butt of a sexual joke.

"Once Upon a Time" is especially notable for its circulation of the attendant anxieties that surround the figure of the Male Mother. Written by Michael Taylor, this episode makes explicit one of the recurring subtextual problems of the series: the schism between Neelix as the Good Mother and Janeway as the Terrible Mother. These archetypal Jungian roles shift fluidly throughout the series; often, Janeway is depicted as the Good Mother while various evil alien beings — the Borg Queen, the Voth lizard queen of Season Three's paleontological fantasy "Distant Origin" — assume the role of the Terrible Mother. Jung describes the differences this way: "[The loving mother's qualities are] ... all that is benign ... that fosters growth and fertility ... [the terrible mother connotes] anything ... dark; the abyss, the world of the dead."[9] "Once Upon a Time" collapses the distinct boundaries of these categories.

In this episode, Neelix threatens to take over for good the role of parenting little, precocious Naomi. There are three family structures against which Neelix's skills are compared: biological mother Samantha Wildman, who may die on an Away Mission; Janeway, who implicitly represents maternal authority and explicitly questions Neelix's handling of Naomi's temporary predicament of motherlessness; and, most interestingly of all, an allegorical interspecies gay male couple, the holodeck characters Treevis (a brownish-green tree-man) and Flotter (a blindingly blue water-man). (In *Trek* lore, holonovels replace books — including children's books, as in this episode — and have the same intergenerational continuity.) The cryptic sexual metaphors here include a moment in which Flotter ejaculates a stream of water from his phallic finger over the flaming Treevis.

An implicit critique of Samantha as the absent, neglectful mother informs this episode. She is the only one of the Away Team who is seriously injured, the one most vividly threatened with death; she may never be able to see her child again. She lives in the world of the dead of Jung's Terrible Mother. Neelix is shown, simply by attentively and omnipresently being there, to be a much more suitable parent to Naomi; he also appears to have no other function than to nurture her. He represents the benignity of the Good Mother.

Then there is Janeway, who in Season Five is at her most frenzied, rigid, and clenched. In her discussion with Neelix about Samantha's likely imminent death and Naomi's need to be told about it, Janeway ends up saying, "Either you tell her about it or I will!" This seems, however sensible, indifferent to his feelings. Then there are the holodeck characters, who bicker like a stereotypical old married couple — their slavish devotion to Naomi doubles

Neelix's and parodies it — they are even more alien than he is, and unreal to boot, being computer-generated programs. But in one scene, after Naomi learns of the danger her mother is in and hides from Neelix in the holodeck, the queer hologram couple team up to refuse Neelix access to Naomi. They posit themselves as her real protectors, signifying the relative normality of the parenting gay couple to the Male Mother, who is a freakish hybrid that makes even the odd gay couple look "normal."

The genuine gendered tensions in this episode simmer underneath its fairy tale surface. It ends on a most interesting note. Samantha, her rightful status as sanctified biological mother restored, returns from the (nearly) dead and to the holodeck with her reclaimed child, the queer holograms, and Neelix. (Samantha has climbed up a gendered rung, from the Terrible to the Absent Mother, by surviving the Away Mission.) After a tearful reunion with the holograms in the holonovel, Samantha takes Naomi and the holograms on a jaunt through the program. Neelix is left behind, staring out almost wistfully at another scene from which he is excluded. But then it is revealed that the figure of Janeway stands behind *him.* Janeway walks up to Neelix and they talk about her old adventures in the holonovel. The childless Janeway and Neelix are left behind. The Childless Mother and the Male Mother are, in these Trekkian social terms, beneath the Absent Mother and the Gay Male Couple in the hierarchy of child-rearing legitimacy.

In light of this episode's sexual stratification, it is interesting to consider that we never again see Samantha Wildman — except for the Season Six episode, "Fury," set in *Voyager*'s *first* season — and Neelix functions for the remainder of the run as Naomi's parent. As Kittay writes, "The actual women who are mothers are subordinated to the men for whom the gifts of the idealized Mother are reserved."[10] "Fury" is specifically set at a time in the series when Samantha Wildman was not yet apparently pregnant. Though "Once Upon a Time" reunites Samantha and Naomi, the remainder of the *Voyager* text would appear to transfer her motherly role to Neelix, who becomes a paragon of the idealized maternal.

It is also interesting to note that Neelix is thereafter firmly locked into place as the nurturer to children. His normally erratic and even violently disagreeable relationship with Tuvok is reimagined as a parent-child relationship in the Season Six episode "Riddles." This episode signifies, too, the overlap between the categories of the homosexual and male-mothering roles embodied by Neelix.

Consistently stoic in the Vulcan manner, Tuvok abhors — though we are always aware that affection must exist in that Vulcan heart, too — Neelix's aggressive cheer, attentions, emotional neediness. In the Season Two episode

"Meld," a startling mediation on violence, Tuvok even murders a holographic Neelix with his bare hands. But in "Riddles," written by Robert Doherty, the tables turn: Neelix guides Tuvok, brain-injured and rendered childlike (like Charly or Forrest Gump), back to health — in fact, Tuvok wants, in a delicious reversal of their previous dynamic, no one *but* Neelix around. Neelix is the only person Tuvok trusts. The infantile state to which Tuvok is reduced here makes him cleave to mommy–Neelix, who is never more explicitly the nurturer than is in this episode: he festoons Tuvok's sick-bay-space with all manner of comforting emblems (e.g., Vulcan flags), plays music for him, until, miraculously, Tuvok wakes up from his coma. He comforts and coddles Tuvok; he brings out Tuvok's inner child, as they romp through the kitchen, making all manner of desserts. This episode is an interesting example of a tender depiction of male-male affectionalism not *explicitly* depicted as homosexual (echoes of John Steinbeck's 1937 novel *Of Mice and Men*). But — much like lumbering Lenny's dependence on George in the Steinbeck novel — it is Tuvok's brain-addled state and childlike dependence on Neelix that facilitates the mass audience's ability to respond favorably to such a depiction — that, and the alienness of the characters. Neelix, who wears alien-male versions of Sixties mumus, presiding over pots, pans, delicacies, now has a child-helpmeet for his nurturing, angel-of-the-home activities. The indefatigably warm and generous Neelix tends Tuvok with unfailing warmth and generosity; he has no other life, no other needs, but the need to nurture — a fantasy of endless love few human beings could ever realize.

"Riddles" extends the cultural work — to use Jane Tompkins's phrase — done by the Season Two "Parturition." It transfers the care of the child by the male couple to the care of the male couple itself by one of its members. Neither "Riddles" nor "Parturition," however, has ever scored particularly high with fans or reviewers. Online critic Michelle Erica Green had this to say about "Parturition":

> This was a pretty harmless waste of an hour ... and an episode which will be remembered largely as the one where Janeway had short hair that mysteriously grew back by the next week. Tom and Neelix are both likeable characters, but the writers have got to come up with better stories for them than insipid stuff like this. We learned nothing new about either of them, the ship's mission wasn't forwarded by these events, we didn't discover an exciting new alien species since we're never going to see this one again ... what was the point?

I think Green missed the point (though she does mention the salient issue of the sign of "hair") about an episode like "Parturition," which interestingly circulates gendered anxieties about birth, empathy, sexuality, nurturing, and male-male tenderness. But episodes like "Parturition" and "Riddles" make intelligent people wince since they privilege sentiment and, worse, allow depictions of male-male relations to be sentimentalized. They also allow men access to the affectionalism and traits possessed, in our culture, by women — hence the discomfort they cause viewers and the pleasure they would have given Bettelheim.

Considering cultural anxieties about homoaffectionalism, sentiment, and the gendered nature of nurture, the character of the Male Mother as embodied by Neelix presents us, then, with an interesting set of critical problems. If the Male Mother is a queer character — in that he is transgendered — what role does homosexuality, if any, play? Is the Male Mother a progressive character, or a reactionary depiction of a feminized male, a sexual other and an unclassifiable gender cast-off? Is the Male Mother an androgyne — a blur of visible markers of maleness and femaleness? Is he hermaphroditic — a combination of male and female elements? I would argue that — for my purposes here — the Male Mother is, in the words of Robin Wood, "an incoherent text" whose "fragmentation ... becomes a structuring principle,"[11] a male with disquieting and unsettling female attributes that elude political valuation — a hybridized male who presents a series of useful problems for culture. He is also the answer — or at least one response — to the challenge Bettelheim put forth in *Symbolic Wounds*.

Homosexuality and Other Worries for the Male Mother

"Riddles" is a male-male version of the film *Regarding Henry* (1991), in which brain-zapped lawyer Harrison Ford goes from unfeeling macho to gentle infantilism, much as Tuvok does here. This episode is also a coded depiction of hurt/comfort slash fiction, in which one character is wounded in some way and another cares for him. The impaired mental state of Tuvok and the alienness of both Tuvok and Neelix palliates the audience, removes the sting of homosexual romance. Yet this suggestive episode resonates, unintentionally or otherwise, with the reality of such situations in the lives of gay men who have had to nurture their partners through illnesses related to AIDS, such as AIDS dementia. In fact, the closest parallel to this episode I can think of is *explicitly* presented as homosexual: the relationship between the characters played by Bruce Davison and Mark Lamos in the film *Longtime Companion* (1990). It is with this episode that the symbolic weight of the title of the first episode — "Caretaker" — presses most heavily on the viewer. On *Voyager*, who is the ultimate caretaker? This becomes an especially charged issue on a series with a woman in the lead, playing a character simultaneously accused of being a phallic, masculinized character and of over-mothering. Neelix emerges as a kind of liminal, compensatory figure, a fusion of male and female that "heals" the split in the characterization of Janeway — or, in another way, enlarges and exposes it.

Voyager opened up new, queer spaces for thinking about gender and sexuality, however inherently problematic the figure of the male mother. In the poignant Season Six episode "Drone," Seven of Nine's nanoprobes fuse with the holographic Doctor's 29th century holo-emitter and create a new creature, One. In a rape-like scene, the emitter-fused nanoprobes pierce the neck of a young male ensign and extract his DNA; penetrated and made mere tissue, the ensign loses all claim to conventional masculine authority. This radical reorganization of gendered roles informs the series. In the series finale "Endgame," two Janeways, the Captain and Admiral Janeway, a much older version from the future, lead *Voyager* home and decimate the Borg. When Admiral Janeway faces off against the Borg Queen, she sinks to the ground as she is assimilated but then rises up in ambiguous triumph; the Queen, though prostrate and defeated, symbolically castrated as limbs shear off her metallic body, erotically envisions her revenge as she dies. These phallic female figures so thoroughly blend "the mother" with patriarchal authority that gender difference comes to seem irrelevant.

Unexpected

Interestingly, no other character from any *Star Trek* series before *Voyager* was anything remotely like Neelix — no male character, anyway. *Star Trek* has famously — infamously, for some — eluded the topic of explicit homosexual identity, working through allegorical treatments of queer sexuality, in episodes that have been celebrated (*DS9*'s "Rejoined") and lambasted (*TNG*'s "The Host"). The original 1960s series had crusty, funny, cantankerous Doctor McCoy, whose warmth comes through as down-home common sense, but there's nothing remotely androgynous about him. *TNG* has a nurturing counselor, the psychic Counselor Troi, but she prefigures Kes, also psychic and sweet, rather than Neelix. *DS9* does have two characters who are *somewhat* like Neelix: its two most alien figures, Garak and Constable Odo. Garak is sinister and secretive and sexually suspect — but he is in no way a warm-fuzzy maternal figure. Literally an elastic shapeshifter, Odo is generally gruff, curt, and surly, though he is revealed to have a romantic soul. But there is nothing maternal about him.

Neelix was, for *Star Trek*, an unprecedented phenomenon — and unrepeated, until the *Trek* series *Enterprise*, set before *TOS*, in the 22nd century. In *Enterprise*, the alien doctor, Phlox, while also somewhat androgynous, and also randy and wry (unlike Neelix beyond the premiere episode), is a kind of warm and maternal figure as well, a dispenser of advice and a counselor. That *Trek* would reproduce, and refine, one of its more controversial and widely disliked characters — it is quite routine to find "Kill Neelix" threads online and in reviews — in a new series that was extremely success-conscious (to the extent that it did away with the usual operatic theme of *Trek* series credits, opting instead for a mainstream country-rock song), that it would specifically reproduce the figure of the Male Mother, signals a striking interest in, and need for, the presence of this figure. In fact, a Season One *Enterprise* episode, "Unexpected," features the pregnancy of resident stud Trip, the good ol' boy engineer, much to his chagrin. Perhaps the new-old interest in Male Mothers should be, at this point, quite expected. But Phlox is a *corrected* version of Neelix's Male Mother: his explicit sexual appetite corrects the sexlessness of Neelix.

The very multiplicity of roles assigned to Neelix suggests the character's indeterminacy as well as the hard time the *Voyager* producers had in "pegging" him. I argue that the role of Male Mother allowed *Voyager*'s creative team to peg him at last — and that there was a gain and a loss in this process. The gains are these: Male Mothers have the capacity to turn gender on its classificatory head, to present one gender in the capacity of a role assigned to another, to thwart the rigid molding of the individual into a clearly defined gender and sexuality. But there are also losses: the obfuscation and erasure of "actual women who are mothers," as Kittay puts it, in favor of a male idealization of the generative power of women. The chilling omission of Samantha Wildman from even the last season of *Voyager*, which strove to include cameos by old-time guest stars (Vorik the Vulcan, Joe Carey the engineer, Q the trickster god, Seska the duplicitous Cardassian), signifies the strangely misogynistic potentialities in the figure of the Male Mother. The very alienness of Neelix was also lost in the process; by becoming a jack-of-all-trades maternal figure, Neelix lost his alien edge.

If Neelix is — as I argue — a queer character, there are troubling complications in his role as well. Male Motherhood becomes a kind of compensation for the losses incurred by queer sexuality. The Male Mother is a construct that allows certain cultural anxieties like homosexuality and the feminine envy of certain men to be negotiated — it is a compensatory figure because it allows men to retain their heterosexual manhood and gendered coherence while still enjoying the benefits of queer sexuality and women's multivalent powers, which the unacknowledged, symbolic figure of the Male Mother allows hetero-manhood to appropriate. (In other words, while ostensibly heterosexual, Neelix gets to enjoy queer male as well as conventionally feminine qualities without sacrificing his hetero-legitimacy.) Does this make Male Motherhood a reactionary strain in representation or a progressive, defiant one?

If indeed a queer character, Neelix becomes the response to gay conservative Andrew Sullivan's proclamation that the usefulness of homosexuals to society lies in their "lack of children." This lack, though some regard it as a "curse," is also

> an opportunity. Childless men and women have many things to offer to a society. They can transfer their absent parental instincts into broader parental roles: they can be extraordinary teachers and mentors, nurses and doctors, priests, rabbis, and nuns ... they can care for the young who have been abandoned by others, through adoption.[12]

Neelix would appear to have fulfilled just about all of these roles on *Voyager*. His parenting *in absentia* of Naomi after Samantha abandons her child by doing her job would appear to suggest that there really is a dark side to Male Mothers: the Male Mother improves on actual female mothers by erasing the need for them at all. And by acting as Male Mothers, queer people can provide a valuable service, one that transcends the perceived uselessness of homosexuals, serving as guardians of and nurturers to generations of the child-populations so crucial to consumer growth.

If disguised Mothers like Neelix can enjoy unprecedented male freedoms and the ability to nurture and nourish without censure in the science fiction genre, why can they do so only in this realm? Science fiction, fantasy, and devotional poetry all allow an unprecedented freedom for the reimagination of gender and sexuality. One wishes that a more generally celebratory response could be offered to these freedoms; yet the difficulty therein is the way genre becomes implicated in the promulgation of coded, *hidden* radicalisms, in the way that genre contains and keeps sequestered any challenges to normativity. Genre's complicity with normativity continues to be its most vexed aspect. Ultimately, Neelix's realization as Male Mother cannot be seen primarily as a radical innovation but as a strategy for the containment of his weird, frightening alien sexuality, and an effective means of relegating him to the sidelines so that the human characters can enjoy Alien-Babe-of-the-Week sexual adventures in which Neelix does not generally participate. And when he *does* find love with a new, exotic female (a shorthand *Star Trek* trope for the establishment of heterosexual legitimacy) in "Homestead," the penultimate episode of the series, she turns out to be a fellow Talaxian—a move that confirms endogamy as an ingenious solution to the problem of emergent alien sexuality. Endogamy functions, then, as the most skillful means of containment.

Disturbing as these resonances are, however, I do not want to leave Male Mothers or Neelix's version of them on a note of despair. For one thing, though acting is rarely considered in theoretical treatments, the performance of Ethan Phillips as Neelix contributed a gutsy sensitivity to the series that remains both moving and unusual — without embarrassment, never telegraphing a lack of belief in the goodness of the character, Phillips imbues Neelix with a genuine interest in extending affection to others. Neelix — despite the troubling aspects of his persona, its losses and lapses — nevertheless also signifies one of the most positive contributions to *Trek* culture: a male character who emphasizes kindness, compassion, tenderness, and love.

Five

THE SEETHING SKIN
Star Trek, Masculinity, and Race

The general argument of this book thus far has been that Trekkian allegory has a radical dimension, especially for the representation of queer sexuality. Allegory becomes a far more vexed issue, however, when it comes to race, especially in terms of black masculinity, the most highly charged, fraught, and contentious category of racial difference in the United States. The vexed quality of *Trek*'s representation of black masculinity can be immediately recognized in the kinds of characters African American male actors usually play on the series. These characters, if they are human, have qualities that denature their humanity; most often, the characters are alien. Examples include the blind, visor-wearing engineer Geordi LaForge (LeVar Burton); the bulbous-browed Klingon Lt. Worf (Michael Dorn) on *Star Trek: The Next Generation*; and the Vulcan-eared Tuvok (Tim Russ) on *Star Trek: Voyager*. In consistently representing black masculinity in a denatured form, as the disguises these black actors all wear suggest, *Trek* has from its inception registered a profound curiosity about and a profounder discomfort with the black masculine. In exploring *Trek*'s representation of black masculinity, I raise questions over not only what racial allegory says about the identities being allegorized, but also the uses of allegory itself. If *Trek* works hard to represent racial difference, why does it almost always cast this difference in the terms of otherness, which is to say, why are the non-white characters almost always represented as literally alien or in some other way denatured?

Mythification, Marking, and Omission

James Snead names three tactics whereby black stereotypes are "forged and perpetuated in all periods of Hollywood film": *mythification* (which relates to the inherently larger than life nature of movie images that we "look up to"), *marking* (the attempt to remove the inherent ambiguity of the black-white division by marking black bodies *as* black to "eliminate any ambiguity"; for example, light-skinned black actors in Original Hollywood like Fredi Washington had to darken their skin to register unmistakably as black), and *omission* (what we don't see becomes as real as what we do: the absence of positive black characters, reinforced by the repetition of this absence, becomes a reality).[1] Thinking about the applicability of Snead's paradigms for popular culture generally, we can establish some of the ways in which *Trek* has cast the racial other.

Mythification. Original *Trek* was a Cold War allegory that dared to imagine not only humankind's survival of the Cold War but a utopian future in which former enemies (such as Americans and Russians) served together peaceably, exploring the universe together. As I argue in the next chapter on the failed *Trek* series *Enterprise*, Original *Trek*'s politics are infinitely more progressive than that of *Trek* in its current incarnation. Original *Trek* made sure to include a Russian character, Chekhov (Walter Koenig), who spoke accented English, prominently in its cast, and, even more daringly, an African American woman character, Uhura (Nichelle Nichols). Both of these characters reflected a future without the Cold War, on the one hand, and without racism amongst humans, on the other.

Despite its utopian premise, racism was alive and well on the series in Kirk's open hatred of the Klingon race. The Klingon empire was clearly readable as a strange fusion of both Russia and China; several other races, like the warring aliens whose faces were black on one side, white on the other, but on different sides of their faces, in the third-season Original Series episode "Let That Be Your Last Battlefield," all but explicitly posed the question of racism in American culture, nearly exploding the confines of allegory. The other Trekkian races all began to demand similar interpretation along allegorical lines: who were the Vulcans — stoically logical yet liable to intermittent rages of furious emotion — supposed to represent, or, for that matter, their coldly sadistic distant cousins the Romulans? Original *Trek*'s most influential legacy may be its poignant and deeply troubling racial allegory, one that was both anti-racist and racist in effect.

Trek's futuristic race allegories are strictly, staunchly tethered to the real-world social, cultural, and political conflicts of their eras. With the fall of the Soviet Union in the early nineties, the political work being done by Trekkian allegory had to be recalibrated: *Trek* races like the Klingons no longer had the same allegorical function and political resonance. The new villains the Borg, the cybernetic race that threatened to assimilate all worlds of the Federation, reflected fears that an increasingly technology-driven culture might erase human individuality; later, the focus shifted from the Cold War to the conflicts of the Middle East and, still later, the post–September 11 "war on terror." The battles between the imperialistic Cardassians and the victimized Bajorans of *Deep Space Nine* seemed to reflect Middle East conflicts, though in incoherent or indefinable ways. Later, the shape-shifting Suliban of *Enterprise* was an all-but-explicit reference to the Taliban and militant Islam. More specialized race allegories reflected the diminishment of Cold War anxieties and a new focus on domestic issues (for example, the Kazons of *Voyager* reflected the intensifying problems of gang violence).[2]

Television, with its comparatively dwarfed image, can't compete with the cinematic screen in terms of the larger-than-lifeness that Snead associates with mythification; yet in another way television is more insidiously influential and more intimate, it could be said, than the big screen. Thinking about myth in a different way from Snead's, and about television as a more insidious infiltrator of the national psyche, we can theorize that, though motivated by a pronouncedly anti-racist agenda, Original *Trek* constructs *a mythification of race*: the concept that race relations and racial difference can *only* be cast in allegorical, distorted, denatured terms, never explicated, always suggested, inferred, symbolically rendered, one thing always represented as *something else*. Ingenious and moving though *Trek*'s racial allegories have been from the outset, they have also blunted and obscured real-world racial conflicts by appearing to suggest that they are unrepresentable in any form *except* the allegorical. *Trek* seems to suggest, disturbingly, that racial conflict is a myth.

Marking. Here is where *Trek* on race gets especially interesting. Not only has there been a paucity of non-allegorized, "human" non-white characters throughout the franchise, but we can also say that, when they do appear, non-white characters conform to a white, liberal standard. *Deep Space Nine* "raced" Captain Sisko by associating him with New Orleans African American culture; it also reified his African Americanness by associating him with a religiosity that, while alien, nevertheless solidified his traditional image as the good, churchgoing black. Yet the series also, to my mind, entirely relinquished any such specificity by transforming Sisko into a non-*human* alien, given that Sisko's origin isn't human at all but otherworldly, his mother revealed to be one of the spectral, wormhole-alien Prophets worshipped by the Bajorans. One can say that, rather than marking its non-white characters, *Trek* mythifies them, deracinating them, on the one hand, and, on the other hand, allegorizing them as the racial Other, an allegorization that is composed of making the racial Other often quite inescapably monstrous, a collection of bulbous foreheads, protuberant snouts, prognathous jaws, scaly skins, and non-human pigmentations. When marking does occur, it serves to reify, not subvert, stereotypes: the Asian ensign Harry Kim on *Voyager* plays the clarinet and is exceptional at math; *Enterprise*'s female, Asian Communications Officer Hoshi is wan, passive, afraid of the unknown, and, conversely, in the alternative, "Mirror" universe episodes, a seductive, sinister siren.

Omission. Omission, then, is one of the most glaring results of *Trek*'s representation of race; though anti-racist, *Trek* renders the racial other invisible. Yet, maddeningly and fascinatingly, *Trek* also makes race almost unbearably omnipresent, as its human characters constantly confront one intimidatingly, tactilely fleshy alien race after another. Nowhere and everywhere, racial difference on *Trek* both models and explodes allegory, just as the series both embeds racism *and* fights for racial tolerance in its treatment of race. In the next section, we will focus on the representation of black masculinity, in terms of the paradigms we've laid out thus far, as exemplary of the problematics of Trekkian depictions of race.

Vision and Black Masculinity

In his study *White,* Richard Dyer critiques the entire cinematic apparatus itself, a critique also relevant for television aesthetics:

> The photographic media and, *a fortiori*, movie lighting assume, privilege and construct whiteness. The apparatus was developed with white people in mind and habitual use and instruction remain in the same vein, so much so that photographing non-white people is typically construed as a problem.[3]

If, as Dyer theorizes, an entire medium stems from racial privilege, the presence in sci-fi films and television shows of characters of color whose vision and appearance are on some level distorted raises a number of questions. Are people of color denied the cinematic and televisual look? Or does their occluded vision signal a kind of awareness of the phobic tendencies of the representation of otherness?

On *TNG*, African American engineer Geordi La Forge (LeVar Burton) wore a visor that hid his eyes. Geordi's hidden eyes allegorize the linked problems of vision and African American manhood in *Trek*. Geordi's visor on *TNG* is a surprisingly clunky symbol of blindness that, while giving him infrared vision, brutally hides LeVar Burton's face and, most importantly, his eyes (the actor's most sensitive, compelling feature). The current *Trek* films have wisely discarded the visor and given Geordi visible eyes through which he can see. These futuristic, bionic eyes, however, are still quite alien in appearance; they expand and contract, seizing on infra-red images like a sci-fi camera. While an improvement, Geordi's sci-fi vision marks him off as Other in a manner that reinforces his distinction from the largely white cast. In a fourth season *Voyager* two-parter, "Year of Hell," Tuvok goes blind (this is an AU, or alternate universe, episode; his sight remains intact in the narrative proper).

Trek joins in with other kinds of popular culture in its representation of black identity as a traumatic engagement with vision and the visual. Vin Diesel's Riddick, the bad-boy murderer-hero of *Pitch Black* (2000) and its sequel, has opaque, "shined-up" eyes that glow in the dark. As played by the racially (and sexually) ambiguous Diesel, Riddick would appear to join the ranks of *Trek*'s men of color whose vision is stymied, occluded, hampered, impaired, or rendered fantastic. On Cartoon Network's animated series *Justice League*, the Green Lantern is an African American man of might with liquid green eyes that match his green-ray ring. To stretch generic lines, in *Suture* (1993), the African American actor Dennis Haysbert is completely facially bandaged throughout nearly the entire film. Given that the access and deployment of her weather-control abilities is demonstrated by the change in her eye color from brown to white, Halle Berry's Storm in the *X-Men* films must also be taken into consideration here as a distaff example of the complicated intersection of issues of vision and African American representation. What's being said about African American men, if they are so often shown, in sci-fi films and on TV, with such strangely distorted vision and optic opacity? It is difficult to tell if this trend represents a statement about men of color as visual subjects, comments on the problematic gaze of men of color, or acts as an intransigent defense against visual scrutiny. As the Storm character suggests, this is a general issue in terms of the representation of African Americans as much as it is one about African American masculinity specifically. Whatever statements are being made, these sci-fi eyes — far from colorblind — pose a glaring problem that demands further illumination.

The black gaze — in terms of both the subject and the object of the gaze, seeing and being seen — is conceptualized as thwarted, compromised, maimed, or altogether blinded. The black body is always seen *in relationship* to the gaze, as reflective of, hampered by, or resistant to the regimes of the visual. Along these lines, *Trek*'s racial Others both openly declare and adamantly defy the white-inflected propensities of mainstream visual media.

Though there is an ongoing need in *Trek* to render the Other's body monstrous, the subject of race doesn't end there. The way in which *Trek* represents race as something literally deposited on the skin (through makeup), or as something that obtrudes from the surface of the body in the form of protuberant appendages, obscures the racial identities of the actors who are often asked to play these allegorical representations of racialized identities.

But in the sheer, messy, cumbersome physicality of *Trek*'s racial Others, those infamous forehead aliens, also lies a kind of *refusal* of the gaze, a resistance to the order of symmetrical bodies that conform to universal (white) standards, of homogeneity and order. These distracting, distorted allegorized bodies refuse as much as they solicit the normalizing tendencies of the colonizing and homogenizing propensities of the gaze, *even* as they loom as evidence of *Trek*'s terrified inability to explore the difficulties of race in explicit, non-allegorical terms. So, in the end, what we have in *Trek* is an ongoing, paralytic deadlock about race and otherness, an uneasy merger between a radical and a reactionary view.

The Black Male Intellectual

Because few African American actors have appeared in *Trek* in any era — Original *Trek* being certainly no more deficient in this regard than its progeny — when there *is* such an appearance, it demands attention. In the second season Original *Trek* episode "The Ultimate Computer," the guest star character, Dr. Richard Daystrom, is a brilliant, though mentally unstable, creator of a computer, the M-5, that has the acumen to run a starship, perhaps even eventually to replace a human crew. This premise leads to the kinds of philosophical conundrums over man versus machine that people associate with Original *Trek*, all of those inadvertently humorous moments in which Kirk rails against the mechanistic dehumanization of humanity, gets the machine to recognize its own absurdity or the severity of its mistakes, and to destroy itself. What's most interesting for our purposes here is the way this episode sets the template for a type that will appear again in the later series, especially *Voyager* and *Enterprise*: the grievously serious, tightly wound, outwardly stoic but inwardly tormented, and, eventually, explosively emotional black male intellectual.[4]

Played by William Marshall, of 1970s *Blacula* fame, Dr. Daystrom is depicted in marked contrast to the rest of the characters in not only narrative but also visual terms. Using Marshall's imposing height and frame with such precision that it's hard to believe these uses were unwitting, the series depicts him — one of the few non-alien blacks in *Trek* — as a *physical* Other while making no mention whatsoever of his race. While this latter touch might appear commendable, the former maneuver, to make him an obviously outsize, corporeal outsider in Kirk's *Enterprise* world, borders, I would argue,

Five — The Seething Skin 103

on the racist; at the very least, it reveals an irresolvable anxiety about the black male body. This continues the Trekkian pattern of a denial of racism in its own futuristic era and a *concomitant* impulse to register race-related anxieties, through allegory or other means, such as the televisual choices made here to depict Daystrom in such sharp contrast to the other—the white—characters.

When we first see Daystrom, we do not *see* him. Crouched beneath a console when Kirk, McCoy, and Spock walk into the Engineering Room, Daystrom is addressed but not visible. The camera then pans to the left from the male group over which Kirk presides to the console beneath which Daystrom works; this allows us to perceive the full effect of William Marshall's looming height as Daystrom rises *up*. The next camera set-up and blocking of the actors establishes the pattern of visual representation for Daystrom's interactions with the crew. Emphasizing both Daystrom/Marshall's spectacular height as well as his adversarial isolation from the rest of the ship, the episode's visual design places Daystrom on the left side of the screen, on one side of a row of computers, and Kirk and his crew on the other side and on the right side of the screen. Most character interactions on Original *Trek* are visually depicted through tight shot/reverse shot medium close-ups, dialogue and reaction shots. While there are such dialogue exchanges between Daystrom, Kirk, and others, the episode's effort to create shots in which several of the characters *and* Daystrom all appear, albeit always separated by some kind of physical barrier, comes to seem an effort to compare and contrast the characters' physicalities. What's troubling is that, while it is Daystrom's intellect that ostensibly towers over the other men, the episode's visual depiction of these conflicts emphasizes Daystrom's towering *physicality* rather than intellectuality. (William Marshall's acting is just as florid and mannered as William Shatner's, yet somehow these two actors, though often in the same visual frame, do not appear to be exchanging dialogue, to be enjoying the chance to share in each other's theatrics. Rather, they seem to be delivering dialogue *at* each other, rarely making eye contact.) Throughout, the episode labors to emphasize Daystrom's physical superiority, almost always shooting Marshall from a low angle when on the bridge and elsewhere so that we can see that he looms over Spock, Kirk, and the rest of the crew. Fascinatingly, the visual schema shifts to register the character's fate. When Kirk and company finally manage to counteract M-5's murderous takeover of the ship, against Daystrom's fervent protestations, Daystrom collapses into Kirk's arms, and the visualization of the scheme now emphasizes the puniness of Daystrom when defeated.

It's almost as if *Trek*, so prone to allegorize and mythicize the non-white subject, when confronted by an actual, non-allegorized non-white character must find some other means to render this character exotic. Kobena Mercer argues that the two prevailing stereotypes for the representation of black masculinity are the supersexual stud and the delicate, feminine exotic.[5] Marshall's Daystrom, increasingly histrionic as his own insanity reveals itself through outbursts of paranoid jealousy (*Trek* consistently seems to view scientists as loonies who can barely keep it together), registers facets of both of these stereotypes, his imposing physical stature undercut by excessive emotionality.

Trek's incitement of allegory encourages us to see the computer as another side of Daystrom. When he speaks to the increasingly destructive computer, Daystrom — who grafted his own memory engrams, his paranoid rage as well as his brilliance, onto the M-5 — speaks to a narcissistic mirror reflection. Given the overlaps between the coldly logical, yet inwardly tormented, computer and the similarly tempered Daystrom, the series may be said to draw a comparison between innovative yet erratic supercomputers and the black male intellectual. As absurd as this comparison sounds, it has a consistent life in *Trek* and in other popular culture works. *Voyager*'s Vulcan Tuvok, played by the African American actor Tim Russ, perfectly fits the mold of the coolly rational yet inwardly seething black intellectual male. Exemplary episodes that feature this type include *Voyager*'s "Meld" (Season Two), "Random Thoughts" (Season Four), and "Repression" (Season Seven), episodes which shatter Tuvok's Vulcan resolve, and *Enterprise*'s "Daedalus" (Season Three) which exposes the scientist Emory Erickson (Bill Cobbs), Captain Archer's family friend and the inventor of the transporter, as a sinister and, ultimately, very sad figure. This odd figure also appears in the 1991 sci-fi epic *Terminator 2: Judgment Day*, in the form of Miles Dyson (Joe Morton), an African American scientist at the computer company Cyberdyne who will be the catalyst for the creation of Skynet, the machine intelligence that will attempt to destroy humanity. At one point in the film, Linda Hamilton's tough-butch action heroine Sarah Connor attacks Dyson, first physically, then verbally: she accuses him, from an ostensibly feminist standpoint, of not "really knowing what it is to create a life, to feel it growing inside you"; yet Dyson is depicted as a warm, loving family man and, finally, a tremblingly emotional male who is a far better embodiment of these qualities than commando, black leather-clad Sarah. The black male intellectual betrays the turbulent emotional life he keeps buried beneath a stoic, taciturn façade, struggling with what we can term *a repression/explosion tension*.

If the M-5 allegorizes Daystrom, the allegorical import of the computer is its representation of Daystrom as *something else*. Brooding to himself, Kirk fearfully contemplates "that *thing*": ostensibly, Kirk is referring to the M-5, but he could also be referring to Daystrom. Kirk has bewildered conversations with McCoy in which Kirk reveals his fear that he will lose his potency if the M-5 takes over. With its visual schema and thematized fears of a loss of masculine potency, the episode suggests an allegory of white male fears over a newly visible, newly intellectually potent, and always already threateningly physical black masculine presence. Allegory here allows Kirk and the series to give vent to fears of this new "thing" without in any way giving explicit offense.

The Seething Skin

Given *Trek*'s incitement of allegory and its conflictual representation of the black male intellectual, we can consider *Trek*'s recurring representation of the black male body in a heightened state of physical distress — sweating, throbbing, bleeding, burning, or melting — as indicative of profound anxieties within not only the depiction of race but also the entire allegorical project. In several episodes throughout the *Trek* mega-text, the black male body undergoes a transformation through a series of traumas that threaten to destroy the body from within and take the repression/explosion tension that is always inherent in the representation of black masculinity to an explicit, corporeal level: in other words, to explode allegory into direct explication.

On Original *Trek*, some of the most affecting moments of the series occur when Spock, suddenly besieged by a force that strips away his fiercely maintained layers of logic, breaks down, piteously or violently railing against or lamenting his lonely, neither-human-nor-alien condition. Spock's repression/explosion tension affectingly speaks to several different, related kinds of experienced racial subjectivity — being non-white, mulatto, or Jewish; desiring across interracial lines; racial, gendered, or sexual passing; being queer; being queer *and* of mixed race at once; or simply any feeling of difference from the normative social order. *Voyager*'s Vulcan Tuvok also poignantly experiences these wrenching assaults on his logical composure. But given that *Voyager* races its Vulcan character by casting an African American actor in the role, the implications are different and, at times, more disturbing, especially given certain aspects of the way the series chooses to depict these breakdowns of black Vulcan composure. In several episodes, Tuvok's explosions are rendered *literally*; they are also depicted as the direct result of a confrontation between Tuvok and a white male identity most often coded as queer.

In the Second Season episode "Cold Fire," written by Brannon Braga,

Tuvok gives psychic-training lessons to the young, blonde, fledgling mutant Kes, whose psychokinetic powers are immense but undisciplined; given the childlike quality of Jennifer Lien, who plays Kes, this pairing suggests the controversial relationship between the slave Tom and the small, angelic girl, Little Eva, whom he befriends in Harriet Beecher Stowe's famous novel *Uncle Tom's Cabin*. In one scene something goes horribly wrong — Kes, her powers out of her control, unleashes them on the Vulcan. In one shot we see Kes screaming in terror; in the next we see what she is screaming at, the image of Tuvok burning alive, blindly clutching at his face, his skin bubbling, his eyes turning as white as two hard-boiled eggs, as his body erupts with green Vulcan blood. Much more than a victim of uncontrollable force, Tuvok resembles a persecuted, lumbering monster here, a black Frankenstein's Monster or the Phantom of the Opera, or the burn-victim-black-man turned titular threat in Stephen Crane's story "The Monster." One of the grisliest scenes ever to appear in a *Trek* show, this scene gives vent to tensions in *Trek*'s representation of the black male body; it terrifyingly enacts *Trek*'s penchant for turning the differently-raced into monsters.

In another Season Two episode, the riveting "Meld," Tuvok, in his role as Security Officer, apprehends a killer onboard the ship, Lon Suder (the superbly strange Brad Dourif). Though a Betazoid — like *TNG*'s empathic Counselor Deanna Troi, who can sense others' emotions — Suder cannot feel. Just about the only feeling that motivates Suder is a desire to kill, to experience the rush — or simply the release — of violence. Fascinated by this white male serial killer — overly fascinated, one should add — Tuvok, driven to understand what motivates an apparently motiveless murder, initiates a mind-meld with Suder. Tuvok comes away from the meld with his own mind disordered, increasingly and finally nearly completely susceptible to Suder's violent impulses but, more pressingly, so the episode suggests, Tuvok's own considerable capacity for violence. In contrast, Suder emerges from the meld Vulcan-like, calmer, more rational — "centered," as he puts it to the now unstable Tuvok.

In Original *Trek*, the Vulcan mind-meld is depicted as eerie, unsettling, otherworldly; in later *Trek*, it's closer to rape. When the now nearly insane Tuvok storms into the brig to effect a capital punishment–murder on the altered, becalmed Suder, Tuvok, sweating and breathing audibly and feverishly, seems positively animalistic. Clenching the pale Suder's face in his hands and grunting, Tuvok could as well be raping as melding with him. The ample homoeroticism and violence of this tautly filmed, disturbing climactic scene intensifies its murky racial politics. One of the powerful implications of the exchange between these men is that male-male intimacy, especially *interra-*

cial male-male intimacy, leads to a total breakdown of the social order, of the custodian of liberalism being reduced to the role of bloodthirsty executioner (liberal *Trek* has no death penalty) and the *murderer* accessing Trekkian rationalist discourse. But the deeper implication is that Tuvok's own latent animalistic rage, only barely submerged, never far from the repressive surface, has found fitting vent.

This episode's sexual and racial logic dovetails with that of African psychoanalyst Frantz Fanon's disappointingly homophobic reading of homosexuality as a white man's disease, one of the negative effects of white colonial rule on the properly heterosexual African subject.[6] But—and here is the weird power of *Trek*—it also goes places other mainstream television works rarely ever do, goes farther; in its transgressive exploration of the boundaries between the normative and the perverse, racial hierarchies, and sexual and gendered identities, this episode has more in common with Robert Mapplethorpe photographs than it does with liberal pieties; it's as liberating as it is phobic.

In the fourth season *Voyager* episode "Random Thoughts," B'Elanna Torres, the fiery half–Klingon, half-human female engineer, is arrested for a "violent thought" on a telepathic planet that has made any violent thought a crime. Absurd as this premise is — it's difficult to imagine any civilization that wouldn't have to incarcerate all of its citizens under such a penal system — the episode eventually develops into something quite fascinating.

Tuvok discovers the real culprit of the thought crime, Guill (Wayne Péré) the ringleader of a black market for violent, perverse thought. As played by Péré, Guill's sexuality appears to lean towards the queer, even as he mentions having to get home to his wife and children. The scenes between Tuvok and Guill occur entirely in dark, nighttime back alleys, suggestive of gay cruising (*Enterprise*'s episode "Stigma" will make the same suggestion). The mind-meld that Tuvok strategically proposes to Guill (a ploy to expose Guill's guilt), given the clandestine nature of their scenes together, is heavily freighted with homoeroticism. The meld scenes expose the depth of Tuvok's inner violence — he represses shocking scenes of horror, carnage, mayhem, all experienced by Guill with a feverish, erotic delight. As with "Meld," "Random Thoughts" collapses homoerotic feeling and racist logic; once again, the implication is that behind the civilized, rational black male's stoic exterior lie writhing, animalistic passions. But like "Meld," the homoeroticization of this exchange also pushes boundaries in provocative ways. In these episodes, allegory powerfully serves as a conductor for queer desire even as it lends itself to phobic suggestions of racism.

During these meld scenes and their aftermath, Tuvok breaks out into a profuse sweat; his green blood bespatters his body; his face, veins, limbs, and torso throb. This emerging Trekkian tendency to render the black male body into a denatured form reaches its apotheosis in the fourth season *Enterprise* episode "Daedalus." Continuing the odd Trekkian tradition of the dubious black male scientist, this episode introduces us to Emory Erickson, the creator of the transporter device, surely one of the most significant features of *Trek* technology. Erickson, however, is as disquieting a figure as Daystrom, hiding a terrible secret and a questionable agenda. Years ago, he allowed his son, Quinn, to be a guinea pig for "sub quantam transportation," which Erickson knew even at the time to be an impossible feat, as he eventually tells Captain Archer (the earnest but woefully miscast Scott Bakula). Quinn's phantomlike, unmaterialized body, a pattern forever encased in a transporter beam, floats through walls and space. Quinn's phantom body exists in a remote area of space called "The Barrens," to which Erickson has schemed to journey while onboard the *Enterprise*. Interestingly paralleling the jealous, competitive mania of Daystrom in Original *Trek*'s "The Ultimate Computer," Erickson reveals that he allowed his son to go on this hopeless mission in order to further impress his colleagues, to find some way to top his invention of the transporter device. The oedipal dynamics here are deepened by Erickson's importance to Captain Archer, who grew up next to the Erickson family, played with Quinn and his sister, and regarded Erickson as a second father. These oedipal tensions hover in the air but aren't explored in any great depth; the chief power of this strangely blank episode is the affecting specter of the denatured black male body.

An Original *Trek* episode provides an interesting contrast to "Daedalus," both in featuring a ghostly *white* male body and in having the counterbalance to that apparitional body be the hystericized body of a black woman. In Season Three's "The Tholian Web," Kirk's transporter beam–encased body hovers in space, unable to materialize, a mournful, ghostlike figure. Yet we see his transporter-beam body floating through the ship, lurking above the grieving crew who believe him dead. In "Daedalus," however, Quinn's unmaterialized, transporter beam presence buzzes and zaps its way through walls and corridors, remaining indeterminate and indistinct, a hazy, sparking blob of energy. It is only when, having captured the energy-specter on film, the crew watches this filmed ghost moving slowly, frame by frame, that Archer can make out Quinn's face within the shiny, throbbing mass. In a suggestive nuance, this technological apparition kills whatever it touches. Quinn's ghost fuses phobias about technology, the black male body, and, I would argue, black male sexuality. His seething skin betrays our culture's fears over race and sex as his phantom transporter beam-body — in which Quinn is trapped, but not conscious — cries out in wordless, ghostly anguish. What's especially troublesome is that, with this episode, *Trek* racial representation gets to a place where the black male is not only allegorized into monstrosity — a distancing, alienating maneuver — but also made lethal to the touch. The black male has become a killing ghost. Given (as I discuss further in the next chapter) *Enterprise*'s pitifully meager interest in its one black male series regular, Travis Mayweather, who gets fewer lines per episode than the black female Uhura did in Original *Trek*, the representation of black maleness as a blank that kills comes to seem even more disturbing.

A Dream of the (White) Phallus: Original Trek*'s Uhura and the Apparitional Kirk*

It is worth pausing for a moment to consider Original *Trek*'s "The Tholian Web" in further depth. In this episode, a Federation ship, *The Defiant*, phases out of normal space and time, and the *Enterprise* threatens to do so as well. (*Enterprise*, the fifth *Trek* series, provided an homage to this episode and to "Mirror, Mirror" in the 2005 two-parter "In a Mirror Darkly.") Kirk, still onboard *The Defiant* when it phases out, appears to vanish along with it. For the remainder of the episode, Kirk continues to appear to various crew members. In his spacesuit, Kirk looks long and tube-like, his helmet giving him a crowned head. Hovering above the crew in his dreamlike, otherworldly appearances, Kirk looks like a ghostly phallus. A floating signifier of his own male power, Kirk as phallus appears to the crew individually, as if he were a divinity appearing before each of his worshippers.

Uhura (Nichelle Nichols), getting ready for bed, sees the apparitional Kirk in her mirror. Elated and distraught, she runs into the corridor, and into the sympathetic embrace of McCoy. Though sympathetic, McCoy interprets her vision of Kirk as a psychotic episode. Confined to a bed in Sickbay, Uhura is the hystericized woman. Once the male crew members on the bridge all see apparitional Kirk, however, Uhura is believed. Flesh and blood Kirk is restored; Uhura seems as relieved that she has been believed as she is overjoyed that Kirk has returned.

"The Tholian Web" depicts the disappearance of Kirk as an event that provokes mass hysteria, one that is conveyed through Uhura, both a woman and an African American. Though the crisis of the loss of masculine power disrupts everything onboard the *Enterprise*— Spock and McCoy are almost literally at each other's throats; various crew members go berserk — Original *Trek* makes the chief point about the magnitude of the loss represented by Kirk's absence specifically through *the body of Uhura*. The black female body becomes the metaphorical body of the *Enterprise*, the conduit through which trauma and terror are negotiated and the ecstatic restoration of order is conducted. Uhura's joy at the reappearance of Kirk allows us to register the joy of having Kirk — white masculine authority — back. The floating signifier of his own manhood, apparitional Kirk reminds the crew that what they collectively crave is the phallic power of his flesh and blood presence. The phallus — apparitional Kirk — is always already everywhere, hovering, omnipresent. Original *Trek* presents the phallus as a nightmarish apparition that demands recognition — that haunts the social world like a mournful, insistent ghost. The flesh and blood Kirk embodies the phallic power his dream-image symbolizes.[7] In contrast, the killing black male ghost of "Daedalus" is an expression of fundamental anxiety over the black male body: not a figure that elicits the orgasmic joy brought on by the apprehension of an angel, as in Judeo-Christian lore (and Tony Kushner's play *Angels in America*), but the eradication of life.

Uncanny Whiteness

My focus thus far has been on the representation of African American masculinity in *Star Trek*. I would now like to consider the possibility that Trekkian racial allegory serves another purpose beyond negotiating anxieties of racial *difference*. One of the largely undiscussed aspects of Trekkian racial allegory is that it functions to negotiate not only fears over racial difference but also racial *sameness*, to reflect back to a presumably white audience a distorted, denatured form of whiteness. Obviously, this has implications not only for representation but also for the kind of audience the monomyth has in its mind as it creates and markets its product. I would argue that this anxiety over whiteness is itself a manifestation of fears over race and difference; moreover, these fears extend to gender and sexuality, especially queer sexuality. If *Trek*'s race allegories also function as an expression of anxieties over racial sameness as well as racial difference, and if black masculinity on *Trek* allegorizes white fears over whiteness itself, what does it mean to cast *whiteness* as otherness?

In the film *Star Trek: First Contact* (1996), the Borg, the cybernetic, assimilating menace, invade the *Enterprise* and kidnap the android Data (Brent Spiner). Like Odysseus on Calypso's island, Data finds himself in amorous captivity, strapped to a bed, captured by the Borg Queen (the indelibly erotic and strange Alice Krige), who coos sexually tinged provocations inside one of the android's ears as Borg drills bore through the other. A master sadist and manipulator, the Borg Queen tempts Data into submission to her cyborg collective, mocking him as an "imperfect being" in his present state. The height of her seductive-sadistic campaign occurs when she bestows a strange gift upon Data: a graft of human skin, a few inches long, over the cyborg circuits of his right arm. The graft-skin glows translucently in the stylized light, and when the Borg Queen brings her moist, veiny, froggy face and lips over the graft and blows on it, the hairs rise and erectly shimmer, leading Data to moan with tremulous pleasure.

The issue of race is only obliquely raised in this scene full of obvious sexual metaphors; but if we insist on considering its racial politics, we can glean some surprising insights into *Trek*. It is absolutely unthinkable that the piece of skin that the Borg Queen grafts on Data's arm could be anything other than white skin. Its pigmentation darker, the gift of skin would look less like a gift, more like a bizarre, unsettling joke. The canny Borg Queen doesn't just give Data the gift of human flesh but *the gift of white male skin*.

The *Trek* universe pivots around the idea of racial equality as a given, humanity having conquered all prejudice and even achieved complete racial harmony in *Trek*'s utopian terms. Neither android Data nor the Borg Queen is, strictly speaking, a *white* character, yet they both *read* as white. So they represent not so much an alternative to established whiteness as they do *a distorted and denatured version of whiteness itself*, an allegorical rendering not of racial otherness but of racial sameness rendered strange. It is a commonplace of *Star Trek* that its aliens represent the racial other, dark skin and difference. While the ape-like, dragon-faced Klingons, leathery-lizardy Cardassians, gooey shape-shifting Founders, discus-eared Ferengi, freckle-covered Trills, and other *Trek* races have all been read as allegorical figures of racial *difference*, they just as resonantly signal whiteness in a denatured, defamiliarized form. In other words, *the chief allegorical function of race in Trek is to reflect back to whiteness a distorted form of itself.* If *Trek* allegorizes racial difference through the alien's appearance, face, body, costume, language, and culture, it also holds up a distorting mirror to its own prevailing whiteness.

Whiteness on *Trek* fits especially well into the Freudian theory of the uncanny—something that is both deeply familiar and deeply unfamiliar *at once*. Especially affecting examples of this white uncanny include characters such as the Borg collective, figured as a zombie-like, mechanized white race that incorporates all difference into its denatured white ideal; the Borg Queen; Hugh from *The Next Generation* episode "I, Borg"; One in the *Voyager* episode "Drone"; the blue-skinned, antennae-headed, white-haired Andorians of Original *Trek*, given a much larger development on *Enterprise*; the new species *Enterprise* introduces in its fourth season, the Aenar, related to the Andorians, but ghostly pale, their skin and hair as white as the snowy world they live in (significantly, they are also blind); the human-like, augmented Klingons of a multi-part narrative on *Enterprise* (the fourth season "Affliction" and "Divergence") in which *Star Trek* accounts for why some Klingons appear white, an anxiety that stems from the Original *Trek* era; and, as mentioned, the android Data.

The blindness of the Aenar tells us something about this white uncanny. If *Trek* often blinds its black characters, the blindness of this allegorized white race similarly alerts us to its function as allegory, as if to say that that which reflects whiteness *to* itself has no ability to see *it*self.

What is interesting about the white uncanny in terms of masculinity is that it introduces an "othered" masculinity on *Trek* that, while reflective of racial difference, more pronouncedly reflects queer male sexuality. The character of Hugh in "I, Borg," is initially an abandoned, damaged drone found on a desolate planet. The away team struggles over whether to assist the drone or leave him on the planet to die, an understandable dilemma given the fearsome nature of the Borg, the greatest enemy the Federation has ever faced. Dr. Crusher (Gates McFadden) insists on bringing the drone up to the *Enterprise* to treat him. Once there, the drone recovers, eventually learning to speak as an individual, to recognize himself as the "you"—or "Hugh"—being addressed. What's especially interesting for our purposes, however, is that the terrifying threat of the Borg, who can, with their penetrative mechanical appendages and tubules, be described as hyperphallic, assumes the form of a young, melancholy man with haunted eyes and pale skin and dark hair, a feminized male who seems far more abject than he does threatening, even as he spouts the familiar Borg threats ("You will be assimilated"). Hugh looks like the sad, touchingly vulnerable male Edward Scissorhands played by Johnny Depp in Tim Burton's 1990 film—a very similar character.

It's almost as if Hugh's denatured whiteness—a relinquished hold on white masculine authority—gives the character access to a femininity *within* his masculine identity. Why would this be the case? Is there a correspondence between an altered racial identity—the mechanized, punctured, transformed, and feminized white male body we have in Hugh—and a queer potentiality? *Star Trek* forces us to consider the ways in which race ultimately cannot be distinguished from gender, as well as the reverse; that race *is* gender, gender race. To explore these themes in greater depth, I will now turn to the notable *TNG* episode "The Offspring."

Beloved in the Language Hindi: "The Offspring"

The mechanically pristine android who aspires to the messy condition of the human, Data (Brent Spiner) is the antithesis of Spock, the stoic Vulcan who rejects his tormenting human side. In the third season episode "The Offspring," Data causes quite a stir onboard the *Enterprise* by creating the titular creature, an android child with a positronic brain much like his own, and in several key respects an improvement. Summoned to the lab to witness the blessed android event are the empathic counselor Deanna Troi (Marina Sirtis), Geordi LaForge, the engineer who wears a sight-giving visor over his blind eyes, and boy-genius Wesley Crusher (Wil Wheaton). The first shot we get of Data's new android offspring is of its footless leg, and of Data attaching the missing foot, turning it like a screw. The complete android we see is androgynous: its bulky face reveals little personality, its bulky chest neither female breasts nor male musculature, and its groin is the smooth, appendageless groin of a mannequin or a Barbie or a Ken doll. Lal, as Data calls his android offspring, glimmers with a faint golden glow; its burnished, metallic quality is a complete contrast from the surprisingly moist, pliant human skin of the android body under construction in the second season Original *Trek* episode "Return to Tomorrow." Its voice is low and indeterminate of gender. But overall, the non-gendered, *unhumanized* android registers in some indefinable way as male, perhaps as a result of its bulkiness and low voice, perhaps because it is played by a male actor, Leonard Crofoot. Moreover, this android offspring registers as a *castrated* male, as suggested by the image of the missing foot.

When Captain Jean-Luc Picard (Patrick Stewart) sees Lal for himself, his reaction suggests irritation, discomfort, and even anger. "I would have liked to have been consulted," Picard says to Data about his creation of Lal. "Why didn't you give it a more human look?" counselor Troi more calmly asks Data. "I have decided to allow my child to choose its own sex and appearance," responds Data. It is precisely at *this* point that Picard seems most uncomfortable, interrupting Data and bringing the conversation to an abrupt halt, telling Data he wishes to speak to him privately. And when he and Data do speak, Picard reveals that he is indeed quite angry over Data's decision to create Lal.

Walking down the corridor with Troi after seeing Lal for the first time, Picard sternly insists "that we do whatever we can to discourage the perception of this android as a child." Troi counter-argues that it is just as legitimate to create a child through technological rather than biological means and that, moreover, Data has the right to create his own child and have it call him "Father." As Data had himself said to Picard, "Captain, I do not recall anyone else consulting you about their procreation." So far, this episode appears to be just as concerned with the themes of non-human kinship, Data's right to create a life and to parent, as it is with the android as *tabula rasa*, ready to be inscribed with an identity.

In a significant scene, the still-unhumanized Lal walks down the corridor with Data and Troi. As the bulky, copper-skinned android observes the people walking past him, he successfully identifies their genders. "Female!" he cries, to which Troi responds, "Yes, Lal, like me"; "male," he next observes, and Data affirms his perception. The people in the corridors pay attention to Lal as well; indeed, everyone who passes gawks at him. After Lal identifies one of these gawkers as male, the male gawker joins a group of other males, all of whom break out in astonished laughter at the spectacle of Lal: these 24th century Starfleet personnel are surprisingly rude and even more surprisingly intolerant in their derisive response to difference.[8]

As Lal walks down the corridor with Data and Troi, he remarks that, in contrast to everyone else, "I am gender neuter — inadequate." Data responds by saying that this is why "you must choose a gender, Lal, to complete your appearance." Troi then counsels (warns?) Lal, "Whatever you decide will be yours for a lifetime. It's a decision that will affect how people interrelate with you." Given Lal's suggested masculinity before his transformation, this scene suggests an allegory of gender-reassignment surgery. Made in the early 1990s, this episode hints at the profound transformation in the public understanding of the varieties of gendered identity that will occur from the '90s forward, as gay identity transformed into "queer," and as the gay rights movement expanded to include transgendered persons as well as gays and lesbians. But still, it is only a hint — the episode insists squarely on the categories Male and Female as Lal's only options, though Data *does* frame gender as a component of one's *appearance*, not of one's essential, core identity. Significantly, the as yet ungendered Lal feels inadequate without a gender; *Trek* is unable to imagine a post-gender world even in a future several centuries ahead of our own.

When Lal does choose a human(oid) identity, "she" chooses that of a young, dark-haired woman, who vaguely resembles, in hairstyle and dress, Disney's animated version of Snow White. This identity is one of several thousand that Lal has considered, and one of four finalists, the others of whom are an Andorian female, a human male, and a male Klingon. Lal's choice of the human woman (who will be superbly played by Hallie Todd) registers most obviously as a choice of gender. But Lal makes as decisive a choice of species and of racial identity. The choice made by the copper-skinned, androgynous male Lal is to become female, human, *and* white.

In creating Lal, Data gives her a "more *realistic* eye and skin coloring than his own"; with his yellow skin and yellow eyes, Data clearly sees his complexion as inferior to that of humans, implicitly inferior to human *whiteness*. As if not only to amplify but also to scrutinize this theme of "enhanced" racialization on a theoretical level, Lal, noticing a landscape painting in Data's quarters, remarks, "Painting: colors produced on a surface by applying a pigment." Lal's clipped, mechanical tones render such a statement ironic; she is clearly, like the painting she studies, a creation, an invention, a fantasy, a copy of some elusive original. Race, like gender, is a matter of applied pigment, a choice, a trick: race and gender are something deposited *on* the skin, like paint on canvas, rather than a manifestation of essence. If Lal, the episode suggests, improves on android Data in terms of species and race "realness," the episode makes it clear, or at least available for interpretation, that it's Data's own sense of android inadequacy that makes him view Lal as an improvement on himself.

The name Lal, in its Hindi origin, signals the connections between the androids' ambiguous racial identity and Orientalist discourse, the view of the East as being, among other things, overly sensual and decadent.[9] With his yellow skin presented as inferior to human whiteness, Data suggests the exotic, yellow Other of Orientalism, a decadent, effeminate male figure that suggests a loss of masculine control as well as queer or transgendered sexuality. Lal possess a clearly defined femininity, at least in appearance; yet, as Hallie Todd plays Lal, she's almost gender-bendingly boyish despite her girlishness. "The Offspring," then, functions both as a queer *and* a race allegory. Much like *Trek* as a whole, the episode positions sexuality and race as *parallel lines* of conflict and interest.

It is the strange, mystically self-satisfied alien wise woman Guinan, played (with insufferable smugness) by Whoopi Goldberg, who guides Lal in the ways of not only human interaction but also human courtship. As always with *Trek*, it is heterosexuality that provides the explicit, visible model of erotic love. As Lal stares at a young male-female couple giggling and making eyes at each other, she learns, from Guinan, that they are "flirting"; in a comedic moment, she cries out in alarm when she sees the man kissing the woman ("He is biting that female!"); later, in a humorously grotesque parody of the kissing she observes, Lal grabs Commander Riker (Jonathan Frakes, who sensitively directed this episode), and places a rough, almost animalistic kiss on him, much to his shock. Assuming the role of masculine seducer with the ship's virile young Lothario Riker, Lal performs heterosexuality, but as the aggressor, in other words and in the terms of conventional gender roles, in a disordered, comedically perverse way that disrupts it.

The inevitable happens: Lal — much like Rayna in Original *Trek*'s previously discussed "Requiem for Methusaleh"—dies once she feels love, for her father Data. These feelings are triggered by a conflict between Data and Picard, on the one side, and, on the other, a staunch, staid Starfleet admiral who myopically wants to take Lal away from Data for sustained research. Picard, having gotten over his initial misgivings, chastises the admiral. Regarding the Federation view of androids, even after the legal and moral victory of "The Measure of a Man," Picard says, "You recognize their sentience but deny them personal liberty." Not while he's captain, says Picard, will the Federation "State" take a father's child from him. The episode places less emphasis, however, on Picard's moral defense of and loyalty towards Data than it does on the issue of Lal's love for Data and what it suggests is Data's inexpressible but no less potent love for Lal.

Earlier in the episode, Data had informed Lal that, being android, neither of them can love, as humans do, the ability to feel not being in their programming. (This is an echo of what the sinister android scientist tells his beautiful android female creation in Original *Trek*'s "What Are Little Girls Made Of?": "*You cannot love.*") "Why emulate humans, then?" Lal quite reasonably asks. "We must strive," responds Data, "to be more than we are." Data's longing for the human corresponds to several different allegorical projects at once—he can be seen as the racial Other who internalizes the racist messages of his culture and longs for privileged whiteness, or the sexual Other who similarly longs for normative heterosexuality, both kinds of longing being similar forms of social abnegation. But what the episode leaves one with is that narrow-minded, dictatorial Admiral realizes, finally, the depth of Data's commitment to his daughter. Noting how quickly Data's hands moved during the surgery to save Lal, the Admiral seems quietly yet palpably overwhelmed by Data's display of doomed parental love.

In the end, "The Offspring," brilliantly written by René Echevarria, emblematizes *Trek* at its best and most problematic. It movingly explores issue of difference, otherness, and sameness rendered strange; it explores the boundaries of gender, sexuality, and race in daring and imaginative ways. It also leaves one feeling profoundly disappointed, wanting more, dismayed at the obviousness, predictability, and deep limitations of this beguiling but frustrating vision of the future.

Racism and Radicalism

Given both the immensity and the thematic tendencies of the *Star Trek* monomyth, one can find ample examples of both racism and radicalism in terms of its treatment of race. Without exculpating *Trek* in any way, without attempting to reconcile its own ever-warring impulses towards both progressivism and phobia, what I will suggest by way of conclusion to this chapter is that, overall, *Trek*'s greatest contribution to an anti-racist project is its depiction of a denatured, decentered white masculinity. White, heterosexual masculinity has, historically, enjoyed the greatest privilege and power; *Trek*'s disordering of this privileged racial, gendered, and sexual category has some profound implications. Figures such as antic, manic Kirk, as played by the joyously wild, overreaching actor William Shatner; the troubled, stoic Vulcan Spock; Data; the holographic Doctor and the male mother Neelix on *Voyager*, all take white masculinity to weird, exciting, disturbing, queer places. That *Trek*'s project to interrogate racism has led to its own racist practice over the years is a sore disappointment indeed; but that, in so undertaking this project, it has yet managed to challenge white hetero-masculinity's stronghold is a valuable achievement. Sadly, as I will demonstrate in the next chapter, the *Trek* series *Enterprise* has largely retooled the franchise so that it *leads* with, rather than critiques, white male heterosexist privilege. And, as I will demonstrate in the chapter that follows the next one, if *Trek*'s critique of white masculinity is a genuine achievement, white masculinity is also an ideal to which the Trekkian universe conforms.

Six

THE TWILIGHT OF IDENTITY
Enterprise, Neoconservatism, and the Death of *Star Trek*

Enterprise, the sixth *Star Trek* television series, aired its first episode, "Broken Bow," on September 26, 2001, the same year in which George W. Bush, the nation's forty-third president, was sworn into office and fifteen days after the United States suffered its deadliest attack on domestic soil. *Enterprise* was cancelled by UPN in the spring of 2005, making it the shortest lived live-action *Trek* series since the first (*Star Trek* ran three seasons, but *The Next Generation, Deep Space Nine, and Voyager* all ran seven years apiece). The loyal *Trek* audience and curious new viewers (both of whom quickly dwindled after very impressive initial numbers) turned away from the series in droves. Numerous and varied discussions were conducted — by the media, *Trek* fans, and general science-fiction audiences — over the reasons for the show's untimely demise, considered metonymic of the end of *Star Trek* as a mega-franchise.

The common explanation given for the shrunken fortunes of *Trek*, which since its reincarnation in the late 1970s with *Star Trek: The Motion Picture* has been a sci-fi cultural phenomenon rivaled only by *Star Wars* (although in recent years it has also been given a serious run for its futuristic money by such shows as *Stargate* and the new version of *Battlestar Galactica*), is that *Trek* is simply a victim of its own extravagant success, and that after so many years of overexposure, fan exhaustion with the franchise has inevitably resulted in the decline in viewership.

Countervailing against this particular explanation for the death of *Trek*, I argue that the franchise has suffered because it replaced its progressive humanist values with a broad reactionary agenda, as evinced by *Enterprise*. *Enterprise* was a neoconservative reimagining of *Trek* that not only "corrected" the politically correct stances of the previous recent *Trek* shows but even retooled the concepts of Original *Trek* to refashion *Trek* in its entirety as a monolithically conservative vision, a fictive universe opposed to diversity and tolerance. Making *Trek*'s masculinist biases explicit themes rather than metatextual, *Enterprise*, in its four year run, manifested itself as one of the most misogynistic and racist science-fiction shows in television history. Examining some key episodes, this chapter exposes the ideological sensibility of *Enterprise* and argues that it was the show's neoconservative agenda that facilitated the seeming "death" of *Trek*. *Enterprise* seems to me much more than *The Next Generation* the chilling fulfillment of neoconservative tendencies in *Trek*, which are always at war with its formerly predominant progressive values. Like HBO's Western *Deadwood*, *Enterprise* is a reactionary revisionist work, a neoconservative fantasy of a return to a time before progressive, politically correct new values ruined things for everybody by policing the expression of good, salty, enjoyable essentialist racist and sexist views.

Discussing the revisionist Westerns of the New Hollywood cinema of the 1970s, J. Hoberman writes,

> The most overtly ideological of revisionist Westerns addressed the subject of the Indian wars [in the United States]. In their open identification with Native Americans, such movies were the equivalent of marching for peace beneath a Viet Cong flag. Hollywood contra Hollywood: Cavalry Westerns [such as *Little Big Man*] were in production when My Lai was exposed, and the revelation of American atrocities only reinforced the argument that the slaughter of Native Americans was the essence of the white man's war.[1]

If, as Robin Wood writes, we can "already look back to Hollywood in the 70s as the period when the dominant ideology *almost* disintegrated," it is far more dubious that the same will be said of our own moment, if television shows such as *Deadwood* and *Enterprise* are any indication.[2] What makes revisionist Westerns such as *Deadwood* and *Enterprise* distinct from '70s versions is their ideological character. In the '70s, revisionism allowed moviemakers to recast conventional genres such as the Western as allegories of the perniciousness of modern political regimes. Today, revisionism does not function as allegory but as political wish-fulfillment, the longing to return to a mythical time of bluntly uncomplicated values in which clear divisions between good and evil—so goes the myth—were clearly drawn. Key programs involved in this current reactionary revisionist project include the re-traditionalization of women, checking the progress of feminism and punishing the ambitious, autonomous woman by reincorporating her into properly normative gendered roles and spaces; the checking, stalling, and ultimate eradication of civil rights movements of all kinds, the foreclosure of movements to end racial, gendered, sexual, class, and other forms of oppression; and the new consolidation of a coherent national identity. *Enterprise*, which goes back to Original *Trek*'s roots as "Wagon Train to the Stars," fits in seamlessly with the projects of reactionary revisionism. It's Wagon Train to the Stars without all of that 1960s liberalism that accompanied Original *Trek*. The difficulty for

Enterprise, however, is that it *still* retains *Trek*'s core liberal values — values hardly mass-affirmed in our own shifting yet still undeniably neoconservative moment — and *Enterprise*'s struggle over overwriting the Trekkian text while still maintaining its character make it a fascinating and disturbing text all its own.

Emerging in the weeks after the devastation of September 11, *Enterprise* shirked the promise and the responsibility of *Star Trek*. To use Robin Wood's term, it "papered the cracks" of American ideology, covering up the fissures in our ever-evolving culture with a racist and sexist program of reaction and retribution.[3] "Gene's Vision" — as the philosophy of Gene Roddenberry, *Trek*'s creator, is often called — has frequently and very often rightly, been attacked for its unfailing and uncritical support of "humanism," a world-view with obvious deficiencies.

> Yet *Star Trek* could also disquiet, disturb, and deconstruct. Its episodes repeatedly challenged unblinking submission to authority, whether that authority was political, economic, social, or religious. *Star Trek* stood for diversity, pluralism, tolerance, non-conformity, and individualism when these traits were not necessarily considered virtues by the masses. *Star Trek* represented rebellion against authoritarianism, rejection of ethnocentrism, and resistance to the status quo. In thinly veiled parables the series addressed diverse issues such as war, slavery, drug abuse, overpopulation, dehumanization, bigotry, ecology, and the misuse of power.[4]

Enterprise shows us a vision of humanity devoid of those very values, values perhaps naive but also still stirring and potentially viable.

Operation Restore America

Racism, sexism, and heterosexism, as Daniel Leonard Bernardi has shown, all work together in the neoconservative moment to "roll back" the political gains of 1960s liberalism, namely in the fields of civil rights, women's rights, and gay rights.[5] Bernardi associates Trekkian neoconservatism with *The Next Generation*, but *Enterprise* is the first *Trek* series openly to represent a break with *Trek*'s core liberal values.[6]

Neoconservatism is associated by many with the 2000–2008 regime of Republican power and its devotion to the philosophy of Leo Strauss. Yet it is most properly understood as part of the curious aftermath of 1960s liberalism and as a phenomenon that began in the Democratic party. As James Mann describes,

> The neoconservative movement that arose within the Democratic party was made up of intellectuals, scholars, and party stalwarts who had originally

been strong supporters of the party's New Deal traditions, [survivors of the Depression].... In the late 1960s and 1970s these Democrats grew increasingly unhappy with the party's drift toward the political left. They were uneasy with Lyndon Johnson's anti-poverty program; they were then enraged when Democratic leaders embraced many of the causes of the youth counterculture of the 1960s, including opposition to the Vietnam War and support for affirmative action.... [Neoconservatives all] believed in the importance of American power; all hoped to revive the assertive, internationalist traditions under which the Roosevelt and Truman administrations had fought World War II and the cold war.[7]

The history of neoconservatism is far too intricate to be elaborated upon here, but for our purposes the most relevant aspect of the neoconservative movement is that it originated as a rejection of liberal values from a liberal base.

Thomas Schaub's study of Cold War literary criticism offers some useful insights into the cultural atmosphere that would produce such a decisive and powerful shift in what Schaub calls the "liberal narrative" guiding postwar thought. For left-to-liberal intellectuals from the thirties, the knowledge of the atrocities being committed in Stalinist Russia was an especially shattering "reality-check." Gradually but unmistakably, the tone of liberal thought underwent a radical change or reversal. By the time he was writing his 1948 study of the work of Herman Melville, Richard Chase could speak of the ways in which Melville spoke to the "new liberalism," the vanguard of which Chase occupied.[8] Bad, "old" liberalism was facile, unimaginative, wavering in its rejection of totalitarianism. The new liberalism, on the other hand, was bracingly new: unequivocally opposed to totalitarianism and the fuller, broader account of human motives it provided; determined to speak of "progress," "history," and "the liberation of the masses" with "the kind of irony that recognized that these ideas could be realized, if at all, with only partial success." Schaub convincingly argues that the liberal narrative treated political issues with a moral ahistoricism. Because conservative dogma seemed confirmed by the recent war, left-to-liberal intellectuals scrambled, in chapter after chapter, to explain recent history as a lesson in innocence and naiveté, in heated opposition to the "unalloyed" liberalism that coursed through American culture, leaving a "dangerous innocence" in its wake. "This habitual and dangerous innocence" was thought to plague American political life, leaving it "insufficiently complicated and disciplined by an opposing conservatism."[9]

Enterprise appears to be a *Trek* series for those who felt *Trek* had undergone an appallingly "sensitive" makeover in its incarnations of the late 1980s and 1990s. The most recent *Trek* series after the first spin-off, *The Next Generation*, featured, respectively, an African American and a female captain in the lead. *Enterprise* set about to restore the Trekkian status quo with a white male captain who, especially in the first two seasons of the series, spouted xenophobic rhetoric and seemed far more uncomfortable with women in command than Captain Kirk ever did in Original *Trek*. Indeed, *Enterprise*'s captain, Jonathan Archer, expressed the same discomfort with strong women espoused not by Captain Kirk but by Captain Pike, the Captain whom Kirk replaced in the *Trek* pilot episode, "The Cage."

In D. H. Lawrence's famous description, the now-mythic character of Natty Bumppo in James Fenimore Cooper's Leatherstocking Tales — the series of novels that features *The Last of the Mohicans*— incarnates "the true myth of America": to "go backwards, from old age to golden youth."[10] One could apply this description to the project of reactionary revisionism generally and *Enterprise* specifically. *Enterprise* represents a neoconservative fantasy of a return to a strong, noble, secure America of tough liberalism, with properly assigned social and gendered roles, all organized around traditional white masculinist values.

Falling Down

Enterprise is about the early missions of Starfleet, the spacefaring military division of the United Federation of Planets, the democratic interplanetary alliance central to the *Trek* universe, but the series is pointedly set *before* the establishment of the Federation. In the premiere episode, "Broken Bow" (2001), Captain Jonathan Archer (Scott Bakula, of *Quantum Leap* fame) spouts extremely conservative, xenophobic rhetoric. He aggressively loathes Vulcans — who in *Enterprise* are the shadowy, cryptic heavies, having held humans back from spacefaring progress for the past one hundred years because the Vulcans have doubts about their fitness and readiness for space exploration — and seems to have serious issues with women in command. Archer shrieks at T'Pol (Jolene Blalock), the Vulcan woman who will become his first officer, that he will "knock her on her ass" if she doesn't do as she's told. Tellingly, Archer fulminates here against an assembly of Vulcans, of whom T'Pol is the only female; yet she is the sole target of his threats of physical violence. Hating Vulcans, thereby nixing one of the great themes of Original *Trek*, the intense love Captain Kirk has for his Vulcan science officer, Spock; hating strong women, thereby nixing the twenty-fourth century feminist Trekkian innovations in gendered relations, *Enterprise* squarely reimagines the Trekkian mythos as a stridently intolerant social system in which male power regained not only validity but unquestionable, even brute, new strength.

Commander Charles "Trip" Tucker III, the chief engineer, a conventional

Southern good ol' boy (played by Connor Trinneer, whose looks eerily evoke George W. Bush), is presented from the start of the series as provincial, xenophobic, and crass. Lieutenant Malcolm Reed, the security officer, is British and given little screen time; it is also revealed in the last season that he works for the shadow conspiracy group of the Federation, Section 31, a "subtle" suggestion of the untrustworthy nature of foreign members of the community. Tellingly, the show's inclusive representation of the "foreign" is an Englishman, whereas Original *Trek* had the Russian Chekhov. Ensign Hoshi Sato is an Asian American linguist and the communications officer. Prone to fearful fits and generally seen as ineffectual in any terms other than the linguistic aspects of her job, Hoshi is the resident screamer. Ensign Travis Mayweather, the helmsman, is African American and a complete blank, rarely getting even one non-technobabble line an episode; without the slightest exaggeration, it is entirely accurate to say that Nichelle Nichols's Uhura on Original *Trek* had more lines of dialog. The most intriguing character, Phlox, is the chief medical officer; this creepy, mirthful alien doctor comes from a species with highly unusual and polyamorous mating customs.

This generally grim and uninteresting cast (except for T'Pol and Phlox) specifically revises the potential and occasional radicalism of previous *Trek* series. There is an ambiguous recurring *Enterprise* character, Daniels, known as "Future Guy." In "Zero Hour" (the Season Three finale), in which Earth and the galaxy itself are threatened (not, incidentally, by androgynous, transdimensional, Third Sex aliens), Daniels asserts that Reed and Hoshi are not crucial to the future of mankind but Archer *is*. In other words, racial and cultural Others and women are not crucial to the future; institutionalized white male power *is*. Comparing the characters on *Enterprise* to those on *Voyager* and *Deep Space Nine* reveals a great deal about *Enterprise*'s overwriting of Trekkian values to fit with an emerging new reactionary national political climate. *Enterprise* systematically overwrote the innovative casting and characterization choices that, to varying degrees of efficacy and radicalism, made the post–*Next Generation* spin-offs progressive Clinton-era shows.

Voyager was a show conceived in feminist or at least pro-woman terms. Conceived by a woman writer-producer, Jeri Taylor, along with Michael Piller, *Voyager* was the first *Trek* series with a woman Captain. Captain Janeway (Kate Mulgrew) was an interesting mixture of Kirk-style heroics, nurturing, maternal sensitivity, and thoughtfully enquiring scientific curiosity (Janeway is a scientist as well as a Captain; unfortunately, this aspect of her persona was downplayed in later years). Whereas *Voyager* had a strong female Captain, Janeway and several other strong women characters, *Enterprise* features two female characters who represent two sides of the debased woman in patriarchy: the tough woman denounced by hostile males and the fumbling, wan hysteric. Patriarchy remains unchanged and unchallenged in *Enterprise*'s twenty-second century; women once again must assume hypertraditional roles[11]; non-white characters are relegated to off-screen space; non-heterosexual characters are non-existent.

At its best, *Voyager* was an epic for women, as the sweeping two-part episode "Dark Frontier"(1995), in which Janeway travels into the heart of Borg space to rescue former Borg Seven of Nine, evinces. (As "Dark Frontier" also makes clear, *Voyager* could be read as a stirring allegory of female same-sex desire. See Chapter Eight for a reading of this two-parter.) Borrowing its great theme of the longing for *nostos*—the return home—from *The Odyssey*, it was a series about a female hero, surrounded by other heroic women. Not so *Enterprise*, which delimited the roles of women and fatally impaired the strength of its strongest female character.

The female characters on *Voyager* and *Deep Space Nine* were tough, empathetic women delineated as heroically complex and daring characters. *Deep Space Nine* was also innovative in having an African American actor (Avery Brooks) in the leading role. *Enterprise* took the two great political accomplishments of the recent *Trek* series — the enlarged visibility and social power of women and racial minorities — and relegated them to the dustbin of pre-history.

The fans, who stopped watching the show in droves, spoke out, and *Enterprise* made hasty changes to redress the show's pugnaciously intolerant early tone. Rather than focus on one of the early *Enterprise* episodes, in which it would be otiose to point out misogynistic, retrograde aspects of the series, since the show in its early seasons was obviously rife with them, I will now focus on the episode "Twilight" (2003), from the show's third season, which many fans view as, along with the fourth, a marked improvement over the first two. Indeed, in terms of storytelling and characterization, the third and fourth seasons do improve on the preceding ones. Yet even at its best, *Enterprise* is a deeply misogynistic, reactionary *Trek* series. To demonstrate my view of the series, I will examine two episodes, "Twilight" and "Bound," at a certain length.

The "Twilight" of Powerful Women

In its third season, *Enterprise* experimented with ongoing, continuous storytelling arcs. The major plot of the third season is Starfleet/Earth's battle against the Xindi, a complex and ingeniously conceived race (on Xindi, several species simultaneously evolved into sentient beings; there are mammalian, insect, reptilian, and avian sentient/humanoid Xindi species) that, having been deceived into believing that humans are their great enemy who will destroy them in the future, misguidedly and preemptively retaliate against the Earth, which they repeatedly attempt to destroy. In the season finale of Season Two, the 2003 episode "The Expanse," the Xindi destroy a significant portion of the northern hemisphere, including Florida, leaving seven million dead. The annihilation of a sizeable chunk of the United States — significantly, Florida, the contested political zone in which the fierce battle between Democratic and Republican parties yielded George W. Bush as president in 2003 — topically reflects national terrors over terrorism. The Xindi, though, displace the more explicitly topical alien metaphorical threat of the first two seasons, the Suliban, a creepy, shape-shifting race able to spontaneously retool their DNA in order to plot against Starfleet and crawl under doors and along ceilings. "Suliban" is almost comically hypersuggestive of "Taliban."

In "Twilight," first aired during November sweeps month in 2003 and (disquietingly) declared the Number One Fan Favorite in an April 2005 poll/re-airing, we see Archer waking up, in the teaser, in his room to the sound of the red-alert klaxon. He is nearly naked, only in boxers. Bewildered, he staggers to the bridge, where the now–Captain T'Pol bellows, "Get him off the bridge!" and orders him back to his quarters. Archer grows more bewildered still as the security officers grab him. As he looks out the viewscreen, he watches as the Xindi weapon, an enormous round grey-silver globe seething with the powerful might of its accelerating weaponry, approaches and then fires upon the Earth, which it swiftly proceeds to destroy. We then get a close-up of utterly befuddled Archer, as nude as a new baby, with apparently similar abilities to make sense of the situation. The implication of this opening sequence is remarkably clear. T'Pol in charge, Archer is reduced to an infantilized, de-sexualized, de-militarized, emasculated baby-male, and the Earth itself is destroyed, by a swirling, circular mass, no less. The globelike Xindi weapon is yonic imagery, an image of female sexuality, in this case retooled as an apocalyptic weapon in the form of, in Barbara Creed's terminology, "the monstrous-feminine."[12] The remainder of the episode only reinforces these initial impressions.

Whereas *Voyager*'s superlative two-part episode "Year of Hell" (the November sweeps episode of 1997) gave us a defiantly determined Captain Janeway intransigently facing off against a similarly apocalyptic threat and restoring order, through her sacrificial death and rebirth, to the universe, "Twilight" gives us apocalypse as the direct *result* of a woman in command.

"Twilight" is, much to the relief of the imaginary *Enterprise* fan (I confess to never having met one), an alternate reality (AU) episode. It's about what might have happened had Archer been forced to relinquish command to T'Pol. Some temporal parasites infect Archer's mind and he, in the fashion of the 1990 film *Memento*, loses the ability to retain any short-term memories. With T'Pol in command of the *Enterprise*, not only do the Xindi destroy Earth but they also destroy nearly all existing Earth colonies throughout the galaxy. Now, only 6,000 human beings remain. Of this T'Pol informs Archer when he wakes up, his mind still teeming with those time-parasites, many years later, on one of the few remaining outposts. In harrowing long shot, we see him stagger out of their makeshift dwelling, anguished, almost unable to contemplate the inestimable significance of the near-total destruction of the human race, the result of his relinquishment of command to T'Pol. T'Pol is now Archer's nurse and lover. Not only has she herself relinquished command but she has also properly, as if in penitence, assumed conventional gendered roles as maternal nurse and heterosexual companion. Adding a layer of perversity to this set-up, Archer has no awareness of his sexual relationship with T'Pol. The implication is that, much like the Salt Vampire succubus of the Original *Trek* episode "The Man Trap," T'Pol preys upon Archer's very body, draining him of life force. T'Pol also assumes the position of automated drone who must chant the same narrative unceasingly, each time Archer awakes. Effectively, the episode turns T'Pol into the Echo to Archer's sleepy Narcissus.

Fascinatingly explicit about its own masculinist agenda, the episode rigs Archer's return to health — through Phlox's new medical procedure, derived after several years of research, to eradicate the time-parasites, which will restore the time-line, giving us back a pre-infected Archer — as the return of humanity's hope for the future. When Archer reboards the *Enterprise* many years later, about to test Phlox's new treatment, and sees his old crew again, he is greeted by Trip, now Captain of the *Enterprise* (and, with age makeup, more intensely suggestive of President Bush than ever), and Malcolm, who informs him that he is Captain of a different vessel. "Did everyone get their own ship while I was away?" Archer wryly asks. "Not everyone, sir"— this comment is delivered, unsurprisingly, by Asian American Hoshi, who almost mutely embraces Archer. African American Travis was killed on the bridge several scenes, and years, back.

In Sickbay, with *Enterprise* now again under Xindi attack, a tense discussion occurs among T'Pol, Phlox, Archer, and Trip, who unswervingly argues that the Archer-procedure cannot be conducted because the ship cannot afford to lose power. T'Pol passionately makes the case that restoring Archer to command in the past is the only chance for humanity. The episode not only posits that white heterosexual manhood is the necessary linchpin and sign of rational power and that its absence results in the destruction of the human race, but also puts this rhetoric in the mouth of T'Pol, who must, in issuing forth, condemn both women and the Other to the categories of agents of social destruction and the extinction of the race. In the words of Judith Fetterley, in a different context, T'Pol — like the viewers who identify with her — is

> co-opted into participation in an experience from which she is explicitly excluded; she is asked to identify with a selfhood that defines itself in opposition to her; she is required to identify against herself.[13]

"Twilight" most coherently realizes the sexist campaign against T'Pol that undergirds the series. Why *Enterprise* felt the need to impair, hobble, and demean its most interesting, well-acted, and exciting character is a saddening mystery. One of the most revealing features of this sexism is the massage techniques T'Pol is forced to administer to Trip in Season Three. The scenes are played as soft-core porn, with gasps and other forms of heavy breathing, partial nudity (we see T'Pol cupping her breasts, Trip shirtless), nighttime atmosphere, and obvious sexual tension. What is most remarkable about these scenes is the ways in which they represent white manhood. Trip not only provides a white male body to be consumed by the viewers' gaze but also a body that exists to be seduced; the series rigs the situation so that it is T'Pol, at Phlox's matchmaker suggestion, who initiates and insists upon the nighttime neuropressure sessions. This is like a rewriting of the classical myth of Selene and Endymion — in which the moon goddess keeps the beautiful male youth Endymion perpetually asleep so that she may adorn him with nighttime caresses — except Endymion here has all the power, Selene the pitiable need. Trip is new-style white heterosexual manhood, as an erotic canvas upon which women's unrealizable and untenable desires are writ large — and as essentially ungraspable as a figure on the page. This version of white manhood represents the extraordinary resilience of the model, its ability to adapt to the pressures and demands of alternative and now more visible and vocal forms of sexuality and gendered identity — feminist, queer, transgendered — while only more effectively consolidating and maintaining its power.

One of the most telling aspects of the series' masculinist bias and misogynistic sensibility is the relationship between Trip and Archer. Trip emerges as Archer's mini-me. In the first two seasons, especially, Trip primarily exists to reinforce Archer's xenophobic and misogynistic traits, often vociferously echoing Archer's castigating threats to T'Pol. Trip's behavior not only crudely mirrors Archer's but also reinforces images of Southern manhood as pugnaciously crude, rowdy, anti-intellectual, coarse. Trip and T'Pol develop a sexual relationship in the third season, in which T'Pol also becomes addicted to drugs and to experiencing emotion, the major druggy high for a wayward Vulcan (all developments much to T'Pol-actor Jolene Blalock's chagrin.[14]).

Despite their burgeoning sexual and romantic relationship, in "Twilight" Trip expresses a characteristic vehement and ungenerous hostility towards T'Pol — and one heavy-handedly overdetermined to lay the blame for the mission at T'Pol's door, as it were. In one military encounter with two Xindi ships, the *Enterprise* is badly damaged and in danger of being completely obliterated. A Xindi vessel clings to their starboard nacelle, facilitating access to *Enterprise* to hordes of warlike reptilian Xindi soldiers. T'Pol makes the gutsy move of ramming *Enterprise* and the parasite-like Xindi ship into the other Xindi vessel, thereby disabling both Xindi ships. The Xindi ships are indeed disabled, but not without doing a great deal of damage to *Enterprise*. Instead of bonding together about the further difficulties they all now face — clearly, T'Pol's military actions have resulted in a calamitous situation, but one not nearly as calamitous as the threat of destruction posed by both Xindi ships if no action had been taken — the crew appear hostile to T'Pol. Trip explicitly denounces her: "Ever since you took command, this mission has taken one wrong turn after another." T'Pol is denounced not only by a senior officer — it is unthinkable that anyone would speak this way to Archer — but also by the man with whom she has become intimate. Clearly, *Enterprise* reimagines *Voyager*'s daring displays of female heroism as dangerous, foolhardy, destructive. Neither T'Pol nor any other woman can command a ship lest apocalypse ensue.

This AU episode makes sure to resolve everything nicely and restore order. Archer's time-parasites are technobabbleishly eliminated by Phlox (actually, in a rousing return to virility, Archer both outmaneuvers Xindi reptiles and implements his own cure) and Archer returns to Normal and his Captaincy. As T'Pol, now properly re-garbed in her Vulcan attire and back to being First Officer (though hardly Number One), leaves Sickbay in the restored *Enterprise* present, Archer, with a faintly leering expression, says to her, "You know, you'd make a great nurse." This line says it all about the sexual and gendered politics of *Enterprise* (and is, to boot, offensive to nurses).

The New Patriarchy

Brannon Braga, the chief creator of *Enterprise*, has received a great deal of flak over the years from *Trek* fans for his flouting of Trekkian continuity. But in my view, his work apart from *Enterprise* — on *Voyager* and on the short-lived CBS sci-fi series *Threshold*— has been provocative and daring, especially in his creation of gritty, intriguing, bold female characters. Considering *Threshold* (available now on DVD) as a counterpoint to *Enterprise* illuminates the choices Braga made for each show. *Threshold* has a heroine at its center, Dr. Molly Anne Caffrey (Carla Gugino), a government contingency analyst whose job is to devise response plans for worst-case scenarios. When an extraterrestrial craft, which emits a horrific auditory signal that transforms those who hear it into aliens, lands in the middle of the Atlantic ocean, Molly and a motley-crew team of government-appointed experts must find a way to battle the alien takeover.

Molly is inventive, humorous, compassionate, and eminently capable. She is that rare action heroine whose brains complement rather than interfere with her tenderness. She also successfully negotiates an almost entirely homosocial world of various government officials, military hotshots, geeky scientists, and corrupt senators. In one of the most poignant moments in the series, an alien-human hybrid little boy, who may represent the hope for the future, tells her that she will indeed save the world, only she won't be around to see it. Like Moses, she can lead humans to the Promised Land of alien liberation but can't enter it herself. Tellingly, this moment, the last in the series, plays as bittersweet rather than as deadening— it makes Molly a complex heroine with tragic stature rather than the inevitably failed female counterpart to hegemonic masculine power. Hearing this mixed-bag prediction, Molly proceeds, emboldened, to her world-saving task.

Given Braga's considerable talent for writing world-making heroines, his misogynistic themes on *Enterprise* appear more vividly as a canny concession to the moods of the nation, complicity with the Bush-era rolling back of feminist power that works to challenge it at the level of premise. *Enterprise* is not alone, however, in its efforts to reinstall women into more comfortably traditional roles. Several series of varying genres from the same cultural moment have striven to corral female authority through various means. Bush-era genre television shows reveal a shared nervousness about strong and powerful women. Most often, the women characters who assert themselves most boldly undergo a transformation through illness, addiction, or some other form of debilitation, that renders them more conventionally feminine, less autonomous, more "sympathetic." The relevance of issues such as illness and addiction loses its urgency in light of the reactionary uses to which the issues are put.

On *Deadwood*, the enterprising, financially independent widow Alma Garrett is depicted, like *Enterprise*'s T'Pol, as a drug addict, as well as an adulteress, and the subservience to strong, often brutal men on the part of several of the women on the series belies their seeming strength and autonomy. It is telling that it is sexually adventurous Samantha on *Sex and the City* upon whom breast cancer is bestowed. The acclaimed new version of the 1970s sci-fi cult show *Battlestar Galactica* promisingly numbers a female president amongst its innovations, yet the president is often depicted as morally questionable (throwing Cylons, the cyborg enemies of the humans, out of the airlock), a stark contrast against the gravitas of the "Old Man," Captain Adama of the *Galactica*. In addition, the president suffers from breast cancer and becomes a female mystic, replacing military authority with occult "feminine" vision.

One of the most disturbing aspects of these retrograde depictions is that they come from television shows acclaimed for their daring and their unconventionality. *Deadwood* has been praised for its raw realism and the garish, heady literariness of its idiolect, *Sex and the City* for its uncensored look at urban sex-lives, *Battlestar Galactica* for its uncompromising vision of a desolate future. All of these series embody a sense of the boldness of postmodern representation. Yet when examined closely they can be read, however brilliantly made and compelling, as reactionary visions of the social order that lock down rather than explore gendered and racial stereotypes.

What all of these shows, *Enterprise* included, have at their core is a male character to whom all the others are subservient no matter how questionable his motives or personality. Al Swearengen on *Deadwood* is a prime example of the new kind of male character whose despicable actions are implicitly condoned by the "complexity" of his characterization. Learning about his childhood woes (abandoned by his mother to an orphanage), we are asked to view Al not as the monster he is but as the victimized child he was. Another technique employed on *Deadwood*—and even more pervasively on *The Sopranos*—is to pit the male character's evil against a higher and more sustained evil. In comparison to other villains of the series, Al comes to seem more thoughtful, compassionate, even benign, just as Tony Soprano does in comparison to the "more" psychotic, lesser gangsters with whom he must contend.

Enterprise disappointingly rolls back feminist progress in the *Trek* universe, but in so doing it is far from alone in Bush-era television. It now seems like decades ago that television brimmed with shows that featured strong women characters at their center—*Xena, Warrior Princess, Buffy the Vampire Slayer, Voyager, Dark Angel, Witchblade, Alias*. The dearth of such series today attests to the cultural shifts with which television shows are complicit.

Vulcans and the Suliban: Or, Jews and Arabs

From its inception, *Trek* has been anti-racist. The Original *Trek* of the 1960s daringly offered an image of racial unity in the turbulent era of civil-rights agitation. The premise of *Trek* rests on constant encounter with otherness and the embrace of it. Many over the years have found this premise alternately hokey and limited; some have read a colonizing agenda in the Trekkian mythos. Nevertheless, it is important to note that, however flawed the attempts, *Trek* has consistently attempted to promote tolerance and critique racism. For this reason, *Enterprise*'s depiction of race causes the greatest concern for the future of *Trek*.

Enterprise's treatment of Vulcans, other than Klingons the most famous alien *Trek* race, most vividly reveals the frightening ideological shifts in current *Trek*. Though always subject to jokes about their staunch, stoic adherence to logic, purgation of emotion, and general lack of a sense of humor ("What's the matter, Spock, change your mind?" asks Kirk in the fourth *Trek* film, *The Voyage Home* [1986]. "No — is there something wrong with the one I have?"), Vulcans have also always been seen as a noble, highly moral race, the intellectual rationalists of the Federation.

Ever since Original *Trek*, Leonard Nimoy's Spock has been taken as a metaphor for racial otherness, specifically for Jewishness in patriarchal white male, Christian culture. Indeed, Nimoy himself has made the connection between his Jewish identity and his portrayal as Spock.[15] His status as "half-breed"—both Vulcan and human—intensified the theme of Spock's loneliness and apartness. Vulcans, though, have come to seem the holy priesthood of *Trek*, one of the signature allies of the Federation, a race who overcame their violent history and now maintain a deeply spiritual, if utterly austere, society.

On *Enterprise*, however, the Vulcans are consistently, throughout the series, villainous — craven, deceitful, profoundly ungenerous, the enemy of humanity. The series makes noises about its Vulcans as *pre*–Original *Trek*— as working towards the moral elevation they exhibit in the later series. But *Enterprise*'s treatment of Vulcans smacks of mysterious phobia. Given the construction of Vulcans as shadowy, duplicitous, and secretly all-powerful — they control humans, their space exploration, much of the galaxy — and the excruciatingly obvious racial allegory of the Suliban, the series seems to have made a coded version of the Jewish (Vulcan)–Arab (Suliban) conflict its chief metaphorical foundation.

Manny Coto, the creative force behind the final season of *Enterprise*, crafted a season that generally exhibited a less reactionary agenda than its predecessors, and even came up with some powerful and affecting episodes ("The Aenar" in particular). Despite Coto's love for *Trek* and his talents, he and his team are responsible for the worst reconceptualization of Trekkian lore in *Trek* history. *Enterprise* rigs the development of the Vulcan race — their passage out of violent emotion into pure logic — as the product of *Archer's* guidance. Surak, the Vulcan visionary who leads his people to their Great Awakening, from a violent, passion-driven, almost animalistic culture to the Stoic severity they now embrace, entrusts the future of his race to Archer. An exotic and mysterious race now has a white, patriarchal Captain to thank for its greatest cultural triumph. (One has only to compare the representations of Surak in Original *Trek* and *Enterprise* to register a profound shift in representation. The Surak who appears in the Original *Trek* episode "The Savage Curtain" is clearly exotic, dark, Other; the Surak of *Enterprise*'s 2004 episode "The Awakening" looks like a Great White Father, a comforting emblem of bland, benign white patriarchy.[16])

"Bound" to Archetypes

In a Season Four episode, "Bound" (2005), the crew are infiltrated by Orion slave women, pea-green sirens who drive men wild with passion and desire. However one looks at it, this is a misogynistic premise. Yet, astonishingly, *Enterprise* manages to resolve the situation far more conservatively than did the '70s *Trek*.[17] In "Bound," the episode strenuously bends the plot in order to allow *Trip* to save the day (though presumably unaffected, T'Pol and Hoshi stand around limply on the bridge as Trip dispatches the green Orion succubi).

"Bound" performs that sexist sleight-of-hand whereby women are mythologized as the more powerful sex even when they maintain no actual social power; female power, then, becomes a compensatory fantasy that enables male rule to continue under the guise of subservience to the all-powerful feminine. The Orion thug-pimp who appears to have dispatched the enslaved green women to seduce and therefore thoroughly unman the men, thereby securing the takeover of the *Enterprise*— because obviously none of the women on Archer's ship, though unaffected by Orion slave girl charms, could ever pose a threat!— reveals that, contrary to popular opinion, *the slave girls are the ones in control*. On Orion, it is the *men* who are the sexual slaves! So *Enterprise* provides us ingeniously with the spectacle of lurid female sexuality — which the trope of enslavement reinforces, enlarges, mobilizes — and the archetypal misogynistic, compensatory legend of female carnality as female power over men, i.e., the lesser sex is truly the mightier, though it may seem otherwise.

Emblematizing neoconservative's deployment of homophobia along with racism and sexism to roll back liberal progress, "Bound" also perpetuates the extraordinary heterosexism of all the *Trek* series. It posits that every single male of the *Enterprise* crew will fall helplessly under the sway of the Orion women's enchanting spell. With bald unawareness of the ironies of its own storytelling biases, "Bound" features a scene in which the males of the crew pound iron together in the weight room, grunting and comparing feverish notes about their sexual frustrations, intensely enhanced by the Orion women, as rivulets of sweat pour down their gleaming, drenched, hypermasculinized bodies. The homosocial was far more knowingly homoeroticized — and undercut — in nineteenth-century American fiction. In Herman Melville's story "The Paradise of Bachelors and the Tartarus of Maids," the split between homosocial groups of men and women serves to highlight the disparity between the social power of men and women: the men in the story enjoy freedom and companionship, while the women, zombielike drudges, must inexorably toil away their days in a noxious paper mill.

Interestingly enough, it is the two most sexually ambiguous figures on the crew — the British secret-spy Malcolm Reed, and the gleaming, chiseled, yet oddly feminized African American Travis Mayweather — who carry on a discussion about their swelling sexual needs and pains. And the episode certainly never considers that some of the women on the ship might experience overpowering sexual desires for the Orion sirens. The Orion women, whose hypnotic dance before Archer and other male crew members suggests the jerky movements of birds (it should be remembered that Homeric sirens had the heads of human women and the bodies of birds[18]), represent archetypal female evil, but they are deployed on *Enterprise* as regulators of sexual and gendered roles.

The Real Neoconservatism

One of the chief lessons provided by *Enterprise* is that a show can be, on the face of it, liberal and open to otherness while, upon inspection, pernicious in its pervasive ideological character. *Enterprise*'s commercial failure also suggests that it is precisely in its "hokey" 1960s liberal values — which include the belief that exploration and the unification of diverse groups are *good* things — that the source of most successful *Trek* lies.

But *Enterprise* also provides evidence for the alarming desire to return to American origins that both covers for and is represented by the reclamation of white American male power in its most masculinist form. It is little wonder that characters like Tony Soprano and Al Swearengen become pop icons in our era. They enable an audience to return to an illusory time before the strictures of "liberalism" in its politically correct form ruined everyone's ability to speak "openly" about blacks, gays, women, and other oppressed groups. Tony, Al, and the early Jonathan Archer of *Enterprise* spoke out explicitly against anyone not of their own raced, classed stature. The failure of *Enterprise* meant that Archer failed to be celebrated for his apparently refreshing racist candor, but the fact that *Trek* producers, desperate for a hit, gave the latest *Trek* this particular new xenophobic spin — that the most current television incarnation of *Trek* could be so openly a rejection of the original's series' basic values — reveals a great deal about the newly traditionalized and once again overtly racist and sexist popular culture age we're watching in.

Seven

WHITE WHALES
Rage and Masculinity in *Star Trek II: The Wrath of Khan* and *Star Trek: First Contact*

At this point, our study comes to a crossroads. We have explored the surprising radicalism of much of *Star Trek*; we have shaken our heads at the equally surprising levels of phobia and suspicion, racism and misogyny. At the end of Chapter 5, I posited that *Trek* is at its most radical in its decentering of white masculinity. This chapter takes that very claim and subjects it to analysis. Several examples exist in *Trek* of a denatured white masculinity that provocatively appears to resist many of the markers of white male privilege, the presumptive assumptions of rationality and coherence that lend the model its power. But for every Data or holographic Doctor, there is a Kirk or a Picard or an Archer: the Symbolic White Father. While we uncovered in Chapter One a Captain Kirk who, far from wielding the might of the white heterosexual male gaze, embodies a position of fragility within the field of the gaze, this Kirk very much belongs to the 1960s TV-world of Original *Trek*; the versions of Kirk that we see in the seven motion pictures in which he, as well as other Original *Trek* characters, appears presents an entirely new set of problems in terms of gender and race. Similarly, the character of Jean-Luc Picard in the motion pictures spun off from *TNG* differs radically from his television series incarnation; as we discussed in Chapter 5, in a film like *Nemesis,* Picard comes to seem, in contradistinction to his television persona, a brutal figure of patriarchal power. This is not in any way to suggest that the film versions of *Trek* shows and the shows themselves are clearly divisible in terms of their political timbre, that the shows present more coherently "liberal" versions of the Captains while the films present the Captains as reactionary—far from it. Rather, the films amplify certain aspects of the television series in their depictions of the Captains, and it is precisely the question of *which* aspects get amplified, and why, that now arrests our attention.

In this chapter, I argue that *Trek* establishes the superiority of white masculinity through a pointed confrontation with an otherness that challenges but does not defeat this white male model. This otherness connotes both racial and sexual difference, and the fear of both. Women's sexuality, queer sexuality, and racial identity all challenge and come close to undermining the stability of white male power, figured here as the militaristic might of Starfleet and the imperialistic might of the Federation, both always already allegories for United States power from the Cold War to the present. These confrontations between white manhood and otherness occur in several different ways. This chapter focuses on three challenges to white masculinity: the black woman; the phallic, alien woman; and the racialized, queer male.

"I Never Read It": Denying the Black Woman a Claim to High Culture

Lily (the great Alfre Woodard) in *Star Trek: First Contact* (1996) is an African American woman freedom fighter in the ravaged Earth of the 22nd century, on the verge of the titular first contact meeting with the Vulcans that dramatically changes, in the *Trek*verse, the course of human history. Jean-Luc Picard's *Enterprise* is only present at Lily's Earth because they have followed a Borg sphere on its journey backwards in time, in an effort to retrocolonize the Earth, so resistant to Borg assimilation in the 24th century. *First Contact* is Picard's Ahab film, in which, in his maddened, vengeful determination to destroy the Borg, who have infiltrated *Enterprise*, he resembles Melville's tormented and terrible anti-hero in his hunt for the mythic White Whale. (The *Moby-Dick* references are nothing new for *Trek*— they also saturate *Star Trek II: The Wrath of Khan*.)

At one point — after Picard has denounced the Klingon Worf (Michael Dorn) as a "coward" and ordered the *Enterprise* crew to fight the Borg hand-to-hand if they have to, anything to avoid blowing up the ship — Lily storms into Picard's ready room. She lights into him, attacking him for essentially ordering the crew to commit suicide by fighting hopeless battles with the Borg, when if Picard simply blew up the ship, they could all at least survive. "I forgot," Lily says, "Captain Ahab always has to get his whale." "What?" Picard angrily responds. "You do have books in the 24th century?" Lily challenges him. After Picard demands she leave, Lily shrieks, "Jean-Luc, blow up the damn ship!" Thunderously, Picard bellows, "No! Noooooo!" With that, he bashes his glass display of model ships throughout the centuries, which loudly shatters. He says, "They invade our space and we fall back. They assimilate entire worlds and we fall back. Not this time. The line must be drawn *here*—this far, and no further. And I will make them *pay* for what they've done!" Interestingly, Picard speaks in the language of postcolonial discourse, accusing the Borg of cultural invasion and colonization by assimilation—charges that have on occasion been leveled at *Trek*'s premise itself.

But his infuriated speech falls on resigned ears. "See you around, Ahab," says Lily. At this reminder that he verges on Ahablike tyranny, Picard iterates one of the most famous passages from *Moby-Dick*:

> He piled upon the whale's white hump the sum of all the general rage and hate felt by his whole race from Adam down; and then, as if his chest had been a mortar, he burst his hot heart's shell upon it.

Picard now realizes what he has been becoming—a tyrant. He owes this revelation to Lily, up to this point represented as the triumphant close reader who can—to the elation of humanists everywhere—marshal the moral power of great literature to stop wars, prevent strife, illuminate human psychology, and force Picard to recognize his own potential evil. But Picard's extraordinary revelation produces another one. About the canonical original she liberally referenced, Lily reveals, "Actually, I never read it." She has quoted from *Moby-Dick* but never read it.

Trek is a mythos that staunchly prides itself—to a fault—on its intertextual and avowed connections with the Western literary and aesthetic tradition. Given *Trek*'s old-fashioned liberal humanist belief in the importance of great literature, it is highly ideologically suspect to have a black woman character simultaneously deploy the Western canon's cultural power and disavow her own familiarity with it. For Lily to announce that she has never read the text is for *Trek* to deny the intellectual, thinking life of African Americans and women in one fell swoop.

I don't write this to make a pro-canonical reading point but to call attention to the way in which this moment strips Lily—the black woman—of an intellectual power she has claimed for herself as it bestows not only this intellectual power but also the entire Western tradition upon Picard, wrenching it loose from Lily in the process. Picard emerges as the rational, learned white male who is the proper, rational custodian of Dead White Male literature—who can effectively quote from it and glean its insights. Lily becomes the conduit for Picard's access to Western cultural power, even as she is disenfranchised from it. What could have been one of the great moments in *Trek*—Picard's angry speech is thrillingly written and delivered—is ultimately a pitiable instance of myopic, naively racist *Trek* thinking at best. The black woman facilitates white male power, a process uncritically replicated throughout *Trek* history.

Star Trek: First Contact harkens back to the Original *Trek* episode "The Changeling," in which a crazed robot erases Uhura's brain, leaving her a *tabula rasa*. Nurse Chapel (Majel Barrett) has to teach her how to be a functioning adult again, from scratch, even teaching her Swahili. By taking away the power of knowledge from the black woman and entrusting it to the white woman, here, the episode is not commenting on the shared history of the oppression of women across color lines — and the shared struggle over civil rights issues — so much as it is rendering a strong, capable professional black woman an infantilized figure in need of benevolent white guidance. A similar maneuver occurs in *Star Trek: First Contact*: after having been challenged by Lily, Picard emerges as the knowledgeable one who has to instruct Lily in the ways of the humanist tradition. Original *Trek*'s lapses are much more forgivable than those of *Star Trek: First Contact*, however, especially when it is considered how much opposition Gene Roddenberry faced in simply having a black character on the series.

Trek has yet to give us a truly strong, resilient African American woman character whose strength and resiliency are supported by the larger series and do not emerge from the power and appeal of an actor's portrayal. Lily, as played by Woodard, is an awkward mixture of intelligence and bravery and stereotypical thinking and role-playing. When she and Picard roam the Borg-infested ship, Lily screams in a panic that is so theatrical as to suggest a minstrel show; though Jonathan Frakes, the director, can be credited with having made in many ways a provocative and intriguing film, his direction of Woodard is offensive at times. But then again, Lily does have many fine, subtle moments, her eyes flickering with growing awareness of Picard's instability. As with all things *Trek*, we don't have one thing or another, but an unwieldy mixture: Lily is both racist caricature and strong, resilient heroine. (A friend of mine once complained that, if anything, Lily is that dread fan archetype, the Mary Sue figure: a character who comes in from nowhere, learns everything about the futuristic environment, and saves the ship.)

So far, the representation of African Americans has not been *Trek*'s most progressive accomplishment, to put it mildly. As the previous chapter argued, it is not as if black men have fared much better on *Trek*, even though *Deep Space Nine* did have an African American actor in the leading role (Avery Brooks as Captain Sisko). When Lily first encounters Worf on the bridge, she gasps. He explains, "I am a Klingon," and then walks away, apparently having resolved Lily's fears. In the exchange of looks between Lily and Worf, there is also a different kind of exchange, one between Michael Dorn and Alfre Woodard, one African American actor looking at another, with mutual bewilderment and a shock of recognition.

"Khan!": *The Racial Other as Queer Threat*

The significance of the 1982 film *Star Trek: The Wrath of Khan*'s numerous references to Herman Melville's *Moby-Dick* has not been lost on fans or critics. What has not been discussed, however, is the significance of making a figure like Captain James T. Kirk — the White Man *par excellence*— into the hunted White Whale and Khan into the Ahab-like hunter.

As discussed in the Introduction, the Kirk-Spock relationship is the most visible tradition of homoerotic love in the Trekkian monomyth. *Wrath* can be understood as a tender and disturbing conclusion to the love story between Kirk and Spock, one that will be renewed in subsequent films. The tenderness is everywhere present in the scenes between these characters (as well as with McCoy). There is no moment in the cinema of the 1980s that more exquisitely conveys love between men than Spock's death scene, in which Kirk watches his friend die behind a wall of glass.

What is also disturbing about this allegorical homo-narrative is that it splits the racial allegory of the Spock character into a good (Spock) and a bad (Khan) racial Other. Much more than the Original *Trek* episode "Space Seed" from which the film was spawned, the Khan of *Wrath* is figured as the racialized Other.

The racial Other both speaks the language of racial consciousness and speaks out against personal ties to race. *Deep Space Nine's* Odo is a good example of a character who is both radicalized into a separatist racialized position ("Chimera") and speaks out against racial consciousness. Odo, the space-station security officer, is a shape-shifter who lives among humans but whose people, a race of shape-shifters known as the Founders, wage war against humankind. When Odo warns a Federation official in one episode against the sinister agendas of his people, his deeply awkward position, in social and moral terms, becomes clear: is he more decisively helping humanity or hurting his own people? Within this social and moral awkwardness lies the chief role of the Other on *Trek*: to represent difference while condemning and dissociating oneself from that difference. In *Wrath*, this process occurs implicitly and symbolically, through the split between the racial Other Spock, loyal to the literal end to the Federation, and Khan, enemy to all the Federation stands for.

Kwame Anthony Appiah explains *racialization* as a modern phenomenon, the belief, which dates back to the mid-nineteenth century and has held since that time,

> that we could divide human beings into a small number of groups, called "races," in such a way that all the members of these races shared certain fun-

damental, biologically heritable, moral and intellectual characteristics with each other that they did not share with members of any other race. The characteristics that each member of a race was supposed to share with every other were sometimes called the essence of that race; they were characteristics that were necessary and sufficient, taken together, for someone to be a member of the race.

Unlike the [ancient] Greeks and the Hebrews, racialists believed that the racial essence accounted for more than the obvious visible characteristics — skin-color, hair — on the basis of which we decide whether people are, say, Asian-American or Afro-Americans. For a racialist, then, to say someone is "Negro" is not just to say that they have inherited a black skin or curly hair: it is to say that their skin color goes along with other important inherited characteristics.[1]

The characterization of Khan is a product of this modern, pervasive tendency towards racialization. Khan's own racial status is both polyglot and heavily, visibly marked as *Other*. To begin with, Khan's appearance suggests the exotic primitive: with his long hair and tribal dress, he connotes a mélange of the indigenous peoples and cultures of the Americas. As "Space Seed" establishes, Khan was the leader of the Middle East before he was deposed and banished, with his followers, into space during the "Eugenics Wars" of the 1990s. In the twenty-third century, Kirk discovers Khan and his crew adrift in the shuttle "Botany Bay." ("Botany Bay" was the name of the first colony, comprised of prisoners, that the English settled in the continent of Australia.) Marla McGivers, the historian assigned to study Khan in "Space Seed," conjectures that Khan is from "the northern India area ... probably a Sikh." Associated with both India and the Arab nations, Khan suggests the exotic Asian of Orientalist discourse as well as indigenous American peoples. It should also be noted that the actor playing Khan, the marvelously impassioned yet cerebral Ricardo Montalban, is of Mexican origin, adding to the polyglot nature of Khan's image. In his fusion of different racial identities, Khan is *a symbolic marker of the concept of race itself*.

As one of the race of genetically engineered supermen who ruled the world in the late twentieth-century "Eugenics Wars" of Trekkian mythology, Khan is also associated with fantasies of racial purity. Given that the most well-known fusion of ideologies of eugenics and a bid for global power occurred in World War II German fascism, the indirect *Trek* suggestion is that Khan is a kind of Nazi. Along these lines, the "Indian" Khan also represents both the colonial subject and the colonizer. Perplexingly and fascinatingly, Khan represents both the racial Other and a figure who attempts to *destroy* racial otherness.

More interestingly still, Khan's grandeur and daring and ingenuity, so grandly conveyed by Montalban, also make him a darkly appealing figure, one the audience roots for. Blake famously said of John Milton and his poem about the fall of Man, *Paradise Lost*, that Milton was of the Devil's Party, even if he did not know it; *Wrath* makes its viewers part of Khan's party, rallies us to his grandiloquent campaign against a Federation god. Khan's scrappy ability to survive on the harsh world of the nearly obliterated, sandstorm-plagued Ceti Alpha 5 provokes admiration and awe; his delight in his own cunning as he outwits Kirk (at least initially) is contagious.

Khan's meld of race and anti-race, of victimization and tyranny, embody the paralytic bind of *Trek*'s disposition towards race, one of mingled sympathy and terror. In this manner, *Trek* recalls American fiction of the nineteenth century, with its similar antithetical attitudes towards race and otherness. On the subject of nineteenth-century fiction, Herman Melville's novel *Moby-Dick* emerges as the economy through which *Trek*'s warring attitudes towards race can be negotiated.

High Culture and Death

Melville's novel, long a high-school staple, has an established meaning as a cautionary tale against obsession and vengeance. Left out of most discussions of *Wrath*'s uses of *Moby-Dick* are two competing but characteristically Melvillean elements of the novel: a troubled and troubling racial politics and a heady homoeroticism. While the novel cannot be called simply racist, it can with justification be called a mixture of racist and ambivalent views of race.

> The question of race in *Moby-Dick* has been a vexed one since the early 1960s.... Since Carolyn Karcher's *Shadow over the Promised Land* (1980) ... the consensus has been that Melville, though occasionally succumbing to culturally ingrained racist stereotyping, created in *Moby-Dick* a radically anti-racist text.[2]

Though a full exploration of how, exactly, this critical "consensus" was established exceeds the parameters of our discussion, it should be pointed out that views of *Moby-Dick*'s politics and race representation are hardly stable and remain controversial. *Wrath*, which emerges at a key point in the cultural and critical re-examination of Melville's original text, overrides the issues of its racial themes with Khan's grandiloquent, Shakespearean-Miltonic-Melvillean revenge narrative. Part of the sleight-of-hand at work in the film's conceptualization of Khan is that, whereas Khan is the film's chief embodiment of the disturbing racial Other, Spock being *the assimilated Other*, Khan is also the one who identifies with the white imperialist colonizer Ahab, seeing *Kirk* as the White Whale, an intriguing inversion of conventional roles.

The racialized Khan functions in the film as a symbol of what Toni Morrison has described as the Africanist presence, in white American culture:

> Africanism is the vehicle by which the American self knows itself as not enslaved, but free; not repulsive, but desirable; not helpless, but licensed and powerful; not history-less, but historical; not damned, but innocent; not a blind accident of evolution, but a progressive fulfillment of destiny.[3]

Though not a "black" character, Khan is virtually black in his symbolic function as a contrast to white male power. As a Starfleet Admiral, Kirk is licensed and powerful. Most importantly, Kirk embodies the Trekkian ideal of historical progress, whereas Khan, adrift in space for centuries and then marooned on a dead planet, is pointedly out of time, narrative, history. Perhaps most acutely of all, Kirk represents innocence, the innocence of American history, which is, paradoxically, not history at all, but a prelapsarian fresh start. Kirk is the Adam of a new American Eden, which the paradisiacal "Genesis Cave" and later planet of the film spectacularly represent. As Kirk says in one of the final scenes, "I know nothing." Though a line Shatner delivers in a bleak register, it nevertheless speaks volumes about the film's retooling of Kirk as the original American innocent, bewildered by the intrigues of otherness. To be sure, the Kirk of this film, fumbling, depressed, and aged, represents an Adam out of sync with Eden; yet the film's narrative returns him to a state of innocence, as Kirk's moving last words evince: "Young. I feel ... *young*."

Though Khan *had* been a great world tyrant, in this film he is much closer to the position of the enslaved or disenfranchised subject. We are on safe grounds to establish that the ultimate sleight-of-hand of the film in political terms is that it figures the abject, colonized subject Khan as the imperialist, colonialist oppressor. The film's chief emphasis is placed on Khan's persecution of Kirk, portrayed as bewildered but indefatigable. But doesn't Khan have a right to complain? In the vaunted enlightenment of the Federation, the condition of those in a penal colony, like Khan and his "Botany Bay" crew, would seem to merit at least occasional inspection. Kirk and the Federation have shirked their responsibility to check up on Khan and his people. Cast off and forgotten, Khan and his crew represent the Trekkian subaltern, erased from history as *Trek* careens towards its mythic fantasies of historical progress.

An interesting aspect of the film's uses of *Moby-Dick* is that Khan can find personal meaning for his own addled quest in Melville's high culture narrative. Harold Bloom, in his famous theory of the "anxiety of influence," posits that the artist of the present is in an *agon*, or conflict, with the artist who came before him. The present day artist competes against his predecessor with a "strong misreading" of that predecessor's text.[4] Khan strongly misreads Melville; he reads Ahab's quest as a narrative of his victimization, not tyranny, and therefore one in which Khan can share. Khan misreads *himself* as Ahab, when it is Khan who is the White Whale of the film, that which must be destroyed.

What is interesting about the film is that its version of Kirk is such a touchingly hapless figure, hardly one worthy of Khan's all-consuming, messianic rage. This Kirk is defensive, sullen, and unsure, downright bumbling in his initial confrontation with Khan. The film is rather like Shakespeare's play *Richard II*, which transforms its fumbling, effeminate, ineffectual ruler into a skilled, securely masculine warrior. But the joke here is that whereas Shakespeare's protagonist is a young, callow man, *Wrath's* Kirk is already quite middle-aged. Kirk's age makes the film's insertion of him into the coming-of-age narrative disconcerting. The film is a kind of early Reaganite elegy for the lost stamina and skill of white males, being overrun by the overzealous racial minorities vengefully angry over their disenfranchisement and social isolation. Ingeniously, though Kirk, especially in comparison to Khan, has all the power, it is *Kirk* who is the underdog, a maneuver that will be taken up again in the later *Terminator* films, in which Arnold Schwarzenegger's T-800 cyborg is an "obsolete model" forced to face off against slicker, more technologically advanced machines.

This odd maneuver, making Kirk the pitiable source of audience sympathy, prepares us for the Kirk of the later *Trek* films with the Original *Trek* cast as well as those with Patrick Stewart's Captain Jean-Luc Picard and the other *Next Generation* characters. In all of the subsequent films, Kirk is portrayed as the put-upon victim of grandiose campaigns on the part of messianic, self-aggrandizing villains or of staunchly unimaginative, conservative Federation officials. The *Trek* films with the original crew anticipate *Enterprise* in the gathering urgency of their overall narrative to restore Kirk, and the once-innocent nation he symbolizes, to his former potency. Kirk comes to incarnate what D. H. Lawrence called "the true myth of America": to "go backwards, from old age to golden youth."[5]

A Sexual Quest

It should be remembered that Melville's novel is also about passionate same-sex ties, albeit ones that cannot be sustained (Ishmael ends up alone at the end, bobbing desolately in the sea, the sole survivor of Ahab's disastrous campaign to kill the Whale). The homoeroticism of Melville's work makes the uses of it volatile, in ways that are highly interesting for this film. In the early sections of *Moby-Dick*, Ishmael, the narrator, must share a bed — in the tellingly named "Spouter-Inn"— with a fearsomely tattooed cannibal man from the Polynesian islands, Queequeg. The major thrust of this comedic and scary episode is that Ishmael learns to love the savage Queequeg, snuggling up to him during their "hearts' honeymoon" at the end of Chapter 10.

This novel also contains an ecstatic paean to homoerotic democratic brotherhood, the sperm-squeezing scene. In this famous passage, a description of sperm whale oil manufacture in Chapter 94, "A Squeeze of the Hand," Ishmael discusses the liberating, transcendent joy of squeezing "the milk and sperm of human kindness" with his fellow male sailors. Ishmael's rapturous description of same-sex intimacy here represents how far he has come from his initial horror at the thought of physical intimacy with Queequeg. His "hearts' honeymoon" with the savage, cannibal Queequeg opens him up to larger connections to the whole race of men. Ishmael and Queequeg go so far as to "splice" each other's identities.

As we have discussed, the loving friendship between Kirk and Spock, complemented by the one both men share with McCoy, goes a long way towards realizing the Melvillean ideal of homoerotic interracial brotherhood. Khan's demonic presence adds something different. If Khan is recognizable as the racial Other, there is also a way in which Khan is the *sexual* Other. As both the racial and sexual Other, Khan's significance deepens. His vengeful hunting of Kirk is also a kind of ravenous desire *for* Kirk. Khan emerges as the relentless suitor, the ultimate version of the lover who cannot accept a "No"; conversely, Kirk is put in the stereotypically feminine position of being the pursued. Chasing Kirk across the galaxy, Khan is like a spurned, vengeful Queequeg, hunting down the ship-bound, Ishmael-like Kirk. (The wearied, melancholy Kirk of this film certainly seems to be feeling an Ishmael-like "damp, drizzly November" in his soul.)

One scene in particular conveys these homoerotic dynamics while also highlighting the theme of white male rage that, I argue, is increasingly prominent in the *Star Trek* mythos, especially the films. Deep within the dead planetoid Regula — where Kirk and Spock trick Khan into believing Kirk is trapped — Kirk and Khan have a telling exchange. Kirk, attempting to goad Khan into giving himself up, tells Khan that he will have to come down and get Kirk himself. Kirk taunts Khan about being a poor marksman, always missing his target. "I've done far worse than that," Khan tells him. "I've hurt you. And I want to go on ... hurting you." At this point, Kirk shrieks — in words that cinematically reverberate across the chill expanse of the dead planetoid — "*Khan*! *Khan*!" Even for Shatner, this moment is deliriously over-the-top. Yet it is more than matched by the reaction shot of Khan, silently moaning, his lips quivering, a shot in which Ricardo Montalban seems to be simulating orgasm. The entire exchange, played on the knife-edge of hysteria, camp, and pathos, allegorizes elements of a failed homoerotic romance: male-male violence, a terrible, unbridgeable impasse between would-be lovers, and wrenching orgasmic release.

As we have seen, queer desire in *Trek* is impossible desire, a desire that cannot be explicitly represented, cannot be realized, but is nevertheless inescapably *present*. *Trek*'s simultaneous obfuscation and suggestion of queer themes makes certain scenes, images, and themes in *Wrath* especially interesting. When Khan quotes (and also distorts) Melville in his declaration of his intent to pursue Kirk — "He tasks me and I shall have him. I'll chase him round the moons of Nibia and round the Antares Maelstrom and round Perdition's flames before I give him up!" — he is declaring fascination with another male character in a manner unusual for a mainstream film. By putting the ostensibly hyper-heterosexual Kirk in the typically feminine position of the woman who must be pursued, Khan scrambles the legend of Kirk as the Great Galaxy Lothario, making him instead something akin to the damsel in the tower who must be won at all costs. Kirk, then, becomes the *object* of the male gaze, now occupying the role of the countless female guest stars in Original *Trek* who fell beneath *his* gaze. In keeping with the Trekkian ban against homoerotic desire, Khan, in his increasingly irrational desire to capture Kirk, ends up destroying himself; desire for another male character has disastrous consequences when explicitly rendered and actively pursued.

The film finds characteristically Trekkian vent, however, for its unrepresentable yet urgent homoerotic desires in the theme of perverse male penetration. When Chekhov (Walter Koenig) and Captain Tyrell (Paul Winfield, who lends every film a welcome dignity) beam down to the hellish Ceti Alpha 5, they are besieged by Khan and his minions. Khan introduces them to the only indigenous life on the planet, the "Ceti Eels" as they are commonly called, grotesque, slimy worms, extracted from a larger creature, that wriggle their way through the ear and into the brain, wrapping themselves around the cerebral cortex; as they grow, they make their victims highly susceptible to suggestion before turning them insane and ultimately killing them. In the grisliest sequence in any *Trek* film, the phallic eels penetrate the men's ears, in close-up, accompanied by thunderous auditory effects that suggest the penetrative power of the eels, an effect complemented by the men's howls of pain. The entire scene suggests a rape — indeed, a gang-rape, as Khan and his followers all stand around the violated men. Khan's books include a worn copy of Shakespeare's *King Lear*, and this scene seems like a nod to another famous Shakespeare play: the eels in the ear suggest pouring poison in the ear, the method whereby Hamlet's uncle Claudius murders Hamlet's father. Later, the eels appear again, this time emerging bloodily from Chekov's ear, the same thunderous cracking sounds and howls of pain engulfing the soundtrack. Kirk zaps the bloody eel with his phaser, destroying its penetrative threat.

I suggest that this entire eel-motif gives vent to the film's inexpressible but intensifying homoerotic themes, rendering the thought of male penetration grotesque, but in so doing also finding a means of suggesting sodomy. Along these lines, it can't be left unremarked that when Kirk and company find Chekhov and Tyrell on Regula, they are in a closet.

Genesis: The Matrix of Heterosexuality

It is fascinating, as our beloved Spock would say, that this failed romance between Kirk and Khan is juxtaposed against a battle over Genesis. Developed by the scientists Carol Marcus and her son David Marcus, the "Genesis Device" creates "life from lifelessness": it transforms a dead planet into new one teeming with life. Of course, it can be perverted into a deadly weapon, since, if deployed at an already living planet, Genesis will destroy that planet "in favor of its new matrix." Khan uses Genesis to destroy Kirk and the *Enterprise*, a plan foiled by Spock's heroic sacrificial death.

"Genesis" is aptly named. Recalling the biblical myth of the world's creation, it also recalls the fundamental narrative of heterosexuality, Adam and Eve. The Genesis Device of the film is a phallic, throbbing torpedo that penetrates a planet, impregnating it with spermatozoa-like new matter. What is interesting is that the biblical creation-myth of heterosexual origins frames a narrative that privileges relations between men rather than heterosexual romance. Though Carol Marcus (Bibi Besch) was an old flame of Kirk's, and David Marcus is their son, and though throughout the course of the film Carol and Kirk have a rapprochement, there is absolutely no suggestion of heterosexual desire or sexual reconciliation between them. Indeed, the closest image of heterosexual fulfillment in the film is the shot of Carol and David on the bridge watching the Genesis Wave transform the dead planet into a living one, a transformation suffused by the impending knowledge of Spock's ghastly death. In the film, heterosexuality emerges as an overarching spectacle, but one regarded ambivalently. The film treats heterosexuality as a strange myth that connotes the *violence* of creation and cosmic change as well as paradisiacal fecundity, figuring heterosexuality as both a mysterious, inscrutable phenomenon and an apocalyptic event. *Wrath's* heart lies instead in the paired narratives of ardent friendship and passionate enmity between men.

A Queer Pair

As we will discuss in the last chapter, *Trek* films like *Nemesis* challenge Freud's theory of the Oedipus complex by critiquing the Father's law and challenging patriarchal authority. *Wrath* does this no less than *Nemesis,* with an especially reparative resonance. The character of David Marcus is, in my reading, one of the most explicitly coded gay characters in *Trek*; his initial conflict and later reconciliation with Kirk is even more deeply moving when the David character's sexuality is considered.

To think of David as gay is to respond to the stereotypical gay qualities the writer-director Nicholas Meyer gives him. But given that the character has not generally been read as gay, the very stereotypicality of the portrayal comes to seem more interesting: this is a queer character who hides in plain sight. A sensitive man of science who hates the military, David particularly dislikes his mom's old flame, James T. Kirk. He is also depicted as being very close to his mother. She seems to be his date much of the time: "Joining me for bridge tonight?" he asks her. He uses phrases that a sensitive boy of a 1950s film might use: "Don't have kittens," he reassures his mother, "Genesis is going to work." Like many of the actors who played those gay-coded sensitive boys of the '50s — Montgomery Clift, James Dean, Sal Mineo, Tab Hunter, Farley Granger, Anthony Perkins — the actor Merritt Butrick was a gay man (heartbreakingly, he died of AIDS in 1989). With his lithe Adonis physique, soft, curly blond tendrils, and sensitivity bordering on hotheadedness, Butrick's David could also be one of the boys Joe Dallesandro played in campy Andy Warhol films.

What is most significant, perhaps, in a reading of David Marcus as gay is that the film makes no gesture whatsoever towards assigning him a heterosexual romance. Lieutenant Saavik, the Vulcan-Romulan woman played memorably by Kirstie Alley, would be the likeliest candidate for the kind of perfunctory, obligatory young lovers subplot we can usually expect in such a film (the previous *Trek* film had one, for example). But this film does not develop a romance between David and Saavik; indeed, it avoids the question altogether. Far from hitting on Saavik, David demonstrates no sexual interest in her at all. He does not even get to play the hero when they are under attack: when a stray phaser beam threatens to obliterate one of them, it is *Saavik* who rescues *David*, deftly reversing normative gender roles.

Adding to the queer coding here, the marvelously unusual Saavik herself is a figure of gender ambiguity. Tall and imposing, she wears her hair masculinely short on the bridge, but at other times lets it hang luxuriantly, sensually loose; she alternates between her butch and femme sides with ease. Meyer exploits something thick and heavy in Alley's screen persona, making her simultaneously rigid and sensual, hard yet voluptuous, a kind of sci-fi Theda Bara.

Adding to this gendered ambiguity is the character's racial one. Though it is never made explicit in the film, the Vulcan Saavik, it is mentioned in the script, is half-Romulan, Romulans being the distant cousins of the Vulcans, but a race whose emotions are not disciplined by the rigors of logic. At Spock's funeral, Saavik cries, defying Vulcan prohibitions on emotional display. She is an intriguing combination of antithetical opposites, and one of *Trek*'s most interesting characters. (On a personal note, as a child and unfamiliar with military terminology and customs, I was really confused when she was addressed as "Sir," "mister," "him": in a way I didn't know how to respond to, something about her character and the actor's performance made it seem plausible to me that this "she" was also a "he," just as, on some level, I felt that David wasn't a typical straight male character.) The characters of both David and Saavik enlarge the sense subtly conveyed by the film of being a world in which same-sex ties and gender ambiguity have a comfortable, everyday visibility.

Revising the Oedipus Complex

Understanding David as a gay character makes his final rapprochement with Kirk all the more notable and moving.

Throughout the film, David telegraphs his contempt for and anger towards Kirk. In their first scene together, David lunges after Kirk with a knife, trying to kill him (David believing that Kirk and his crew actually murdered their fellow Genesis project-scientists). This scene is crucial in setting up the conflict between Kirk and David as an unresolved Oedipus complex, in which the already adult David still experiences murderous rage against his father. For Kirk's part, he hardly wields anything like the Oedipal father's frightening wrath and power to castrate the son, at least insofar as his relationship to the human characters goes. Fumbling and unsure, this Kirk walks around in a sluggish state. It is precisely the disparity between David's *view* of Kirk as the ultimate autocratic paternal entity and Kirk's own insecure, faltering demeanor that makes their conflict poignant.

When the two do, finally, have a rapprochement at the end, it is, significantly, after Spock has died. David comes into Kirk's quarters; Kirk is seated alone, with an untouched drink, which he offers to David, who doesn't take it. David reminds Kirk of what he told Saavik: "How we face life is at least as important as how we face death." When Kirk tells him that those are just words, David firmly but sensitively corrects him, telling him that they are nevertheless good words, words from which "ideas begin." (This whole discussion is surprisingly philosophical.) They then discuss the Kobayashi Maru test with which the film began, an impossible, no-win scenario that Starfleet candidates for a captaincy must take. Kirk is the only one known to have beat the no-win scenario: he reprogrammed the test itself to make it possible to win. "You really never have faced death," David observes.

During his experience of the Oedipus complex, the son believes that the father will castrate him, and, moreover associates the father with death, the power to take away life. As a figure who attempts to *cheat* death, Kirk emerges as a different kind of father-figure, one caught between the Oedipal son and the Father himself. As the entire scene is played, it feels like a coming out scene, one already familiar to audiences who watched television dramas of the 1970s like the ABC series *Family*, in which a teenage best-friend of the family's son Willy comes out (in a 1978 episode entitled "Rites of Friendship.") But what's interesting is that it feels as much like a scene in which the *father* comes out to the *son* as it does the reverse. As David is about to leave, Kirk seems to be verging on some kind of statement of his own, even though he is apprehensively waiting to see if *David* will make one. David does turn around and tell Kirk that he's proud to be Kirk's son. The two men tentatively, awkwardly, and poignantly embrace.

Given the enmity between the two men throughout the film, this achieved closure is truly remarkable. Each of these men finally recognizes and connects to the other. If we read David as a gay character, not only Kirk's acceptance of him but also David's desire for Kirk's approval and recognition that Kirk is his father is significant. But *David's* approval of Kirk is also important. "I was wrong about you," he tells Kirk. Along these allegorical lines, David can be seen as a gay man who must reconsider his broad view of patriarchal masculinity as murderous and hatefully opposed to him. The feminized Kirk and the strong, solid gay son David reject assumptions about gender and straight-gay interrelationships, while they take Oedipal conflicts to a different level; the healing reconciliation between father and son here rejects the view of the Oedipus complex as fundamentally illustrative of all male-male relationships in our culture: an enduring model of male-male enmity throughout a man's life.

If, as I suggested in the Introduction, this film can be read as an anticipatory elegy for gay loss during the AIDS crisis that would sweep the Reagan 1980s, with Spock's death and Kirk's mourning of him uncannily suggestive of AIDS-related gay grief, this scene between David and Kirk bears some similarity to themes in David Leavitt's masterly, heartbreaking novel *The Lost Language of Cranes*, about a young openly gay man whose father is a closeted gay man. If the Kirk-Spock relationship has been the open secret of homosexuality, to use Eve Kosofsky Sedgwick's useful paradigm, in the *Trek* saga, this secret is exploded in the public scene of Spock's death and Kirk's mourning witnessing of it. If Kirk, then, is the closeted gay man of an older generation who struggles his way towards openness about his sexuality later on in his life, the scene between David and Kirk is truly as much a coming out scene from the father's perspective. What makes it also the son's coming out scene is the apprehensive, unsure expression on David's face when Kirk approaches him. David, as Butrick plays him, seems to be wondering if Kirk will punch him or hug him. Luckily for us all, the scene ends with a healing embrace.

Queering The Wrath of Khan

If Khan is indeed the other in both racial and sexual registers, the particular elements of his demise demand attention. He dies quoting Melville: "From hell's heart, I stab at thee. For hate's sake, I spit my last breath at thee." (Montalban delivers these dying words superbly, as if he were aware that they were his last chance at cinematic glory.) Khan dies still attempting to appropriate high culture for his own outsider purposes. Khan then deploys the Genesis Wave against the *Enterprise*. If the Genesis device is a kind of spectacular symbol of heterosexual reproductivity — one in opposition to the queer family Khan leads — what does it mean for a queer villain like Khan to deploy this reproductivity against the symbolic representation of all that is lawful in the universe, a Federation ship?

If the Genesis device represents the matrix of heterosexuality, it is also tied to the normative, rational, imperialist order of the Federation. Khan deploys heterosexuality against the very symbolic structure that maintains heterosexuality as the normative sexual and, indeed, the human standard. The Genesis device is shown to be reproductivity in its most explosive form. But the device is also the explosion of the *death drive*, which Freud posited as a mythic psychic force that hastens us to our own destruction; what we want, fundamentally, is to die, or to return to a state of fetal calm. The death drive has been read more generally as the cultural movement towards death and destruction, war and suffering.

Lee Edelman argues in his study *No Future: Queer Theory and the Death Drive* that queer people have been associated with the negative: with anti-life, with death; he goes further, though, arguing that this is actually precisely the role queers *should* play, in perpetual mockery and defiance of the social order.[6] Yet *Wrath* more provocatively suggests that it is compulsory heterosexuality — which absolutely maintains heterosexuality as the only sexual standard of our culture — which is the death drive, a decimating force that obliterates every trace of otherness and difference in favor of its ever-new matrix. A queer martyr, Khan sacrifices himself to the cruel knowledge about the social order he accesses in death. Despite its conservatism, *Wrath* is ultimately a daringly queer film, maintaining an attitude of ambivalence towards normative heterosexuality, refusing heterosexual closure, and suggesting that compulsory heterosexuality, which institutionalizes heterosexual reproductivity as the ultimate goal of being human, is a death force.

Not So Fast

No sooner do we discover a radicalism in *Trek*, however, than we also find a phobic dimension within this very radicalism. The reconciliation between white men that climactically occurs in films like *Wrath* and *First Contact*, two films that are mirror images, comes at the cost of the annihilation of otherness. Kirk and David movingly reunite, but both the good racial Other (Spock) and the bad (Khan) must die. Indeed, Khan loses *his* symbolic son: his chief crewman, Joachim (Judson Scott), a filial figure also represented as young, handsome, and blond. One of the most poignant moments of the film comes when Joachim dies in Khan's arms; his dying words to Khan are, "Yours ... is the superior..." Khan vows to avenge him. In *First Contact*, the closure achieved between Picard and Data comes at the expense of the annihilation of the phallic alien woman, the Borg Queen, as well as the Borg drones she commands.

If we consider Khan and the Borg Queen as complementary villains who both combine the threats of sexual and racial otherness, we can better understand how films like *The Wrath of Khan* and *First Contact* restore white masculinity to a state of coherence and stability precisely by confronting this masculinity with the threats of otherness that, however threatening, prove to be no threat at all, which is especially true of *First Contact*, in which no regular character dies.

The Phallic/Alien Woman: The Borg Queen

In his 1974 essay "Violence and the Bitch Goddess," Stephen Farber examines the figure of the *femme fatale* in film noir, calling her the bitch goddess.[7] Farber links the bitch goddess to the desire for materialistic success. Clearly, though, as Farber himself notes, there's more to this cruel woman than the drive for economic gain. Like the film noir *femme fatale*, the Borg Queen of *Star Trek: First Contact*, played with sublimely seductive skill by Alice Krige, conforms to the misogynistic mythos of woman as seducer associated with death. Her desire far exceeds a craving for material success; she wants to consume entire worlds and the people that live on them.

The Borg Queen recalls archetypal female figures of destruction and sexual menace, figures with deeply misogynistic overtones. The biblical Eve of Western tradition is a figure that fuses sexuality and death. "Greedily she engorged without restraint/And knew not eating death" (IX. 791–92): this is Milton's description in *Paradise Lost* of Eve eating the fruit of the Tree of Knowledge after Satan, in the form of a serpent, has seduced her. The Borg Queen fuses Eve, Woman as erotic harbinger of death, and Satan, the irresistible seducer, with resonances from classical myth as well. As Calypso does Odysseus in *The Odyssey*, the Borg Queen captures and keeps Data in amorous captivity.

Eve-like, she tempts Data with a promise to fulfill his deepest wish: to turn him human by giving him human skin. (Interestingly, the human is therefore merely a matter of surface covering, all externals.) With the graft of pink human skin stitched to his arm — hovering, like an exhibit, above his mechanical arm-electrodes — Data is in the position of submission to the bitch-goddess, his sexuality fixed upon and limited to one piece of organic material that is not even his own. When the Borg Queen blows on the swath of human skin, the hairs on it rise; the skin dimples into gooseflesh. "Ooooo," Data orgasmically moans as the greenish-black Borg Queen smiles accommodatingly and knowingly. She tempts him with flesh, the price being his android soul.

If the phallus is overdetermined as the principal sign of male power, the penis being only an approximation of the phallus, here Data's sexuality is figured as anything but phallic. The effect of the skin hovering over the exposed section of his metallic endoskeleton is to suggest a kind of castration, a wounding; it is also an orifice that can be penetrated. As a figure who must involuntarily *submit* to pleasure, Data is an example of the new kind of Hollywood masculinity that dates from the era of the first President Bush (elected in 1989) to 2009, in which masculinity itself becomes a sexual spectacle. This spectacle has both narcissistic and masochistic dimensions; here, Data is a prime example of the masochistic, in which watching the male being *forced* to experience sexual satisfaction — as opposed to being the phallic sexual seducer who domineeringly has his way with his erotic objects — becomes the focus of the cinematic gaze.[8] In this regard, the film corresponds to the thesis of Gaylyn Studlar, in which she provides an alternative to Laura Mulvey's view of spectatorship as a mode of male domination, exemplified by Mulvey's now-familiar paradigm of the oppressive male gaze. As discussed in Chapter One, Studlar dissents from Mulvey's view, arguing that film places the spectator not in a state of narcissistic omnipotence but in one of masochistic powerlessness that resembles the child's position to the looming, all-powerful pre–Oedipal mother. Data's fetishistic regard for the Borg Queen is the chief expression of his masochism.

Ultimately, in framing the appearance of the Borg Queen as one the masochistic male watches from a position of childlike helplessness, the film creates a version of *powerful womanhood as pedophilic*. The Borg Queen as mother flaunts her sexuality, forces the male child to witness its full awe and terror, and imposes it upon him. The theme of pedophilia here is deepened by all of Data's prior associations with childlike innocence throughout his appearances on *Trek*: Data is always figured as the child awaiting proper socialization. (As if in a compensatory attempt to restore him to this state of childlike innocence, the next *Trek* film, *Insurrection* [1998], will make Data's chief role that of playmate to a male child.) Clearly, pedophilia is a highly disturbing theme to discover in this film, one that will have even more disturbing implications on *Star Trek: Voyager*, which will figure the former Borg drone, now human woman Seven of Nine (Jeri Ryan), as daughter to two perverse mothers, the masculine, authoritarian Captain Janeway (Kate Mulgrew) and the phallic Borg Queen (Susannah Thompson, Alice Krige).

Fetishism and the Borg Queen

The Borg Queen is a riot of Freudian images of the phallic woman and of fetishism. Recalling our discussions of Freud's theory of fetishism from Chapters One and Three, we can see that the Borg Queen easily fits into this Freudian model. As Freud theorized, the male child initially believes that his mother — a being infinitely more vast and powerful than he — has a penis. This mother with a penis is Freud's model of *the phallic mother*, a figure who resolves gendered anxieties by fusing both sexes. But the boy discovers that the phallic mother only exists in his fantasy. The discovery that the mother is without a penis — i.e., castrated — is profoundly traumatic for the boy. If this immense, powerful being, his mother, can be castrated, than surely *he* can be as well. Even after the boy has consciously accepted that his mother has no penis, in his unconscious life the image of the phallic mother never goes away.

Freud theorized that one of the ways in which some males cope with the profound trauma of the discovery of the penis-less mother is fetishism. (Another is homosexuality.) The fetishist gives the mother back her penis, if you will, by endowing certain objects — a shoe, a nose, even the shine on the nose, or even sexy underwear — with a special sexual significance, a phallic quality. The man who worships women's boots, for example, tracing their sleek outline and pointed tips with his fingers, is re-endowing his mother with that phantom phallus.

However one feels about these Freudian paradigms, however much one chafes against their prescriptive application to experiential life, one must concede that *representation* certainly seems to evoke Freud. Lying on the Borg gurney and forced to watch as the Borg Queen is assembled, Data is the symbolic boy watching his mother dress, seeing her naked and donning clothing, just such an episode in which knowledge that she does not have a penis would emerge.

The fetishist makes up for the mother's perceived penile lack by phallicizing everything associated with the mother and with women. The Borg Queen is just such a fantasy of woman, so deliriously hyperphallic that she seems a parody of fetishism. With rods that pop out of her head; protuberant tubules; long, mechanized limbs; strong, gloved hands that threaten to pulverize anything in their grasp; and black rubber-sheathed metal legs, the Borg Queen is a particularly phallic version of *the spatialized woman*, a representation of woman as a body that is cut up into components, each component having a distinct identity of its own. Each component of the Borg Queen is equally phallicized, as if each part of her body were a distinct phallic symbol.

The Borg Queen can be called, in the words of Ann Pellegrini writing in the context of the female bodybuilder, "a body whose Herculean development has already been cut into discrete parts: abdomen, deltoids, quadriceps, biceps, pectorals."[9] Discussing the hypermuscular woman, Pellegrini critiques overly "neat" attempts, in her view, to "reintegrate the hypermuscular" female body into the logic of patriarchy and phallic authority. But surely, whatever the limitations of such readings might be, they apply to the Borg Queen, precisely because she is a male fantasy, the creation principally of the screenwriters, Brannon Braga and Ronald D. Moore, and of the director, Jonathan Frakes. Pellegrini provides an apposite description of the Borg Queen, even if it is precisely such readings that Pellegrini disputes: "The phallus is everywhere on the muscle-bound body, because every part of his or her body has been transformed into a phallus. S/he has become *a fucking penis*."[10]

If the Borg Queen is indubitably a male fantasy, she is also no less interesting for being that. She represents the terror of female sexuality but also threatens masculinity with her appropriation of phallic power. She can be read as an expression of unresolved male fear specifically of the mother's sexuality, not of her *lack* of sexual power but of her access to it and the way she uses it to dominate defenseless men. In other words, the Borg Queen represents a fear that the mother's sexuality will overwhelm, crush, *vanquish* the male.

Barbara Creed's thesis in her provocative book *The Monstrous-Feminine* is that key science-fiction and horror films depict ancient, archetypal images of woman as a monstrous force, specifically as the archaic mother who will engulf her child and reabsorb it into her own system, clearly a misogynistic but also a deep-rooted fantasy.[11] These themes will have an entirely new resonance when presented in the context of the female Oedipus complex on *Star Trek: Voyager*, to which we turn in the next chapter. In *First Contact*, they expose the presence of ancient sexual anxieties in the pristine, orderly, hygienic *TNG* world, a world that is overturned in this violent and disturbing film, filled with lurid tableaux.

Lurid Oedipus

In its depiction of childlike Data, the Borg Queen as monstrous mother, and, as I will show, Picard as the retooled Oedipal father, the film represents an especially lurid version of the Oedipus complex, one that brazenly exceeds any model of normative psychosexual development. Yet what *First Contact* devises here is really only an idealized, sentimentalized version of the Oedipus complex as Freud theorized it. Despite its normalization and familiarity in our culture, Freud's theory of the Oedipus complex is a peculiarly gruesome account of familial relationships and individual development. It is telling that Freud took his view of family life from Greek tragedy. In the male version of the Oedipus complex, the boy, when he begins to desire his mother, looks upon his father as a hated rival. But he also — when confronted with castration anxiety — begins to fear the father; if he took away the mother's penis, surely he can take away the boy's as well. So the boy comes up with an ingenious solution: he identifies with the father rather than competing with him, and desires women who *resemble* the mother. Misogynistic views of women and ongoing castration fears are the grim legacies of the process.

First Contact is a deeply oedipal film that ultimately resolves father-son rivalry — their mutual enmity and conflicted desire — and preserves misogyny as the achieved result, if we understand misogyny as the repudiation of the feminine. The bonds between men apparently can be forged only through this repudiation, as Freudian theory illuminates and *First Contact* dramatizes.

To repeat, the son resolves the Oedipus complex by *identifying* with the father and *internalizing* his wrath. I have been arguing that Data is the oedipal child victimized by a predatory *mother*. The Picard of *First Contact* is a retooled version of the oedipal father: in his annihilation of the monstrous mother, he is the savior of the son (Data), dispensing with the question of female sexuality altogether.

The Oedipus complex works to ensure exogamy (relations outside the family) rather than endogamy (those within it), to ensure, in the male's case, that he realize that the father is the proper ruler and the mother his inferior; the mother will provide a *model* of a proper sexual object but cannot be desired herself. What is fascinating about *First Contact*'s version of the Oedipus complex, however, is that so extreme is its repudiation of the mother's sexuality that it obliterates the thought of woman as sexual object altogether. When Picard and Data, in a discussion that feels post-coital, discuss the now dead Borg Queen, their nostalgic tone ("I'm sorry to see her gone," says Data; "She was unique," says Picard) seems like an elegy for Woman, for sexual difference itself. So determined is this film to restore male-male oedipal bonds that it threatens to install these bonds as the only ones imaginable. This is a threatening maneuver because it implies homosexuality as the only available sexuality once sexual difference has been obliterated — a disquieting maneuver indeed for the ostensibly heterosexual world of *Star Trek*.

As White Men Unite, the Other Ignites

The film ends with Picard on the bridge alone, having sent the crew away in escape pods because he has finally, thanks to Lily, decided to blow up the damn ship. Suddenly Picard hears the haunting, ghostlike whisper of the android Data, summoning him to Engineering, where the Borg Queen holds Data captive. What is interesting about this moment is that what draws Picard to danger and death is the internalized sound of a male voice, a theme that the last *TNG* film, *Nemesis*, will make central, as we discuss in the last chapter. Such a voice — a voice that beguiles one towards death — is normally associated with the Sirens of Greek myth. Data is a kind of male siren here, drawing Picard to his irresistible doom. This moment bears reflection because the much more conventional gesture would have been to have the Borg Queen, a version of the siren-like film noir *femme fatale*, whisperingly bewitch Picard into embracing his own death. That it is Data, not the Borg Queen, who bewitches Picard is even more striking when we discover that the Borg Queen did, actually, once have sexual designs on Picard. When Picard enters Engineering, the Borg Queen reminds him of his past as Locutus, when he was made the Borgified intermediary between the humans and the Borg. (Picard was assimilated into the Borg collective in the original *TNG* two-parter "The Best of Both Worlds," the third season climax and fourth season opener.) In a striking flashback shot, we see the grotesquely assimilated Picard-Locutus deep within the Borg collective, as the Borg Queen whisperingly and erotically caresses his tubule-laden face.

Taunting him about his prior submission to her and her collective ("Have you forgotten our song?" she asks, with characteristically wickedly relish), the Borg Queen all but tells Picard that he'd been her sex-slave. Though the Borg Queen is a figure of intense gender ambiguation, this scene now figures her as heterosexual siren. When she sexually teased and tormented Data earlier, she was the sadistic seductress who uses sex as a weapon, in *any* way appropriate to her present plans. The climactic scene in Engineering, however, fixes her sexuality much more decisively. "You wanted a counterpart," Picard remembers, someone who could be by her side, as an equal. To his quiet horror, Picard further realizes that the truly perverse aspect of it was that he had to submit to her deadly designs *willingly*. "But I didn't," Picard manfully insists. "I fought you." The Borg Queen, with transparently wounded hostility, tells Picard that she no longer needs him, having found her true counterpart in Data, now revealed as the Queen's apparent minion and the product of further skin-grafting experiments. Half of Data's face is covered in human skin — with his pale-white synthetic skin on one side, the pink human flesh looks a garish red, an image suggestive of a racial makeover or a split in racial identity, with Data paleskin and redface at once.

Skin Shows

First Contact is the first *Trek* incarnation of the Borg Queen. Before the film, the Borg, originally developed on *TNG*, were a race that seemed to consist entirely of males, visually rendered a denatured bone-white, a hue made starker by the contrast to the grays and blacks of the *TNG* Borg costumes. The Borg of *First Contact* and *Voyager* have, instead, the "decaying, mottled" skin of the zombie.[12] When the Borg Queen, the Borg drones, and Data are captured in the same shot, we see a fascinating array of skin tones and complexions, even though all of these characters are typed as white characters. The Borg Queen's translucent, moist, greenish-white amphibian skin; the drones' ashen, corpse-like white; and Data's olive-yellow android hues all convey the sense of whiteness as otherness — as a continuum of colors and types, a broad spectrum of effects — that we discussed in the previous chapter. Thinking about the Borg as a race opens up an entire new level of racial complexity in *Trek*.

The Homosocial Collective: The Borg as Queer Race

Thinking about the male homosocial aspect of the Borg, and the ways in which the Borg Queen simultaneously disrupts and extends the homoerotic implications of this homosociality, only deepens the questions of the intersection of race and sexuality here and elsewhere in *Trek*. *First Contact* is truly heir to *The Wrath of Khan* in its foregrounding of this intersection.

As Mark Dery writes of the Borg, they are a "cartoonish" totalitarian antithesis to Trekkian liberal humanism.

> And, horror of horrors, they're queer! At least, that is, in the alternate universe of *Science Friction* [a slash fiction journal], which highlights the gay subtext of the Borg episodes. Once "outed," the Borg appear to be so obviously and so variously wired into gay myth and metaphor that it seems almost unthinkable that the connections could have gone unnoticed.[13]

Slash fiction — stories, with varying degrees of sexual explicitness, that pair same-sex characters in romantic and sexual situations, e.g. Kirk/Spock — is, interestingly, mostly written by heterosexual women.[14] Dery interprets the slash phenomenon as a feminist maneuver designed to right the inherent power imbalance of heterosexual relations: with two men in a sexual relationship, there is a new equality in terms of gendered power. Or so goes the fantasy. (With all due respect to the ingenuity and the ardent passions of slash, the utopian belief in homosexuality as democratic in ways heterosexuality is not is, quite frankly, just that, a utopian fantasy.)

"Like sailors, bikers, cops, and other stereotypical characters in homoerotic fantasy, the Borg are an all-male society living in close quarters. They are in constant physical communion with one another, literally bonded by electronic interconnection," writes Dery. In an observation as relevant to our discussion of race as it is to homosexuality on *Trek*, Dery notes that the "Borg's cadaverous pallor evokes urban nightcrawlers — sybarites who come out only after dark, like the androgynous vampires in Anne Rice's best-selling homoerotic novels." The Borg Queen emerges as a kind of queer matriarch, a female ruler of a race of queer men.

In his study *Totem and Taboo*, Freud theorized that, in the primeval horde of ancient times, a band of brothers killed the Father in order to gain access to Woman/the Mother. (Their sense of guilt forced them to develop prohibitions against murder and incest, prohibitions from which the concepts of law and order sprang.)[15] The Borg of *First Contact* are a primeval horde with no Father, only a phallic, erotically fulfilled and libidinally plenteous Mother. The appearances of the Borg Queen can be seen as, in Brett Farmer's words in another context, the "triumphal assertion" of the "pre-oedipal mother filling the space of the screen, and, by extension, spectatorial desire with the absolute plenitude of her delirious jouissance."[16]

If the Borg are an allegory for a queer subculture, they are specifically an allegory of queerness as *a race*.[17] The question of whether the Borg can be understood as a race is raised in the *TNG* novel *Spartacus*. As Picard muses in it,

> "They are highly organized. But are the Borg a race?" The thought had been much on his mind. He had been captured and incorporated forcibly into the Borg.... "Up to now, we have treated the Borg as a race because that is how they manifested themselves to us — as invaders."[18]

As Robin A. Roberts argues, the ex–Borg Seven of Nine maintains a "mulatta" identity that is both "biracial and bi-gendered."[19]

"Anonymous and continuous," Mark Dery writes, "the exchange of fluid data among the Borg conjures the fleeting, faceless sex, in bars, bathrooms, and public parks, of the gay sexual demimonde in the '70s and early '80s." As Dery points out, in the slash world the Borg assimilation of Picard is a sexual assimilation as well: Picard is forced into the endless homosexual "link" of the hive mind as well as made witness to prosthesis-enhanced, cybernetically heightened queer Borg sex.

If the Borg are a race of invaders who suggest the racial, gender, and sexual Other, the welter of allegorical modes they embody may represent their particular, peculiar fearsomeness in the Trekkian world; like no other race, they cannot be rehabilitated, remaining staunchly, resolutely Other. In this regard, Picard and Data both may be said to enact a symbolic purgation of their fused racial and sexual threat at the climax of *First Contact*, a kind of ethnic, gendered, and sexual cleansing at once. The authoritarian white male and the bi-racial male — Data here being both android and human, and always the android aspiring to the condition of the human — unite to eradicate the threat of otherness.

Balletic Violence: The Homoerotic as Spectacle

I want to conclude this chapter by resisting the end-directed trajectory of most academic criticism, however. If Picard and Data purge their pristine world of this complex threat of otherness, the film itself has trafficked headily in this otherness. In one sequence in particular, in which Picard, Worf, and a newly introduced young Lieutenant, Hawk, must thwart a Borg plan to use the deflector dish to contact more Borg (through an "interplexing beacon"), the film stunningly synthesizes its simultaneous attraction and repulsion towards queer, raced desire.

The first thing to mention here is that, since his appearance in *First Contact*, Lt. Hawk has unexpectedly become a queer *Trek* icon. According to *Memory Alpha, the Star Trek Wiki*,

> While rumors have persisted that Lt. Hawk was originally intended to be Star *Trek*'s first openly gay character, the producers of *Star Trek: First Contact* and actor Neal McDonough have denied this. However, Hawk is indeed depicted as being gay in the novel *Section 31: Rogue*, which has been referenced again in the *Star Trek: Titan* novel series, where his partner, an unjoined Trill male named Ranul Keru, serves as the Titan's Chief of Security.[20]

Neal McDonough, who would go on to be a brilliant actor in the sadly short-lived television series *Boomtown* (2002–2003), gives Hawk a brooding intensity that manages to exceed the limitations of the role and suggest hidden depths. Obviously, something about Hawk and McDonough's portrayal of him has spoken to queer *Trek*kers across the lines of prohibition.

The deflector dish sequence is also significant because it involves Worf. As Michael Dorn plays this character, a Klingon who was raised by humans, he is an intriguing mixture of the formidable and the vulnerable. Played by an African American actor, Worf is an interesting allegory for black masculinity, especially in the context of whiteness. Blacks fit into the terrain of white (male) desire, argues Kobena Mercer,

> by being confined to a narrow repertoire of "types" — the supersexual stud and the sexual "savage" on the one hand, or the delicate, fragile and exotic "oriental" on the other.[21]

Throughout his appearances on *Trek*, Worf oscillates between these modes, Dorn ably managing to suggest qualities of both martial Klingon might and a surprising vulnerability. The series and films depict Worf as a split character. On the one hand, as a Klingon, he is depicted as a fusion of two stock types: the mystical Asian warrior and the scary, switchblade-wielding black street tough. On the other hand, he is an estranged, butt-of-everyone's-jokes character who provides reliable comic relief. (Riker ribs Worf about the *Defiant*, "Tough little ship." "*Little?*" Worf growls.)

Before heading out to the dish, Picard asks Worf if he remembers his "Zero G" training, and Worf says, "Only that it made me sick." Then Worf, as Dorn plays him, wears a pitiable expression and says in the voice of frustrated, frightened child, "Oh no, what are you suggesting?" Part of the comedic pleasure of the scene and of Worf moments generally would appear to be the sadistic kick of torturing Worf.

Worf's version of the switchblade is the Klingon *bat'leth*, or "sword of honor." In a particularly telling moment in the deflector dish sequence, the bat'leth figures prominently. As they attempt to thwart the Borg in their appropriation of the dish, the *Enterprise* must restore manual control to the "Mag-Locks," which once turned off allow the dish to float away into space, rendered useless to the Borg. As Worf is fiddling with a Mag-Lock, one of the drones perceives him as a danger and proceeds to move towards him in the inexorably slow but steady manner of Michael Myers in the *Halloween* films, or George A. Romero's zombies, clearly models for this version of the Borg. Worf fires his phaser at the drone, to no effect. "They've adapted," Worf warns the others. As the drone approaches him, Worf reaches behind his gravity suit and pulls out the bat'leth, which action is accompanied by a blade-sharpening sound on the soundtrack. Aurally as well as visually, the film conveys Worf's prowess as a warrior, that character type with which Worf is so obsessively associated.

What is especially interesting is that the particular drone that attempts to assimilate Worf is shown to be a gender-bending figure in precisely the manner Mark Dery described in his article on slash fiction appropriations of the Borg. With his stylized makeup — black eyeliner especially prominent — and a certain feminine quality, this drone, whom we first see in close-up, suggests a drag performer. The intent, unflinching gaze that he fixes upon Worf as he implacably approaches him suggests that of a lover, or a rapist, intent on his sexual prey, an implication deepened by this particular Borg's gender ambiguity.

As Jonathan Frakes stylishly directs this sequence, certain moments have a balletic quality, which adds to the sense that the sequence is a kind of meditation on something beyond the action being represented, an allegorical rendering—but of what? (Indeed, though *First Contact* is widely regarded as the best *TNG* film, some fans complain about the dish sequence being slow and "out of place.") As Worf battles the Borg, he and his adversary seem to be engaging in a peculiar, stylized dance, a kind of formal ritual. First Worf slices off the Borg's right hand, then the Borg slices into Worf's suit, the weightlessness of the Zero G atmosphere giving these gestures the solemn gravity of a ritual performance. Indeed, the entire scene has an oddly languorous quality.

That *Trek* cannot explicitly represent homosexuality is not to say that it cannot represent queer desire. Other popular culture texts *do* explicitly represent homosexuality, to *Trek*'s shame. But something that almost no Hollywood film or television series ever dares to represent is actual sex between members of the same gender. The inability to represent something—the repression of a particular mode of identity or reasonably common human act—is a kind of pressure-cooker, one that eventually explodes like a stew left too long under a lid. The repression of sex between men, or at least the possibility that it might exist, must find some form of vent in representation. I argue that, in general Hollywood terms, repressed same-gender sex finds vent in onscreen violence between men, violence that is usually stylized and ritualized. In terms of homoeroticism, Hollywood representation inscribes the economy of violence over the economy of sexuality. In this manner, *Trek* follows suit.

We can see this overinscription in the balletic, murderous dance between Worf and his menacing cybernetic suitor. When Worf slices into the Borg's phallic arm, cutting it in two, blood gushes out in a stream that, in the weightless atmosphere, emerges in slow motion and in thick gobs. When the Borg slices into Worf's leg, we then get a close-up of Worf's face, and hear Worf moaning "Ahhh...." The contorted look on Worf's face in relation to his moan lends itself to speculation. If the economy of violence stands in not only for itself but for sex, everything about this moment suggests orgasmic release as well as the pain of inflicted violence. Gasping for air, Worf sounds curiously contented, as if he were floating off into pleasurable post-orgasmic sleep.

It's almost as if each of the men—Picard, Worf, and the homoerotic icon Hawk—must have his dance with homoerotic threat, since each of the men faces off with a Borg male. All of the Borg in this sequence, as in the film, are male. Given his homo-pedigree, is it any wonder that it is Hawk who does not survive his encounter with a Borg? Or, more properly, succumbs to assimilation? When a Borg first approaches Hawk, Hawk shoots his phaser at the deflector surface, which sends the Borg spinning out into the atmosphere. If this is indeed a sexual allegory, Hawk could be fending off the unwanted advances of an amorous male. For the Borg aren't killers, but lovers, wanting to envelop the objects of their desire in an assimilating embrace. Like the vampire, or like queer AIDS subcultures in which men deliberately inject themselves with their infected lover's blood so that they will contract his HIV, the Borg want to share the same viral load.

It's a bizarre kind of mating dance, in which an object is seized, embraced, and made to be the suitor's possession by sharing his blood. The penetration of one male by another is depicted in terms of violent attack, Borg tubules penetrating the vulnerably exposed necks of writhing men. Borg blood is filled with nano-viruses that colonize the corpuscles of the blood of those they infect. On a cellular level, the same process of embrace and penetration and possession occurs, infinitely. The homoerotic metaphor of assimilation makes all such scenes especially loaded, such as the earlier one in which a young, handsome ensign is assimilated by a male drone. As the Borg blood courses through his body, turning it into a writhing, pulsating machine-human hybrid, the assimilated ensign cries out to Picard for help. Picard's response is to kill him with a phaser blast. As Picard had warned, "Don't let them touch you."

Hawk is attacked by another Borg, who — in a suggestive gesture — picks Hawk up and carries him away. The shot of Hawk being carried is a long shot, from the back; from this perspective, it looks uncannily as if Hawk were being carried over the threshold. Picard eludes a Borg attempting to assimilate him by flying above him, in a curious, limb-waving dance. As he attempts to complete Hawk's work with the Mag-Lock, a strange figure appears above Picard, standing with one leg raised above Picard's head (suggestive pose). The strange figure is Hawk, still in his gravity-suit; when he turns his face around, we see that he is in the process of being assimilated. He pushes Picard, whose transparent visor begins to crack, to the ground, and is about to crush Picard's visor with his foot when he is shot by Worf, who survived the Borg attack by using the dismembered Borg limb and its tubules to stanch the escaping oxygen. Hawk-as-Borg floats off into space, and the now de-magnetized deflector dish, the Borg drones hanging from it, floats off into space. "Assimilate ... *this*," Worf says, in a line that would appear to restore his threatened phallic authority: he shoots at the dish, blasting it into smithereens.

The scene that follows this one comes between it and the scene in which Lily shrieks at Picard to blow up the ship. After being told that the Borg are taking over the ship, adapting to all weapons, and that the situation is utterly hopeless, Picard, in full Ahab mode, berserkly orders his crew to stand their ground, "fight hand to hand" if necessary. Worf takes it upon himself to tell

Picard that he is wrong, to which Picard responds that Worf is a coward. "If you were any other man I would kill you where you stand!" Worf rebukes him. This dramatic but also silly, nonsensical moment — calling *Worf* a coward? — conveys, I think, the maddening but undiscussable, unnameable homoerotic tension throughout the film, especially in the previous deflector-dish sequence. Homoerotic tension becomes a virus that infects gendered relationships, that calls masculinity into question. Picard's attack on Worf is a self-accusation, a rupture in the text between allegory and explication in which the homoerotic secret of *Trek* threatens to spill out, finding vent in a questioning of gendered stability.

The homoerotic as well as racial crisis in *First Contact* makes the film a fascinating mixture of the radical and the phobic. As I will demonstrate in the next two chapters, the *Star Trek: Voyager* telefilm "Dark Frontier" and the tenth Star *Trek* film, *Nemesis*, both go well beyond *First Contact*, to say nothing of the reactionary series *Enterprise*, as radical treatments of gender and sexuality and, to a certain extent, race.

Eight

AN EPIC FOR WOMEN
Star Trek: Voyager's "Dark Frontier"

More than any other *Trek* series since the first, *Star Trek: Voyager* explored an astonishing range of same-sex desires. There are several other radical or at least politically interesting dimensions to the show—the race consciousness of hybrid B'Elanna Torres, the half-human, half–Klingon woman engineer, for example—but in this chapter I will focus on the show's consistently interesting depictions, in allegorical terms, of same-sex desire. What makes *Voyager*'s intensely readable queer metaphors so fascinating is their relationship to the show's seeming heterosexism. This heterosexism finds its most powerful visual expression in the curvaceous cat-suited form of Seven of Nine, widely seen as a vulgar heterosexual male fantasy of woman. Within this denunciation of a more than admittedly questionable conceptualization of woman lies another form of heterosexism: the negation of lesbian desire for the figure of Seven of Nine, to say nothing of the negation of gay male desire for this eye-popping display of spectacularized femininity. Assuredly, this last point will give some of my readers pause; rest assured, I will return to it. In this chapter, I make the claim, one that counters several critical assessments, that *Star Trek: Voyager* was one of the most daring representations of femininity in popular culture. By examining the two-part Season Five episode "Dark Frontier" closely, I will demonstrate that *Voyager*'s feminist accomplishment lies in its determination to grant women access to epic narrative. *Voyager* is one of the few television programs to give us *femininity on an epic scale*. Before turning to a close reading of "Dark Frontier," I will first establish the terms through which I discuss *Voyager* as feminist epic. To do so, I will explore the following themes: the epic as journey; *Voyager* as an extension of the Hollywood woman's film; the evolving persona of the leading protagonist of the series, Captain Kathryn Janeway (Kate Mulgrew); lesbian/queer motifs; and the usefulness of a psychoanalytic framework for reading the series.

Epic Journeys

In the view of the Hungarian Marxist philosopher and literary critic Georg Lukács, the epic of classical antiquity endures as the ultimate art form; in contrast, the novel is a puny attempt at epic grandeur. What the epic captures and conveys is the totality of life. "The epic gives form to a totality of life that is rounded from within," he writes.[1] Lukács articulates the prevailing view that the classics of ancient literature, in particular the epic, provide us with unparalleled access to the truths of human experience. If Homer's *The Iliad*, in its recounting of the Trojan War, tells us everything we need to know about war, courage, and human suffering, his *Odyssey* illuminates the fundamental human yearning for *nostos*, or homecoming, the ardent desire for which impels the wily trickster protagonist Odysseus to make his mazy way back home from the Trojan War to his ever-faithful wife, Penelope.

Voyager instructively accesses both the view of classical epic as the greatest of art forms and the intensity of nostalgia that permeates *The Odyssey*. Recasting Homer's homeward-bound epic in feminist–sci fi terms, *Voyager* gives us an epic narrative about a *female* hero who seeks — with increasing obsessiveness — to bring her crew back home to Earth. In doing so, it grants a female protagonist access to the grand human truth of epic.[2]

Voyager *and the Hollywood Woman's Film*

To be sure, many critics have viewed *Voyager* as a failure and the character of Captain Janeway as a failed attempt at a strong woman character. Janeway makes most sense as a larger-than-life representation of femininity, a feminine icon or archetype, rather than a realistic, "round" female character. If we read her in terms of the latter, Janeway will surely appear to be a failure; but in the terms of the former, she emerges as one of the most exciting female characters in any sci-fi work.

Another character who has been popular with fans but troublesome for critics is the ex–Borg-drone-turned-human-woman Seven of Nine (Jeri Ryan). Many critics have complained that the treatment of Seven/Ryan has been misogynistic, rendering the character and the actor a cyborg bimbette in tight-fitting outfits. The interesting aspect of the characterization of Seven of Nine has been the show's ambivalence over her: the more she resisted and chafed against the Trekkian humanism of the series, the more compelling Seven was; the more "human" she became, the less. Nevertheless, despite the unevenness of her development, Seven of Nine remains one of *Trek*'s greatest characters, the focus of some of the best *Trek* scripts (even if this meant that other characters unfairly got short shrift as a result).

If one sees *Voyager* as a narrative about the awakening of queer desire in the heroine, *Voyager* can be plausibly read as a narrative of sexual awakening that does *not* lead to sexual fulfillment. In this regard, *Voyager* returns to the themes of the original woman's film melodrama, albeit with a queer edge. *Voyager*'s gendered themes correspond to those in (avowedly heterosexual) women's films such as *Alice Adams* (1935), *Now, Voyager* (1942), *The Heiress* (1949), and *Summertime* (1955). In many key women's films, the protagonist is an independent, autonomous, deeply singular woman who enters, in the course of the film, into a struggle between the social order and herself. This struggle can be defined as a question: Will she submit to the marriage plot and become a "normal," married, and therefore properly socialized woman, or will she hold onto her odd if not altogether eccentric personality and independence? For she cannot have both, these films suggest, only one or the other. The woman's film dramatizes what the feminist literary critic Carolyn Heilbrun termed the "the marriage plot"—the socialization of women into properly marital roles—as opposed to the "quest plot" that Heilbrun associated with men.[3] *Voyager* fuses the marriage plot and the quest plot in its characterization of Captain Janeway. *Voyager* is a show whose sensibility, then, is fascinatingly pitched between the classical epic and the Hollywood woman's film.

Transformations of the Feminine: Janeway through the Seasons

One of the prevailing themes of the woman's film genre is transformation. Over the course of the film, the female protagonist will transform into a new version of herself. This phenomenon is in spectacular display in a film like *Now, Voyager*, in which Bette Davis's spinster heroine, Charlotte Vale, transforms from overweight, bespectacled woman to a stunning, svelte, fashionable one—in conventional Hollywood movie terms, from an ugly duckling to a swan. While this transformative feat has been read by critics as a misogynistic "makeover," the way it plays out in the film is more complex and more unsettling than critical accounts would make it seem. The "ugly" Charlotte is a woman of dark wit whose emotional turbulence disrupts the ice-bound repression of her patrician Wasp household, and the "beautiful" Charlotte continues to seethe with anxiety and conflictual desires. The spiky qualities of this woman's film are worth mentioning here because *Voyager* inherits some of the same problems that have bedeviled this genre—a perceived inability to represent a woman's life accurately or without falling into stereotypical patterns.

Perhaps the woman's film transformation most relevant for our analysis of Captain Kathryn Janeway is that undergone by Catharine Sloper (Olivia de Havilland) in William Wyler's great film *The Heiress*, based on the stage version of Henry James's novel *Washington Square*. The heroine is an awkward, shy (but quietly strong) young woman regarded with contempt by her father, a physician obsessed with the memory of his witty, beautiful, now dead wife, and seduced by a mercenary man who wishes to marry her for her money. Betrayed by this faux suitor and her father both, Catharine transforms throughout the course of the film into a steely, unflinching woman, a kind of Fury of retribution. Kate Mulgrew's Captain Janeway follows a surprisingly similar trajectory; the contrast between her tremulously, endearingly nervous energy in the first season and her stately, steely calm in the last is truly striking. Mulgrew, who gives one of the great television performances as Janeway, has remarked that she felt that Brannon Braga, the upstart young *Trek* writer who presided, along with frequent writing partner Joe Menosky, over *Voyager*'s fourth-season reboot, understood Janeway better than Jeri Taylor, who originally conceived the character; if this is the case, the brash, almost pugnacious Janeway we intermittently see in the first two seasons more authentically spoke to the character as Mulgrew conceived of it than the flighty, nervous Janeway of Taylor's early conceptualization.

Indeed, in these first two seasons Janeway seems more like an homage to an earlier feminine type than a futuristic woman. The holodeck program she enjoys indicates as much: a *Jane Eyre*–style gothic mystery that, tellingly, never gets resolved. Her hair a prodigious bun that she twirls as she twitters, with her eager, vital energy and determination to be involved in everything, the early Janeway seems like a Victorian woman of science, a New Woman with an eagerness to display her gumption as well as her scientific zeal. Though Mulgrew seems to have been hampered by the producers, whose anxiety about their new female captain led them to reshoot scenes in the pilot so that Janeway looked more "Captain-like" (hence the creation of that infamous bun, which replaced Mulgrew's original, longer hair style), she yet manages from the start to suggest the depth and range with which she would endow Janeway throughout the years. The early Janeway is touching and appealing.

For certain critics of *Voyager*, Janeway's evolution masculinized her, made her tougher and less likable. Yet what Mulgrew always managed to do was to show that Janeway was a mixture of conventionally masculine and feminine qualities, oscillating as she did between maternal warmth and determined, almost absolutist, resolve. Janeway's gender fluidity makes her one of the most provocative of sci-fi characters; in her ability to be warm and sensual one moment and a stone-cold scourge the next (online commentaries often refer to the Janeway "Death Stare"), Mulgrew explored the range of feminine identities, giving viewers an ever-shifting series of Janeways that could speak to different audiences at different times.

There are several ways to read Janeway's transformation over the years. I would argue that the series allows us to see the evolution of a mass-culture, heterosexually-typed heroine into a queer one. If overall *Voyager* is a show best understood as a feminist version of an epic quest narrative, whose central characters are archetypal, another aspect of the show that must be considered in order for its achievement to be recognized is the lesbian subtext that became an increasingly potent theme, at times almost threatening to be explicated in the text itself. With increasing pathos and urgency, the show ultimately suggested that the great love of Kathryn Janeway's life was not her First Officer, Commander Chakotay (Robert Beltran), but, instead, the once mechanical, now painfully human Seven of Nine.

If the complaints about Mulgrew's Janeway from different circles can be summarized with the phrase, "She plays her like a man," what many commentators overlooked is the heterosexist bias within the complaint; what if her "masculine" qualities are precisely what make Janeway exciting and interesting? Mulgrew's characterization affords the viewer the pleasures of the masculine woman, who combines the appeal of masculine authority with femininity. But of course this is only one part of the story; her feminine warmth, conveyed through Mulgrew's acting choices (placing her hands comfortably on the other characters or looking sensitively into their eyes) was just as crucial to the development of Janeway's character. She provides, in other words, a dizzyingly pleasurable array of gendered and sexual styles and affects.

One Season Two episode, "The 37s," captures the pleasures of early Janeway exquisitely. In this episode, the *Voyager* crew discover human beings in cryogenic freeze on a human-run planet, a surprise given that the ship is 70,000 light years away from Earth. These humans, the titular 37s, were abducted by aliens in the year 1937; amongst them is the aviator Amelia Earhart, the famed first woman to fly solo across the Atlantic Ocean. Within the hokey plot lies a powerful feminist narrative of shared female aspiration and daring. The scenes between Janeway and Earhart (played wonderfully by Sharon Lawrence), in which Janeway tells the American pilot how much she's inspired her, provide the kinds of suggestive opportunities only possible in science fiction. With Janeway's retro-futuristic look and Earhart's brash, 1930s feminism, these scenes play like a new myth of female heroism, making nostalgia and futurity indistinguishable.

Season Two reflected the warring impulses in the creators' conceptualization of Janeway — was she a scientist, thoughtful and precise? A nurturing maternal figure? A tough, militaristic disciplinarian? Several episodes tried out these distinct approaches. In one of the most politically astute episodes of the series, "Alliances," Janeway struggled over whether or not to retain her "almighty Starfleet principles" in the face of social and cultural conflicts that threaten *Voyager*. "Alliances" foreboded the later, absolutist Janeway who adamantly stuck to her principles even if it meant potentially harming her crew ("Thirty Days," Season Five). This season also saw the emergence of "Action Kate," the thrilling, heroic Janeway of battle, as showcased in the terrific episode "Deadlock," in which two different *Voyager*s must work together to defeat the diseased, organ-stealing Vidiians. This episode anticipates the series finale "Endgame" by having two Janeways. The doubling of Janeway allegorizes the duality of her character.

As the series progressed and changed creative hands from Jeri Taylor to Brannon Braga, "Action Kate" took precedence over the other versions of Janeway. The episode that most decisively marks this transition is the two-parter "Scorpion," the Season Three cliffhanger. In this episode, *Voyager* is caught between an apocalyptic conflict between the Borg and a new species, known only by its Borg designation as "Species 8472." Through this conflict, a new series regular, Seven of Nine, was introduced in the Season Four opener "Scorpion, Part II," and her own transformation from Borg back to human became the focal point not only of the series but of Janeway's character, in that Janeway was her chief mentor throughout this process, a role that would become the chief drama of Janeway's character. Initially depicted as hotly conflicted, their relationship develops into one of deeply loving mutual admiration and concern. When Janeway promises to take the seemingly dying Seven to the Grand Canyon when they get back to Earth ("Imperfection," Season Six), the way Mulgrew plays the scene, standing sensually against a wall, the declaration has distinct erotic overtones.

Like some, I read the relationship as a coded lesbian one, but other viewers have seen the relationship strictly in terms of mother-daughter. It should be pointed out, of course, that both can be true at once, but even as I make the case for a lesbian subtext here, I am respectful of those viewers who felt that an emphasis on lesbianism distracted from the representation of powerful bonds between women.

From what I have gathered from speaking to fellow *Voyager* fans who have disputed lesbian readings, lesbian subtexts are often read into powerful women's relationships as an attempt to undermine the women and the relationships, as if to suggest that the only way to be a strong woman or to have a strong bond with another woman is to be a lesbian. While I think that such a presumption itself springs from homophobia, I do understand why some would chafe against being made to feel that strong womanhood can derive only from a particular sexual type. With all due respect for these concerns (insofar as they do not flow from a homophobic source), I will proceed with a reading of "Dark Frontier" that makes a case for the lesbian as well as the mother-daughter dynamics of the series generally and this narrative specifically.

Freud's Women

My reading is a psychoanalytical one that understands this *Voyager* narrative within the context of Freud's theory of female oedipal development, albeit from a queer-feminist perspective. The title of the two-parter seems to raise a Freudian question, if we remember Freud's infamous description of female sexuality as "the dark continent." What do women want? Freud asked. "Dark Frontier" provides an answer.

In his 1925 essay "Some Psychological Consequences of Anatomical Distinction between the Sexes," Freud explores masculine and feminine identities within patriarchy. Writing of penis-envy — a theory that can only be recuperated as desire for power in our culture, as Freud's French re-interpreter Jacques Lacan did — Freud remarks that one of its consequences "seems to be a loosening of the girl's relation with her mother as a love-object." In the tragic terms that Freud lays out, the development of femininity derives from

> the narcissistic sense of humiliation which is bound up with penis-envy, the girl's reflection that after all this is a point on which she cannot compete with boys and that it would therefore be best for her to give up the idea of doing so. Thus the little girl's recognition of the anatomical distinction between the sexes forces her away from masculinity and masculine masturbation on to new lines which lead to the development of femininity. [The thus far unseen manifestation of the Oedipus complex now occurs when] the girl's libido slips into a new position by means — there is no other way of putting it — of the equation "penis = child." She gives up her wish for a penis and puts in place of it a wish for a child: and with this purpose in view she takes her father as a love-object. Her mother becomes the object of her jealousy. The girl has turned into a little woman.[4]

Reading Freud against the blindnesses of his own argument, we can posit that he theorizes the *emotional and social consequences of the construction of fem-*

ininity within patriarchy*, the *enforced* separation between mothers and daughters (which also must occur, with equally traumatic but differently registered resonances, between sons and mothers). If the Oedipus complex provocatively illustrates the male process of socialization, what Freud might have more properly been describing here — had he not attempted to shoehorn femininity into his oedipal narrative — is the *Persephone Complex*, the inevitable, ineluctably tragic dissolution of the daughter-mother bond necessitated by the daughter's journey away from the mother into the social order, which the Greek myth of Persephone's abduction hauntingly symbolizes.

"Dark Frontier" is an exemplary narrative through which to study the Persephone complex. In the Greek myth, Persephone is the maiden daughter of Demeter, the earth-goddess of grain, fertility, and the seasons. Hades, the god of the underworld, abducts, Persephone, rapes her, and later makes her his queen. Demeter roams the earth, searching for her daughter; in her grieving wrath, she turns the world to ice. Finally, in this myth about the origins of the seasons, a pact of sorts is made: Persephone will spend half the year with her mother and the other half with Hades. "Dark Frontier" takes this myth as well as the inherent mother-daughter conflict in patriarchy to a rich level of symbolic complexity all its own.

The Mother-of-Enjoyment

"Dark Frontier" begins with a scene in which *Voyager* is endangered but displays its mettle in battle. A Borg scout ship discovers and attempts to assimilate *Voyager*. We learn immediately that this will be no ordinary bout with the Borg. When their collective voice recites its usual ominous refrain, "Resistance is futile," Captain Janeway shoots back, "Is it?" *Voyager* proceeds to retaliate, although they exceed their intentions when they end up destroying the ship. Though Harry Kim (Garrett Wang) will express regret at the destruction of the Borg, Janeway seems devoid of any regret at all. Indeed, she's exhilarated: "I don't know about the rest of you, but I feel lucky today!" Her euphoria is exciting but unsettling; later, *Voyager* will correct it by making her mournful over the loss of Borg ("Unimatrix Zero Part II," sixth-season opener). In "Dark Frontier," Janeway's relish for battle and for evening the odds against the Borg reflect an instability in her persona, a determination so intense as to be dangerous, one that will be present again in other epic episodes such as "Year of Hell" (Season Four) and the series finale "Endgame." Oddly, this dangerous quality lends her a sexual bravado not usually associated with the character. In the briefing room discussing the plan to infiltrate a damaged Borg sphere to steal a transwarp conduit for speedier travel back to the Alpha Quadrant, standing Janeway sidles up behind seated Tom Paris (Robert Duncan McNeil) and Chakotay, negotiating her space and theirs in a master class of eroticized body language.

What are we to make of this horny and hellbent Janeway? In this episode, Janeway is a cross between the maternal superego, the female enforcer of law and custodian of power, and a female version of what Jacques Lacan calls the "Father-of-Enjoyment."[5] Janeway represents a perversely pleasurable female appropriation of the Law of the Father, which Lacan theorized as the Symbolic order of law, language, rationality, and the Father. (In contrast, the mother's realm is that of the *pre*-linguistic.) Janeway takes her Starfleet rigidity, those "almighty principles," to a delirious, obscene height in this episode, reveling in her autocratic power while also openly defying the misogynistic strictures of patriarchy with her brazen display of female bravado.

The complexity here is that Janeway is also the oedipal mother whose child must reject her and assume an uncertain place in patriarchal order. The daughter's oedipalization, as Freud confesses, is an ambiguous process. Devoted to the father but unsure of his disposition to her, uneasily identifying with but also rejecting the mother, the daughter — in Persephone-like fashion — is a being of two worlds, wanting a share in social power while being made to feel the social opprobrium heaped on femininity. The girl identifies with her mother but also blames her for having bestowed the same troubling gendered status upon her. Heterosexual relationships and having children are compensation for being "marked" as female, attempts to possess the father. In Freud's tragic terms, patriarchy breeds in women not only social inferiority but also the psychic inculcation of this inferiority (to read Freud as reparatively as possible).[6]

As feminist critics have shown, Freud infamously leaves the mother's own experiences out of the questions he provocatively raises. The Janeway of "Dark Frontier," very much figured as Seven of Nine's mother, dramatically, defiantly reinserts a woman's own needs and sexual autonomy into the patterns of the Oedipus complex and its experiential aftermath. Janeway may be Seven's mother-figure but she is also on a personal mission that far exceeds her maternal role.

Family Romance

Janeway's focus on the *Voyager* "family," reiterated throughout the run of the series, would appear to locate *Voyager* within the normative ideology of the nuclear family as conformist social model. Yet the series deemphasizes the idea of the biological family, emphasizing instead the *chosen* family, a theme it shares with *Buffy the Vampire Slayer*. If Janeway inserts her crew into a normative social category when she insistently calls them a family, she also conceives family in non-normative ways. Kinship on this series is not a matter of blood but of unity, shared ties forged through adversity. If the queer elements of *Voyager* stem from the gendered challenge of placing a female protagonist within a franchise with misogynistic elements, thereby challenging those elements, they also stem from the series-long development of the theme of the non-biological family.

I would also argue that *Voyager* exhibits a profound ambivalence towards the concept of "the family," an ambivalence that deepens "Dark Frontier." This ambivalence towards family deepens into an almost open declaration of contempt in its depiction of Seven's biological parents, the Hansens. The human Seven was born Annika Hansen; her parents Magnus (Kirk Baily) and Erin Hansen (Laura Stepp) were scientists who boldly studied the Borg, the first to do so up close. They would surreptitiously beam into a Borg cube to observe their culture (Borg anthropology studies). But they also recklessly brought along the young Annika on this scientific mission, during which the entire family was assimilated.

Janeway all but forces Seven to read through the Hansen's memory logs, the ostensible reason being that they invented a technology that can help *Voyager* remain undetected by the Collective. Again, this is an example of Janeway *not* being particularly maternal, hastening Seven's emotional development for the Captain's own ends. Juxtaposed against its maternal themes, *Voyager* exhibits a genuine ambivalence about mothers. Janeway's mothering can be a source of great frustration ("The Disease," Season Six), and female figures of authority are most often regarded on the series with a very skeptical eye (Season Three's "Distant Origin" and "Favorite Son"; Season Four's "Scientific Method"; the character of the Borg Queen). The ambivalence towards mothers characterizes the episode's critical view of the Hansens. While both parents are in error, the episode does show Annika being much closer to her father; he is, if anything, much softer and more conventionally maternal, as Baily plays him, than her mother. At the climax, when Magnus returns, revealed as a Borg, Erin Hansen is nowhere to be seen and never discussed.

Maternal Madness

When Janeway does indeed show genuinely nurturing feelings towards Seven, it is already at a point deep within the "Dark Frontier" narrative.

Janeway realizes the toll reading her parents' journals has taken on Seven, and tells her that she will be given an assignment other than the Away Mission to steal the transwarp coil. After having been contacted by the Borg Queen and told that *Voyager* will be assimilated if she does not agree to return to the Collective, Seven begs the Captain to let her go on the mission; reluctantly, Janeway agrees, but senses something is wrong. "I know you, Seven," the Captain says.

The emotional intimacy between the Captain and Seven is unlike that of most *Star Trek* relationships, which is not to suggest that there aren't other relationships of great intensity (we can track the affectionalism between Kirk, McCoy, and Spock from the original series all the way up to the first six *Trek* films for an example of ardent love). But the relationship between Janeway and Seven has a distinctive urgency all its own. The closest analog is the Picard-Data relationship, fatherly Picard often serving as the human-aspiring android's mentor, but it does not have an especially homoerotic character. The special quality of the Janeway-Seven relationship derives from the ways in which it is both a mother-daughter relationship and a lesbian one simultaneously, or at least alternately. In this narrative that will bring both of these qualities dramatically to the fore, especially by contrasting the Captain's relationship with Seven to that between her and the Borg Queen, the questions raised are complex. Is the statement being made that an erotic potential inheres within parent-child relationships? Or is it that a series like *Voyager* can solicit two different kinds of audiences and, concomitantly, two different kinds of readings, at once?

As Robert Ray has argued of Hollywood film, popular representation plays to the ironic and the non-ironic audience at once, which is certainly true, I argue, in *Star Trek*'s case.[7] We can say that queer allegory is the domain of the ironic audience, whereas the experience of the series and films in which no question of same-sex desire impinges can be understood as that of the non-ironic audience.

Critiquing the depiction of lesbians in popular culture, Melissa M. M. Hidalgo writes that queer female sexuality "gets folded into a discourse of temporary erotic adventure-seeking or as just another fashionable accessory" to adorn the heterosexual status quo.[8] Given the homophobic climate of representation, allegory, despite its limitations, gains force as a means of depicting non-normative forms of desire. The appeal and the power of allegory in this regard is that, because it has no clear-cut, explicit representation that can be critiqued as such, lesbian narratives such as "Dark Frontier" can unfurl to their full thematic length, under the radar of representation's policers. Following these lines of argument, allegory is an ironic form of representation, implying a level of aesthetic experience entirely distinct from the explicit aspects of narrative.

Persephone's Return

When the Away Team is finally scrambling out of the Cube, transwarp coil in hand, Seven suddenly reveals to Janeway that she is not returning with them. "I wish to return to the Collective," Seven tells her. "Seven!" Janeway yells, pointing her enormous phallic phaser at her. "I'm giving you an order." Seven still refuses to yield, as a force field goes up, now truly blocking any connection. "Go," Seven tells her. "I'm not leaving without you!" Janeway says. When she realizes that she really must leave Seven behind, the look Janeway gives Seven is truly wrenching (an effect created through Mulgrew's sublime performance as well as the brilliant writing by the crackerjack team of Brannon Braga and Joe Menosky, who wrote most of *Voyager*'s epic two-part episodes). A momentary expression, it combines bewilderment, regret, fear, longing, and an inexpressible loss.

This moment is an indelible symbolic expression of the loss of the daughter in the Persephone complex, the necessity that the mother must give up her daughter to the social order, the gulf between them, the mother's loss and the daughter's anguished but resolute decision to leave the mother's side. *I wish to return,* says Persephone-Seven. This is Persephone declaring she wishes to go back to Hades, and leave Demeter behind.

Of course, the perversely interesting aspect of "Dark Frontier" is that, far from leaving the mother's side, Seven is only returning to a different mother, the Borg Queen, whose Hades is her cyborg domain. What awaits the Persephone-like Seven is not marriage with Hades, the King of Hell, and not, therefore, compulsory heterosexuality, but a reunion with *the original, pre-oedipal mother. Never forget who you are,* the Borg Queen whispers in Seven's mind before she decides to return to the collective. Seven has two mommies. The differences but more importantly the similarities between these two epic mothers will be discussed below.

Queer Love

"I'm not leaving without you." This poignant line expresses maternal longing. It also expresses, in my view, queer desire, Janeway's erotic love for Seven.

The second half of "Dark Frontier" (narratively stronger than the first, rare in a *Trek* two-parter) demonstrates both the depth of Janeway's love for Seven and the bewilderment this love inspires in the crew, a bewilderment that amplifies the sense of strange — queer — love between these women. Janeway is specifically a mystifying object to her crew in "Dark Frontier." At the start, when the bridge crew is perplexed by how they managed to destroy the Borg scout ship, feeling obviously uneasy about having annihilated all those on board even though they acted in self-defense, Janeway's relish for their triumph seems really out of place, even unseemly. After she tells them how lucky she feels today and walks to her ready room, the baffled looks exchanged by those still on the bridge suggest that they view Janeway as a bewildering figure.

B'Elanna is stunned to hear Janeway chastising her for having read the abducted Seven's memory logs. Explaining that B'Elanna has violated personal-privacy protocols, Janeway admonishes her that in losing Seven they have "lost one of our own." "She was never one of us, Captain," B'Elanna staunchly insists, more with a tone of puzzlement than insurrection. When asked if they should shut down Seven's power-draining alcove, Janeway says, "No, leave it on," a moment later looking up at Chakotay, as if either daring him to question her or saying, "Please, don't ask me why." Later, talking to Chakotay as they read the Hansens' journals, Janeway wonders aloud why the Borg would have picked this moment to abduct Seven. "You should have assimilated us when you had the chance," Janeway weirdly exclaims. "Captain?" says Chakotay, not for the first time with a genuinely befuddled but also alarmed expression. Janeway doesn't explain what she meant, proceeding to make further plans to mount a rescue operation for Seven. Janeway's strangeness throughout this narrative is interpretable as code for the effect her emerging, newly revealed lesbian desires have on the crew; estranged from them yet determined all the same, Janeway fights for the right to express her desires, whatever effect they have on others.

Orpheus and Eurydice

I can think of few works of popular culture in which a woman's desire for another woman is so dramatically conveyed on the screen, or in such mythic terms. Janeway's rescue of Seven is a feminist, queer reimagining of the classical myth of Orpheus and Eurydice. Orpheus, a great musician, loses his beloved Eurydice when she dies after being bitten by a snake. Overwhelmed with grief, Orpheus descends into the Underworld. He plays his sublime music and moves even Hades to tears. Orpheus is told that he can have Eurydice back, but on one condition: as they are wandering out of the underworld into the world of the living, Orpheus must never look back to see if Eurydice is behind him: he can only look at her once they have walked out of hell. Just at the last second of their journey back into life, Orpheus does look at Eurydice, who vanishes, lost to him forever. "Dark Frontier" takes this myth to a different level altogether. Janeway's journey into hell, the infernal nether regions of Borg space, has a happy ending. If Seven is Eurydice as well as Persephone, Janeway is an Orpheus who wins back his love.

The Return of the Phallic Mother: The Borg Queen on Display

The versions of the Borg Queen that we see in *First Contact* and in "Dark Frontier" differ strikingly in several respects, first in terms of the way they are visually introduced, with equal theatricality but from very different perspectives. The Borg Queen is a creature that deconstructs the cyborg's fusion of human flesh and the machine — literally. A human-like woman's head and bust, with a long, snaky spinal cord dangling beneath them, are placed atop and joined to a metal-robot torso, arms, and legs, all of these disparate parts clanking into place and becoming one body.

In *First Contact*, the Borg Queen is introduced from the android Data's perspective as he lies on a bed. Seen from high above him, the Borg Queen's human head and bust are transported on long, black, snaky wires, an image redolent of the Medusa and Freud's theorization of its symbolic meaning as representative of the "terrifying genitals of the Mother." (The same snaky wires will descend in aid of the Borg Queen at the climax, but Picard uses them to rescue himself as Data drags the Borg Queen to her destruction.) As Data watches — as I argued, from the symbolic perspective of the male child watching his naked mother dressing — the Borg Queen's head and bust moving across the screen from a low angle, we are put in his position, watching both a spectacle of female sexuality and a deconstruction of this very sexuality. For the Borg Queen is a rejection of corporeal and genital sexuality as much as she is, especially as Alice Krige wittily plays her, overpoweringly sexualized. In awe, we gape at her dismembered body and the power its deconstructed parts wield over our gaze. We are put (in a heterosexist way) in the position of the boy looking up a woman's dress, another version of the boy who watches his mother dress. All of this adds to the disturbingly pedophilic quality of the scene.

What we are asked to experience in such sequences is the perverse spectacle of woman's dismemberment; moreover, we are asked to condone it by falling under this creature's queenly will. Which we do—she is an undeniably mesmerizing, fascinating spectacle. Overall, the sequence visually represents the creation of a phallic woman. An erect, metal shaft awaiting a head, the Borg Queen once created is woman as penis, primed for penetration, aiming for death.

"Dark Frontier" takes a different though obviously complementary approach. While witnessed from the same low angle, the Borg Queen's metal body is itself something that must be constructed and assembled, its halves rising up from a kind of trapdoor and snapping into place. Her corporeal upper half is not the gruesome morgue-gray, torn-off one of *First Contact* but a green-lit, pale version devoid of any suggestion of living human flesh, more like a disembodied spirit caught in an uncanny green glow that makes her flesh look ghostly. Her metal spinal cord glints and shimmers in the green light, like a rope of jewels.

The most important distinction from *First Contact* is that, whereas Krige looks at and speaks to Data in her wickedly teasing way as her head floats across the screen, a spectacle of decapitated yet voraciously verbal womanhood, the Borg Queen of "Dark Frontier" does not speak and for the most part does not look at Seven. Instead, her eyes are closed as her face and upper body descend, and her expression bespeaks a serene, meditative calm.

This distinction serves the purpose of de-eroticizing this Borg Queen. This is not in any way to suggest that she is not an erotic presence, only that her eroticism takes a different form. "Dark Frontier" makes the decision not to present the Borg Queen from the outset as hypnotic sexual spectacle but rather as a figure of precision and power whose force derives from calibrated effects, mechanisms locking into place, orderly movements culminating in clarity and cohesion.

This sense of orderliness is matched and reinforced by Susannah Thompson's equally brilliant but very distinct version of the role. Cerebral and precisely modulated, her Borg Queen is not the lascivious sexual seducer of *First Contact* but a Machiavellian, cerebral strategist with surprising reserves of quiet feeling beneath her literally steely calm. No less sadistic than Krige's character, Thompson's Borg Queen expresses her sadism in different ways. She doesn't tempt Seven with offers of fleshly pleasures but, rather, with an offer of kinship, of family, of being a part of a vibrant culture that Seven left behind. *Never forget who you are.* Ethnicity, not erotic stimulation, is what this Borg Queen offers Seven. (Although not my present focus, the theme of Borg-racialization, which we touched upon in the previous chapter, is a very important one that deserves further exploration.) At the start of the later episode "Unimatrix Zero Part I," the Borg Queen's body-construction scene will be more like that in *First Contact*, when she speaks to a rogue drone as her head, bust, and body are being joined. But, in her measured tones as she tells the rogue that he has a "disease," attempting to obtain his involvement in his own destruction as well as that of the rebel Borg faction, the Queen comes off as a savage parody of the nurturing psychotherapist, not a sadistic seducer.

Not Now, Voyager

Reinforcing the correspondences between *Voyager* and the woman's film, the first scene between Seven and the Borg Queen is extraordinarily reminiscent of a similar scene in the Bette Davis melodrama *Now, Voyager*.

In that film, Charlotte Vale, a former frumpy spinster, now glamorous but still troubled, returns home after an overseas trip in which she has had an affair with a dashing but unhappily married man, Jerry (Paul Henreid). This trip has represented her liberation — sexual as well as psychic — from the stifling confines of prim New England and her mother's icy, repressive Boston-Brahmin rule. During the course of her trip, Charlotte has lost over 25 pounds and had her hair cut short. To our eyes, Charlotte looks fascinatingly modern and attractive (in a proto-lesbian way), but to her mother her appearance is freakish. Eager to show her mother how much she has accomplished and transformed, Charlotte is instead met with her mother's most icily critical assessment of her. "It's worse than I've been led to believe," Mrs. Vale says to Charlotte, adding, "Come, let me look at you," forcing Charlotte to "walk up and down." Completely ignoring her physical transformation, Mrs. Vale tells Charlotte that she will be wearing one of her old dresses. "But I've lost over 25 pounds, mother," Charlotte counters, to which her mother responds that she had already had the old dress altered to Charlotte's new size. "You seem to have thought of everything, haven't you Mother?" Charlotte responds, already sadly resigned.

This achingly poignant sequence foregrounds the gulf between Charlotte and her mother, Charlotte's humiliation and disappointment, and the mother's mystifying coldness and cruelty, which culminates with the mother telling Charlotte her apparently freakish appearance can be explained to others as the result of a long illness — as if Charlotte, transformed, wants to *apologize* for her newly self-confident appearance! Bleakly, Charlotte cannot give a final response, slowly walking in defeated fashion out of her mother's bedroom and down the hall back to her old room. (Later, Charlotte will defy her mother with aplomb, but her rebellion also seems to cause her mother's death.)

"Dark Frontier" replays this scene in the Borg Queen's examination of Seven. "They have remade you in their image," she contemptuously tells Seven. "Hair, garments." She chastises Seven for having forfeited her Borg claim to perfection for the trappings of human inferiority.

As played by the stunningly beautiful Jeri Ryan, who portrays Seven with intelligence, wit, and sensitivity, Seven of Nine has always been subject to criticism for her eye-poppingly curvaceous, eroticized physicality. No doubt, Seven's body-clinging get-up was designed to appeal to coarse, misogynistic tastes. But what detractors never consider is the remarkable heterogeneity of the Trekkian viewing audience. What one viewer might find in Seven, another viewer may see entirely differently. In Ryan's Seven, I see an echo of the Hollywood femininity of the 1950s, of Grace Kelly, Marilyn Monroe, but also the Kim Novak of Hitchcock's *Vertigo* (1958), a touchingly ghostlike, blank, yet tremulous presence, as well as one of gendered ambiguity. Ryan's Seven captures some of the vulnerability within Marilyn Monroe's physical plushness. In contrast to the steel-plated, formidably mechanized Borg Queen, with her moving limbs that sound like spinning gears, Seven looks particularly vulnerable, soft, corporeal, *human*. Her dolled-up looks make her look more like a girl than a *femme fatale*, reinforcing the mother-daughter theme of the narrative. But she also has a boyish quality that takes these exchanges and the contrasts between both figures to yet other levels.

Freud (in his typical universalizing manner) draws on various cultural traditions to theorize the human fascination with the phallic mother, the mother with a penis. In "the vulture-headed Egyptian goddess Mut," he writes, "we find [a] combination of maternal and masculine characteristics as in Leonardo's phantasy of the vulture."[9] Freud refers here to the dream Leonardo had as a child of his mother descending upon him in his bed as a vulture and putting her tail in his mouth. The early Church fathers, looking for a precedent to explain the Immaculate Conception, drew upon the myth of vultures as a female species that reproduce by opening their vaginas in mid-flight and being impregnated by the wind.[10]

Likened to the queen of an insect colony, the Borg Queen is a variation on Freud's phallic mother, not a vulture but an insect mother. When the Borg Queen places one of those formidable, black-gloved rubber-metal Borg hands on Seven's face, the moment tingles. Its erotic charge stems from the fetishistic nature of the Borg Queen and the juxtaposition between her phallic apparatus and the comparatively soft, pliant flesh of Seven's body. I say comparatively, because boyishly beautiful Seven is herself a remarkable mixture of hard and soft, her body phallically rigid and softly feminine at once. But in contrast to the Borg Queen, Seven looks like an emblem of conventional femininity. A female otherness contrasts against an even more powerful version of female otherness.

As a phallic woman contrasted against a female character who takes that quality of phallic femininity to the *nth* power, Seven seems like the excess of the human, what was squeezed out of that hard, streamlined body the Borg Queen brandishes. Between them, the female characters form an allegory not only of the varieties of womanhood but also of gendered identities generally, ranging from the masculinely phallic to the softly, conventionally feminine. It is precisely in that between them they suggest the varieties of gendered identity that the radicalism of "Dark Frontier" lies. The narrative suggests that gendered sameness is also gendered difference, that qualities associated with gender need not be confined to one gendered body alone. Between them, the Borg Queen and Seven suggest and encompass the continuum of human gender roles and sexualities. When Captain Janeway is added to the mixture, normative assumptions about gender and sexuality begin to seem quite limited indeed.

The Varieties of Phallic Womanhood

The gender liminality of *Voyager*'s women is extraordinary. The fiery human–Klingon B'Elanna Torres, as Roxann Biggs-Dawson acutely plays her, is a fascinating mixture of aggressive toughness and vulnerability. Ryan brings a kind of androgynous sexual charge to her embodiment of knockout femininity. Mulgrew's Janeway is the most complexly fascinating of all, a dazzling blend of the feminine and the masculine. In "Dark Frontier," her own gender ambiguity takes on further ambiguation; her gendered performance is truly complex here, combining a renegade machismo, a bureaucratic, order-barking efficiency, maternal anguish, and, finally, the fully accessed dimensions of what Judith Halberstam has called "female masculinity."[11] Janeway emerges in the climax of the episode as one of the great embodiments of Halberstam's concept.

What is fascinating about Janeway's masculine qualities here is that they are always contrasted with her equally feminine ones. In comparison to the steel-plated Borg Queen, Janeway appears almost Juno-esque, a figure of pleasing maternal amplitude. As Michelle Erica Greene (by no means a *Voyager* fan in its Braga years, it should be added) writes, "next to the too-skinny Borg Queen, [Janeway] had a reassuring strength and solidity that was attractive in the earthy, maternal way being emphasized."[12] Green makes a series of points about this episode that we should consider:

> I want to write something about the fragmented female bodies in this episode: Janeway announces at the start of the episode that she likes her Borg in pieces, which is exactly how we see the Queen when she first arrives, and the portrayals of good mothers and bad mothers, dutiful daughters and deceptive ones, an exobiologist who has to drag her scientist-husband away from research to eat his dinner, a child who suggests to the captain a plan very similar to the one ultimately proposed by a Starfleet officer to find a missing crewmember. Pretty much everything about this episode concerned women, with the pathetic patriarchy of Annika's youth replaced by the warring matriarchies in which even little Naomi Wildman wants a place. "Keep your shirt tucked in, go down with the ship, and never abandon a member of your crew," says Janeway to the little girl, explaining what it takes to be captain.[13]

As Green's analysis makes clear, "Dark Frontier" is so deeply grounded in women's worlds that it makes patriarchy seem pitiably pathetic.

"Dark Frontier" truly corresponds to Halberstam's concept of female masculinity in making the female the site of all possible gendered identities, different forms of masculinity as well as femininity. Janeway and the Borg Queen, in particular, can be said to oscillate between different kinds of masculine as well as feminine roles. When the Borg Queen places her gloved hand on Seven (doubling Janeway, who finds Seven an equally irresistible tactile site), she is a tender mother figure, and also a suitor wooing his love. When she demands her male Borg minions to assimilate Janeway and Seven, she is like a general commanding his troops. Formidable but diminutive, Thompson's Borg Queen doubles Seven in having a strangely boy-like quality.

With Janeway and the Borg Queen being such fascinating mixtures of maternal warmth and autocratic masculinity, the climax, in which they confront each other, takes gender liminality to further extremes. Warring over the body and mind of Seven, these distinct yet complementary maternal figures each challenge the other with their defiance of normative gendered standards.

"You sound like a mindless automaton," the Borg Queen chastises Seven, in a surprising echo of Janeway's own staunch rhetoric of individuality. In the understandably negative Federation view, totalitarian groupthink is most closely associated with the Borg. But the Borg Queen seems to want Seven to think for herself—provided that in doing so she thinks *as* a Borg. While Janeway speaks from the liberal humanist perspective that most *Trek* shows share (*Enterprise* being a very stark exception), her own rhetoric of individuality is so dogmatic as to be obsessive. Moreover, with the full monstrousness of Borg culture taken into consideration, the emphasis on eradicating every last scrap, literally, of Borg culture from Seven is analogous to a kind of racist reprogramming. Seven is conscripted into femininity and specifically into white, liberal, Federation femininity. With their black-veined, denatured white skins, irregular bodies, and green-lit uncanny hues, the Borg are a metaphor for otherness on several levels; in contrast, the Federation is a metaphor for the same groupthink it ostensibly abhors. The Borg Queen wryly insinuates as much in her criticism of Seven's thinking.

All of this is to say that, between them, the Borg Queen and Janeway represent the Symbolic order of language, law, and reason, the Law and the Name of the Father. Structurally, the Borg Queen occupies the position of the pre-oedipal mother whose imaginary, pre-linguistic realm must be rejected for the individual to enter the father's Symbolic order. Certainly, everything about Borg space connotes such an image of the feminine and of maternity: dark and amorphous, it is a realm of yonic symbols,[14] of orifices which open up to receive or emit other yonic forms, such as Borg spheres. Everything about the interior of Borg ships signifies the womb — the sense of enclosure, of circular spaces, of maturating Borg bodies or bodies that regenerate, receiving nutritive manner umbilically. The Borg assimilation tubules evoke umbilical cords, even as they phallically penetrate.

But the Borg are the pre-oedipal, maternal feminine thoroughly reconceived in terms of the Symbolic. While Borg spaces and bodies and customs connote the mother's realm, their ideology (of conquest) and manipulation of the body (the phallic tubules and hard, impenetrable body armor) reorder the maternal with the logic and symbology of the Father's phallic order. The Borg Queen is ultimately the representative of the Symbolic order, even as she seems to be a steel-plated matriarch.

Similarly, Janeway, blasting in heroically to rescue Seven, speaks the Father's language as she totes the phallus in the form of her huge, long phaser. "Forget about her, Seven," Janeway says of the Borg Queen. "*She's irrelevant.*" This is a succinct depiction of patriarchy's relegation of mothers and the maternal to the sidelines of social power and cultural recognition. Janeway commands Seven to follow her instructions, instructions with which Seven complies, allowing Janeway to succeed in rescuing her prodigal daughter/lover.

Phalluses That Matter

But whose phallus is it that Janeway wields? We can concede that the two matriarchs are symbols of the Father. But they are also more than that.

If read from a queer perspective, the entire scene of the climax begins to feel very different.

Janeway's looming phallus, which associates her with the Father's Symbolic realm of law and language, could be *the lesbian phallus*. In Judith Butler's words, this lesbian phallus could be the promotion of "an alternative imaginary to a hegemonic one." Butler makes special note that it is not the penis but the lesbian phallus to which she refers, for "what is needed is not a new body part, as it were, but a displacement of the hegemonic symbolic of (heterosexist) sexual difference and the critical release of alternative imaginary schemas for constituting sites of erotogenic pleasure."[15]

If queer individuals produce an alternative imaginary to the hegemonic one, are we merely reproducing, in alternative guise, the same heterosexist, patriarchal schemas? If Janeway is the queer phallus and not the patriarchal one, the phallus is nevertheless still employed for killing. The wild perversity of queer desire cannot break free of patriarchy's hold. Yet the exhilarating proposition *Voyager* makes here is that the phallus is up for grabs, a free-floating signifier appropriable by anyone. Janeway's phallus is hers alone, and in wielding it she need not be masquerading as the Father. However one feels about the *uses* of this phallic power, especially being tied, as it is, to the rhetoric of the Symbolic, it is nevertheless an achievement to make it accessible to characters like Janeway, an achievement deepened by the queer resonances of her character.

Indeed, I can think of few narratives in which actual male characters play so unimportant a role, as Green pointed out, yet which foregrounds the phallic as prominently as "Dark Frontier" does. The diminishment of masculine authority reaches its height in the shot of Seven's Borgified father Magnus, obediently stepping forward to display his own abjection to Seven at the Queen's behest. When the Borg Queen reveals her plan to assimilate humanity with a virus, a plan for which she demands Seven's help, she summons up a visual display of the species. We see a hologram of a tall, muscular man in his underwear, revolving in a way appropriate to a display. Masculinity has been objectified, made visual spectacle here, and made irrelevant in the face of formidable female power; in addition, the homoerotic valences of this male apparition derive from the radicalism of gender ambiguation in this narrative, the acquisition of all gendered power by the feminine. In the end, at least in "Dark Frontier," the phallus becomes a utopian symbol of gender liminality, at least in feminist and queer terms.

The narrative ends with Janeway checking up on Seven, who should be regenerating but is instead working after hours. Janeway teasingly chides Seven to go to bed. Then she demands that she do so ("Now. That's an order.")—

yet the teasingly affectionate tone is still there as well. The episode suggests that there is something pleasurable in wielding and submitting to female power. With these implications of submission and domination, of teasing and tenderness, the narrative blurs the lines of maternal and queer desire, affirming its power as a multifaceted, new kind of epic for women that is also an epic for all viewers.

Nine

THE ECHO OVER THE VOICE
Star Trek: Nemesis and the Challenge to Patriarchal Narcissism

In this final chapter, I return to several of the questions that have motivated this book. In the first chapter, I suggested that, while associated with Captain Kirk's infamous skirt-chasing, Original *Trek* rejects its own heterosexism by making the encounter between the male protagonist and the women he meets a defamiliarizing, uncanny occasion. In response to the general impressions that *Star Trek* refuses to represent queer desire, I have suggested that the franchise does represent queer desire, if this desire is read in allegorical terms. And, while also subjecting this contention to a critical scrutiny, I have argued that *Trek*'s most provocative achievement in terms of gendered representation has been its decentering of white hetero-masculine subjectivity (though in the previous chapter it truly began to occur to me that the powerful women of *Voyager* far surpass this achievement). To weave together all of these argumentative strands — and in a way that allows me to end this book on a happy note! — I now turn to a discussion of a film that I believe foregrounds the most radical elements in *Star Trek*'s depiction of gendered and sexual identity.

The *Star Trek* monomyth has provided a consistent challenge to stable, implicitly heterosexist constructions of masculinity. *Star Trek: Nemesis* (2002) is the apotheosis of this politically valuable disordering of and challenge to the codes of normative masculinity, especially in that it exposes an apparently impeccable figure of white liberal values, Captain Jean-Luc Picard, to a stern ideological critique.

The central theme and conflict of *Nemesis* is this: an older and more powerful man's anguished contemplation of an alienated mirror image. What is striking in *Nemesis* is that this mirror image — the copy, but in a younger guise — also engages in a reciprocally anguished contemplation of the older man of whom *he* is a reflection. The copy looks back at the original looking at him, a defiance of the normative order of things, in which copies must accept that they are inferior to their originals. There are many precedents for the themes central to this film. With its prohibitive originals and intransigent copies, *Nemesis* plays like Milton's epic poem *Paradise Lost* meets queer theory.[1]

In this chapter, I examine *Nemesis* as a significant example of queer politics in popular film. (I do not claim that this queer discourse in the film is consciously generated. But who knows? It might be.) I read the film as an allegory of queer manhood and a critique of institutionalized heteromasculinity. That it can be both such a queer and a thoroughly mainstream work, intended for consumption by the widest possible international audiences, reflects what has been one of the central themes of this study: that popular culture can have a radical vision fully integrated with its most craven commercial designs.

Though this will undoubtedly strike many readers as an outlandish comparison from any angle, *Nemesis* reimagines, albeit with a queer twist, many of the key themes of *Paradise Lost*, Milton's magisterial seventeenth century poem about the war in Heaven (between Satan and his fellow rebel angels and God, the Son, and their loyal angels) and the fall of Man. The linkages between the texts include the dubious nature of power (God/Picard); the intransigence and mysterious motives of a passionate rebel against this power (Satan/Shinzon); an obsessive interest in the nature of originality and imitation; and the anguish of the copy, which both Milton's poem and this *Trek* film depict as a state of social abjection.

To orient my reading, I will first explore some of the relevant moments in *Paradise Lost*, drawing on Freudian theories of jealousy, homosexuality, paranoia, narcissism, and oedipal conflict. One of my strategies here is to denature the Trekkian specificity of *Nemesis* in order to appreciate its place within the broader cinematic construction of American manhood. If since the late 1980s queer themes have not only become increasingly visible in dominant culture, such as Hollywood cinema, but have profoundly reshaped the way we view even normative masculinity, *Nemesis* emerges as an important film in several ways, chief among them that it stages a conflict between a queer manhood and the normative masculine identity that conforms to the social order.[2] The film's staging of this conflict does not sentimentally ennoble its queer antagonist, but it also does not leave the social order unscathed.

What is most interesting about Shinzon's campaign against Picard is that it is left so muddled, mysterious, unresolved. His motivations are as queer as he is — unresolved, unfulfilled, unknowable. For Shinzon, Picard is truly a "sight hateful, sight tormenting," as seeing the prelapsarian Adam and Eve, "imparadis'd" in each other's arms, is for Milton's Satan (IV, 505–6). *Nemesis*, at heart, is about the copy's desire not to mimic but to *obliterate* the original. In this way, it takes Satan's radicalism in *Paradise Lost* one step further. Rather than wishing to be Picard's preeminent reflection, what Shinzon wants is to elevate the *copy* to the supremacy of the original by erasing the original altogether and positioning the copy in its place, a shift with the potential to destroy hegemonic masculine authority altogether. For these reasons, I claim *Nemesis* as queer and resistant cinema.

Toppling Tradition

Nemesis introduces a new *Trek* race, the Remans, an off-shoot of the Romulans, who are themselves the distant, warlike cousins of the pacifistic and eminently logical Vulcans. The Romulans consider the Remans genetically inferior and use them as chattel, forcing them to work in stifling, sooty mines. The subaltern Remans, with their batlike faces and reptile eyes, do indeed look sub-human, bestial, whereas the Romulans continue to look like arch, evil Vulcans. Into this contentious climate enters Shinzon (Tom Hardy), the film's villain. Shinzon was raised a Reman but is genetically human — in fact, he is the clone of none other than Jean-Luc Picard (Patrick Stewart), captain of the *Enterprise*, himself, albeit about half Picard's age.

The film opens with the destruction of the Romulan Imperial Senate by Shinzon's faction. The reactionary senators, who loathe the Remans, gulp in poisoned air pumped in by a terrorist device the Shinzon-led rebel faction plants. Dying, the Romulans transform into statues of stone that topple to the ground and disintegrate with a crash. This opening brilliantly evokes Western images of traditional power on the wane: the lawmakers of classical Rome crashing into oblivion. Watching tradition topple prepares us for a film that will interrogate hegemonic power's gendered self-conceptualization as white, heterosexual, and male.

Shinzon's closest affectional bond is shown to be the one he maintains with his male Reman Viceroy (Ron Perlman, doing customarily well under tons of makeup). The frequent scenes in which the Viceroy massages Shinzon's bald-dome head — a match for Picard's — suggest a stylized form of erotic connection, a sanctioned form of male-male Eros in Reman society, much like intercrural sex between the *erastes* and the *eromenos* in the Hellenic Greek world.[3] The film makes the strong suggestion, then, that their bond was initially a pederastic one, as the *erastes*-like Reman rescues the *eromenos*-like boy Shinzon, dumped into the bowels of a mining colony, from a tormenting Romulan guard. The mock-classical style of Romulan society in this film charges the pederastic relationship suggested between Shinzon and the Viceroy with extra significance. (This is a different kind of pederastic relationship than that suggested in the relationship between the Borg Queen and Data in *First Contact*, but no less interesting for being a distinct kind.)

The Member of the Wedding

The film proceeds to give us a wedding scene between Riker and Troi, with Picard making a speech in which he embraces Riker, Troi, and the *Enterprise* crew as his family. These lines resonate tellingly throughout the film. *Trek* debunks the notion of family as biological, positing instead a new vision of the family as the result of extended, continuous ties of friendship. (This theme of "chosen families" powerfully informs the series *Star Trek: Voyager*.) While not a subversive model of family — one would have to dispense with the concept of family altogether — *Trek*'s friendship-family model at least enlarges the concept. It's a queer model of family, family reimagined as a network of friends joined together by shared experiences; most *Trek* characters have little contact with members of their own families, and, when they do, these meetings are most often comical or tragic (*TNG*'s comically ribald and vexing Lwaxanna Troi, *Voyager*'s Admiral Paris, troubled Tom Paris's staunch father).

Data, making a celebratory speech, begins it with his salutation of "Ladies, gentlemen, and invited transgendered species." This is a remarkable moment for *Trek*. Given *Trek*'s utter inability to deal with queer issues explicitly, in anything other than an allegorical form — though allegory, paradoxically, may be the most resonant, the most suggestive, manner in which queer themes find expression — Data's nod to the reality of the transgendered body and social identity signals sensitivity and progress. It is especially noteworthy that Data — who could be seen as a himself a model for queerness, and not in spite of but perhaps because of his fumbling experiences with the opposite sex (recall Tasha Yar's question about Data's sexual performance capacities — "You are fully functional?" in an early episode, "The Naked Now" [1987] and his goofy attempts to be the perfect boyfriend in the *TNG* episode "In Theory" [1991]) — utters the welcome to transgendered guests. Though this film begins with a wedding, the still enduring cultural sign of normativity, the film perversely tweaks even this socially sanctioned and legalized union by reminding us that, on the complementary wedding Riker and Troi will also have on Betazed, telepathic Troi's home planet, the wedding party and guests must all be in the nude, like Adam and Eve in prelapsarian Eden. There is a positively randy atmosphere onboard the *Enterprise* when Picard, scoffing at Worf's predictable discomfiture at having to be publicly nude on Betazed, chidingly says, "A big strapping fellow like you?" and informs him that he, like the rest of the principal crew, will all comply with compulsory Betazed wedding customs. Though it is through a wedding that this film initially presents its take on the *Next Generation* family — a family of friends — *Nemesis* dispenses with conventional heterosexual narrative and explores, instead, queer themes of selfhood and identity, serving as a pop culture forum for the investigation of subaltern sexualities.

Myself Am Hell: Or, Gender's a Drag

When Picard gazes at Shinzon, he confronts an uncannily youthful mirror image of himself. What does Shinzon see when he gazes upon Picard? Picard is the embodiment of Establishment power. Does Shinzon feel jealous of Picard's power and stature? Shinzon certainly seems driven by interior frenzies that seem intensified by the gaze, frenzies that lead Shinzon to wage a war against Picard that is as enigmatic as it is obsessive. Yet *Nemesis* refuses to provide a clear, definitive rationale for Shinzon's campaign against Picard, whom he appears to love and hate, abhor and desire, at once; the film leaves Shinzon's actual motivations murderously ambiguous.

Freud postulates that within the process of jealousy lies a sense of terrible grief. "It is easy to see," writes Freud, "that essentially [jealousy] is compounded of grief, the pain caused by the thought of losing the loved object, and of the narcissistic wound; further, of the feelings of enmity against the successful rival, and of a greater or lesser amount of self-criticism which tries to hold the person himself accountable for his loss."[4] Freud postulates that the bereft lover who cannot possess his beloved will turn the pain of this loss and the enmity he feels towards his rival against himself. Freud's view of jealousy is one aspect of his larger theory of inextricable connections among jealousy, paranoia, and homosexuality, connections that are vividly present in *Nemesis*. If Shinzon is indeed driven by jealousy for Picard's power, the very embodiment of normativity, what *Nemesis* adds to Freud is the *political* potentiality of the processes of grief-stricken jealousy. In *Nemesis*, both the loss of the beloved object and the enmity Shinzon experiences towards the successful rival are directed against Picard, who is another version of ... himself. He has already lost what he fears losing — his normative gendered and social identity, embodied in a most powerful form by Picard. But Shinzon confronts the masterly original whom he reflects; in a reversal of Freud's schemas, Shinzon holds *Picard*, not himself, "accountable" for his loss. His campaign against

Picard, the *Enterprise*, humanity itself—while admittedly redolent of psychopathology—is a critique of Picard and the power he embodies, a power that *always already* disenfranchises the other as embodied by Shinzon. Simply by existing as himself, Picard negates the very existence of Shinzon. His gigantic and mystifying campaign against Picard can be read, in Lacan's terms, as a "*passage à l'acte*, a temporary ritual 'cure' and self-punishment for psychic pain," except that the punishment is directed not at himself but against the masculine power of which Shinzon is a discontented copy.[5]

Shinzon's mysterious war against Picard is a war against male power. As a copy with an attitude, Shinzon strives to force Picard to recognize the copy's legitimacy. Moreover, he seeks to elevate the copy to a status *superior* to that of the original, whose own legitimacy is contested, embattled, challengeable, as Shinzon's abilities to rattle Picard evince. As Judith Butler wrote on the subject of drag performance in her groundbreaking essay "Imitation and Gender Insubordination," "Drag ... implies that all gendering is a kind of impersonation and approximation. If this is true, it seems, there is no original or primary gender that drag imitates, but *gender is a kind of imitation for which there is no original.*"[6]

Nemesis treats the concept of gendered identity as a performance, staging a battle between competing performances of *one* gendered identity, Picard's. The film explores drag's dizzyingly deep and multivalent levels. "I am who I am," the rallying cry of *La Cage aux Folles* and its cross-dressing ilk, takes on a new resonance here, since neither Picard nor Shinzon can lay claim to uniqueness, to singular selfhood, Shinzon because he is a copy, Picard because he has *been* copied. Yet, while Picard's hold on the title of authentic selfhood is shaken by Shinzon's campaign, it is only shaken, never really stirred. Shinzon can don Picard-drag—"I know *exactly* what you feel" Shinzon tauntingly tells Picard (Tom Hardy's performance as Shinzon is provocatively taut). But ultimately Picard occupies a zone of autochthonous "realness"—that elusive quality so intensely prized by the drag queens of Jennie Livingston's superb 1990 documentary *Paris Is Burning*—that Shinzon can only imagine. Shinzon exposes the process of maintaining one's own prescribed gendered identity—to say nothing of the effort to mimic that of another gender—as a form of drag. If he is a homoerotic threat to Picard, his paranoia—why, exactly, does he mistrust Picard so adamantly, with so little direct contact with him?—and his jealousy do not, as classical psychoanalysis would have it, evince the pathological nature of his queer desires but, instead, come to seem plausible, if off-putting, attempts to understand his enemy, on the one hand, and understandable frustration with his socially abnegated status, on the other.

Narcissism and Oedipal Conflict

Gender, sexuality, and selfhood all pivot on desire — but desire is always already predicated on the possession, the consuming, the incorporation of the other. *Nemesis* gives us figures who view the self as Other. It is therefore a retooling of the Ovidian Narcissus myth — the beautiful boy who desires himself. When Narcissus stares at himself, he sees — at first — not him*self* but a beautiful young man so beautiful that he instantaneously falls in love with him. The heartbreaking joke here is that Narcissus now experiences what he has been putting everyone else through — the pain of gazing at his own overwhelming, entrancing beauty. The moralistic trajectory of the myth is Narcissus's eventual discovery that what he sees is a reflection of himself, which makes his predicament no easier to bear. Narcissus has been specifically cursed for his cruel rejection of the desiring needs and longings of his female *and* male aficionados. A site of polyamorous desires he refuses to satisfy, Narcissus is an unpityingly and determindedly inviolate male (the type of which I discuss in my study *Men Beyond Desire*) who is violently conscripted into desire, forced to *experience* desire, which is synonymous here with anguish and death.

Nemesis retools the Narcissus myth by widening its political dimensions, since Shinzon's narcissism is indistinguishable from his vengeful campaign against institutionalized white male power. (Nemesis, who inflicts the punishment of his hopeless desire on Narcissus, is the goddess of revenge.) *Nemesis* politically enlarges the Narcissus myth by having Shinzon see not a mirror-reflection but the Establishment version of a normative self he will never be: stately, official, privileged, respected, legitimate, moral, *loved*. What does it mean to desire your own ego ideal, especially if this ego ideal represents the power and the privilege that you lack?

In his 1914 chapter "On Narcissism: An Introduction," Freud universalizes narcissism within his discussion of the two types of infant sexual object–choice, which he distinguishes as the "anaclitic" and the narcissistic. The first, the anaclitic, or attachment, type of object–choice focuses on "those persons who have to do with the feeding, care, and protection of the child ... in other words, the mother or her substitute." The second, the narcissistic, can be found "especially in persons whose libidinal development has suffered some disturbance, as in perverts and homosexuals, that in the choice of their love-object they have taken as their model not their mother but their own selves. They are plainly seeking themselves as a love object and their type of object–choice may be termed *narcissistic*."[7] Freud, in his inconsistent and subversive way, then goes on to disrupt his own argument by positing a primary narcissism in all people. As much as anything, *Nemesis* is an elegy for a lost access to primary narcissism (that state of total oneness between self, mother, and world) and an allegorical exposure of the cultural fate of socially disruptive desires (such as narcissistic homosexual desire).

In the scene in which Shinzon first introduces himself to Picard and his Away Team (Riker, Troi, Data), Shinzon, draped in an odd, regal purple-blue-green gown (it makes him look like a gender-bending vampire), magisterially descends a long set of stairs, shrouded in darkness to make the big reveal of his appearance all the more striking. He poses a sexual threat, first directed at Troi but then extending to all the members of the Away Team, if their mutually apprehensive body language is taken as evidence. When Shinzon does reveal his face, the face of the young Picard, Picard, now dramatically shown in close-up, looks both stricken and frightened. The fluid ease with which identity can be transferred from one body to another deeply unsettles Picard: it's the ultimate identity theft.

Picard demonstrates the original's hostility towards the copy, always figured as a pale imitation, lacking authenticity. Judith Butler, writing of "the homophobic charge that queens and butches and femmes are imitations of the heterosexual real," argues that "this notion of the origin is suspect ... the origin requires its derivations in order to affirm itself as an origin, for origins only make sense to the extent that they are differentiated from that which they produce as derivatives."[8] Through Shinzon's affront to Picard's claim to authenticity, *Nemesis* exposes Picard's anxiety as the original's destabilized access to the power of *realness*.

Shinzon takes out a dagger, a gesture that initially appears to threaten the Away Team. Instead, he cuts his own hand, handing the dagger to Data for genetic testing. Dr. Crusher (Gates McFadden) will confirm that Shinzon, for all intents and purposes, is Picard. Shinzon has been made *from* Picard, and in this scene of their initial meeting, the power dynamics most strongly suggested are oedipal, with Picard as, in Lacanian terms, the Symbolic Father to Shinzon's unruly Son, who transgressively desires the maternal/erotic Troi. (Very briefly put, in Lacan's formulation, the world of the mother is the pre-oedipal realm before language, a realm of sensations, feelings, and connection to the mother's body; the Symbolic, which we enter once we acquire the ability to speak, is the realm of the Father, of language, law, and rationalism.)

This scene surprises, however, by ultimately *revising* Oedipus. In Freudian oedipal theory, the son not only feels murderous aggression towards the father, but also fears that the father will castrate *him*. Ostensibly, then, when Shinzon cuts himself, he effects a symbolic castration, an enactment of his psychic fears of Picard the father. Yet Shinzon authorizes his own castration. In cutting himself, he is not demonstrating his own lack or fear. Rather, he cuts himself bodily to demonstrate that *Picard* was cut, castrated, in order to produce Shinzon. Shinzon's false castration is a mocking reflection — an exposure — of Picard's original one. In other words, Shinzon reminds Picard that the core of his normative, masculinist subjectivity is the original trauma that produced it: the fear of castration, first noticed in the mother's missing phallus, then felt in the fraught psychic life of the child as his own.

Shinzon reflects the weird, unsettling nature of Freudian oedipal theory — namely, the peculiarity of the superego. What are the origins of the superego, that authoritarian voice inside our heads that commands us to follow the Law of the Father? As Leo Bersani describes it,

> The superego is the child endowed with the father's authority *and* with the child's aggressiveness against that authority; and this monster of moralized violence unreservedly attacks its own double — the child's ego as the father — with all the violence perhaps originally projected onto the real father (and which may indeed have been nothing more from the very start than the "real" scenario necessary in order for the child to replicate it as a psychic scene).[9]

Nemesis inverts that parenthetical schema, turning a psychic scenario into a real, enacted one, a literal acting out of these oedipal issues. Shinzon can be read as a figure for the psychic struggle between father and son, the living embodiment of the psychic battles and processes that produce a superego in the child's mind. An allegorical figure run amok, he acts out the oedipal allegory, giving it flesh and blood.

"I am a mirror for you as well."

Shinzon evinces no clear, direct motivation for his campaign against Picard. Though Shinzon suffered a terrible childhood in the Reman slave colonies, he has obviously risen to the top of the Romulan ranks, now enjoying tremendous power as Praetor. While one could argue that Shinzon's childhood left painful scars that, unhealed, leave him eager constantly to reenact the causes of his trauma, *Nemesis* leaves Shinzon's motivations, much to the chagrin of *Trek* fans, murderously nebulous.[10] It is precisely the nebulous nature of Shinzon's motivations that make them so fascinating. It is clear, however, that his motivation is not merely a matter of competitiveness.

Although Captain Picard, as ever in *Trek*, is ostensibly the hero and Shinzon the villain, the film undercuts this traditional structure. Picard is shown to be, like Milton's God, the Ruler who "laughs" at his suffering enemies.[11] Beaming down to a desert planet upon which lie the scattered parts of B-4 — Data's subpar sibling android and doppelganger — Picard exhibits a boisterous energy that seems entirely out of place with the seriousness of their discovery and their predicament. His responses to Shinzon are alternately smug and condescending ("You're not a *Reman*"). In a blandly humanistic manner, he encourages Shinzon to be more like him. "I am a mirror for you as well," Picard informs Shinzon. *Nemesis* gives us white male power as self-aware and buoyantly playful, but, more deeply, white male power as the ultimate *jouissance*, ecstatic pleasure linked to death. If whiteness and maleness are the standards that otherness should emulate, Shinzon finds the idea that he should mirror Picard abhorrent. Intrigued by but ultimately dismissive of Picard's realization of heteromasculine whiteness, Shinzon determines to destroy it. Shinzon simultaneously places himself in the subaltern social, gendered, and theoretical position *and* claims this position as the superior one: "You will see the triumph of the Echo over the Voice," Shinzon informs Picard.

The film conveys the homosexual desire that Freud linked to narcissism and paranoia through increasingly violent metaphors. Picard certainly labors to maintain his status as a total top to Shinzon's unruly bottom. When Picard rams the *Enterprise* into Shinzon's vessel, the scene plays like space-age sodomization. Penetration imagery intensifies in the climax of the film, as Shinzon impales himself on Picard's makeshift lance. But Shinzon ups the queer ante by *further* impaling himself on the lance, dragging himself along its length so that he can come face to face with Picard. Mesmerized by this dazzling display of his own beautiful, dying youthfulness, Picard stares with narcissistic longing at his distorted mirror image. This is a significant moment because, while Picard should be deactivating some apocalyptic weapon aboard Shinzon's ship that will destroy the *Enterprise*, he is instead mesmerized by Shinzon's mesmeric reflection, which is to say, Picard is at once self-mesmerized and mesmerized by his copy's own image. Picard's own narcissism becomes synonymous with his death-drive: he is willing to destroy himself, everything he knows, and everyone he loves for one last lingering look at his idealized younger self. He is like Ovid's Narcissus, staring at himself even in the river Styx on his way to the underworld.

Echo, Narcissus, Nemesis

Nemesis is one of the few *Trek* films to feature a feminist sensibility. Like the diabolical dandy who embodies a decadent, non-normative form of heterosexuality, Shinzon, his telepathic Reman Viceroy serving as conduit (how queer is that?), invades the lovemaking scene between Troi and Riker.[12] Troi looks up and sees not her grunting, bearded husband but coolly implacable, smooth-faced Shinzon. He whispers the Betazoid term of endearment that had been the sole enunciatory property of Riker: "*Imzadi.*" Terrified, she screams at Shinzon's invasion of her mind and body (and, implicitly, properly marital sexual domain).

Rather than leaving this rape at that, *Nemesis* allows Troi to retaliate. She uses her *own* telepathic powers to locate, through Shinzon's telepathic Reman aide, Shinzon's cloaked ship. Her program of retaliation is depicted as being no less intense and implacable than Shinzon's. As Stuart Baird brilliantly directs the sequence, the editing closes in on Troi's eyes — her shockingly Medusan gaze — as the concentrated essence of retaliatory feminist justice.

If *Nemesis* gives women the power of the gaze, the intensified power of the avenging *feminist* gaze, what kind of power does it give Shinzon? I argue that it gives him the power of the *queer Voice*. Shinzon is a defiant, queer male version of the mythological Echo. Thus the film blurs the lines between the feminist and the queer, allowing perverse Shinzon to counter Picard's normative manhood with *a feminist queer campaign* against it.

This is certainly an odd argument to make: after all, Shinzon did violate Troi. But, oscillating between the sexual roles of heterosexual rake and queer male, Shinzon enjoys a perverse range of pleasures. The dimension of his characterization with the most radical edge is his rewriting of the Echo myth as a narrative of queer male transgression, a rewriting that hinges on the themes of echo and voice in the film. Ovid's version of the Narcissus myth helps us to understand not only male subjectivity but also women's place in patriarchy, as well as the queer implications of Shinzon's campaign. Taking a moment to recall the particulars of Echo's myth — a part of the Narcissus myth, but so poignantly powerful a part that it has a relevance all its own — will help us to understand the film's treatment of Shinzon more fully.

Ovid's Echo: Myth and Feminist Film Theory

Obsessed with Narcissus, Echo is constantly "following him," as Robert Graves limns the myth, "through the pathless forest, longing to address him, but unable to speak first," forever iterating her plea, "Lie with me!" In terms of the action and themes of *Nemesis*, Narcissus' rough shaking off of poor Echo, and adamant dismissal of her advances — "I will die before you ever lie with me!" — are eerily relevant.[13]

Echo becomes Echo because of female rage against male power. A loquacious, charming nymph, Echo distracted Juno while her spouse Zeus was off philandering with another nymph. Upon discovering Echo's duplicity, Juno punishes her by denying her the ability to speak — now, Echo can only repeat what someone has said to her. One of the most poignant figures from classical myth, Echo can be used, in feminist terms, as a figure to represent women's problematic role within patriarchy. If the position of Woman in the West, as Hélène Cixous argues, is one of decapitation — the denial of mind and voice — the myth of Echo encapsulates this position.[14] By explicitly and repetitively designating himself as Echo to Picard's Voice — voice being analogous to phallus and therefore male, patriarchal power, as psychoanalytic theory demonstrates — intransigent Shinzon both identifies with woman's subject position in patriarchy and transforms his campaign against Picard into queer activism.

Riffing on Laura Mulvey's influential 1975 essay "Visual Pleasure and Narrative Cinema," in which she argues that the dominant Hollywood cinema is organized around the patriarchal white heterosexual male gaze, which spectacularizes and objectifies women's sexuality, Kaja Silverman lays out the problems in film's gendering of the gaze and the voice. The male viewer wishes to "disburden himself of the various losses which organize his subjectivity," to "displace his discursive lack onto women." Women are excluded "from symbolic power and privilege," an exclusion "articulated as a passive relation to original cinema's scopic and auditory regimes." Moreover,

> the female subject's gaze is depicted as partial, flawed, unreliable, and self-entrapping.... Women's words are shown to be even less her own than are her "looks." They are scripted for her, extracted from her by an external agency, or uttered by her in a trancelike state. Her voice also reveals a remarkable facility for self-disparagement and self-incrimination.... Even when she speaks without apparent coercion, she is always spoken from the place of the sexual other.... She is [also] what might be called a synecdochic representation — the part for the whole — since she is obliged to absorb the male subject's lack as well as her own.[15]

If voice is a metonym for the phallus, woman's castrated, self-hating, maimed voice represents her subjugated status. It is precisely for these reasons that both the myth of Echo and Narcissus and *Nemesis*'s deployment of it are so valuable. In its privileging of the Echo over the Voice, *Nemesis* complexly engages with the simultaneously empathetic and misogynistic Ovidian categorization of women as the second sex. In wishing to demonstrate to Picard the supremacy of the Echo over the Voice, Shinzon positions himself as Woman to patriarchy as well as queer threat to Picard, a spellbinding fusion of feminist and queer positions.

Jean-Luc Picard's Body: Bodies That Matter in Nemesis

To move from voice to body, Shinzon's corporeal transformations are of great significance as well. As Judith Butler has influentially demonstrated, the body is both a text awaiting inscription from hegemonic power and one always already inscribed. As Butler writes, "Heterosexuality is always in the process of imitating and approximating its own phantasmatic idealization of itself—and *failing*."[16] Social construction—the "constitutive constraint"—not only produces the "domain of intelligible bodies" but also "unthinkable, abject, unlivable bodies." "The latter domain of [those abjected bodies] is not the opposite of the former, for oppositions are, after all, part of intelligibility; the latter is the excluded and illegible domain that haunts the former domain as the spectre of its own impossibility, the very limit to intelligibility, its constitutive outside."[17] "Abject" bodies only serve to haunt the normative domain of intelligible bodies; Shinzon's abject body haunts Picard's intelligible one.

If biological sex confers gendered identity, for Butler, even the term "sex"—as the sign of gender—is normative: regulatory and privileged. The source of the regulation is heterosexual hegemony. "Sex" is a performative ideal, and actively monitored by regulatory power. "Performativity must be understood not as a singular or deliberate 'act,'" though, "but as the reiterative and citational practice by which discourse produces the effects it names."[18] The "heterosexual imperative" is such that it requires that a subject being formed identify with "the normative phantasm of 'sex,' and *this* identification takes place through a repudiation which produces a domain of abjection," a repudiation which is essential for the subject's emergence *as* a subject. For Shinzon, abjection is as much an identity as intelligibility.

"Sex" is not the only restrictive category. Another constructive trope, "gender," which Butler distinguishes from "sex," operates "[as] the social construction of sex ... [which is] absorbed by gender, [becoming] something like a fiction [that is] ... installed at a prelinguistic site to which there is no direct access."[19] The "heterosexual imperative" is synonymous with "compulsory heterosexuality." "Construction is neither a subject nor its act, but a process of reiteration by which both 'subjects' and 'acts' come to appear at all." As Butler argues, there "is no power that acts, but only a reiterated acting that is power in its persistence and instability."[20]

If gender is a performance, an unceasingly "reiterative and citational practice," Picard's encounter with Shinzon provokes a crisis because Shinzon represents a disruption in Picard's own performed masculine identity, an interruption, a frozen, isolated frame in what becomes a stalled gendered performance. Shinzon presents to Picard an identity that halts and then disrupts the process of normative socialization: he chooses queer abjection rather than the assurances of a normative, properly socialized gendered identity. What Shinzon specifically refuses is the *repetition* of gendered identity, the constant and continuous acting that would allow him to perform, inhabit, and *become* the role of Jean-Luc Picard. Shinzon enacts Guy Hocquenghem's theory of queer desire as "an arbitrarily frozen frame in an unbroken and polyvocal flux."[21] Shinzon threatens because he freezes the frame, holds it up defiantly against what is meant to be an unceasing flow of endlessly reiterated and citational practices, practices that then constitute a normative, stable gendered identity.

Picard must repudiate Shinzon because Shinzon is the *not-him*, what Butler describes as the "excluded and illegible domain that haunts the former domain as the spectre of its own impossibility." Shinzon is not the *opposite* of Picard but what Jonathan Dollimore has described as "the proximate," a key trope within Dollimore's theory of the "perverse dynamic."[22]

Picard as a symbol of normativity relies upon an always already unquestioned and implicit heterosexual presumption, although he has no moments of romantic or sexual intrigue with anyone in the film — other than Shinzon. As Picard gazes upon the dying Shinzon at the climax, his expression both blank and bereft, we see Power mourning its own necessary abjection, haunted by its own repudiated, spectral knowledge of its own impossibility, even as it consolidates itself through the destruction of the evidence of its illegibility.

Shinzon — though much more of a rakishly heterosexual presence than Picard in terms of his actions in the film — both occupies the queer zone of illegibility and indeterminacy of the film and bears the marks of this queerness: the Marks of the Queer Cain. As Paul Morrison argues in his book *The Explanation for Everything* — a Foucauldian study of the discursive uses of homosexuality as rationale or logic for cultural failures, such as fascism — AIDS discourse concretized the homophobic elision between bodily and moral corruption, disciplinarily determining our view of "the gay death skull beneath the youthful skin" of the beautiful/ravaged gay male/AIDS–stricken body.[23] The body ravaged by disease came to symbolize the retributive and inevitable retaliation of Nature against the moral abjection, the sheer depravity, of homosexuality. Shinzon's young–Picard beauty gives way to genetic disease, his face grotesquely mapped by crisscrossing black veins.[24] *Nemesis* marks queer abjection on the body. A spectacle of queerness, abjection, incoherent and murderous rage against power, and death, Shinzon emerges as the perverse dynamic of the *Star Trek* universe. Despite Shinzon's staggering and stirring effrontery, *Nemesis*, through his death, restores the social order, safely recirculates and contains Shinzon's perverse energies. But the echoes of his intransigence resound ominously.

Queer writer Willa Cather's "Paul's Case" is a story, widely interpreted as a gay allegory, about a young man who commits suicide. Discussing the story, Judith Butler writes that "Paul's body refuses to cohere in any ordinary sense, and the body parts which nevertheless hang together appear discordant precisely because of a certain happy and anxious refusal to assume the regulatory norm."[25] One could say of Shinzon that he exposes the wrenching difficulties inherent within the maintaining of the regulatory norms of male identity. "His pleasure is split," writes Butler of Paul, in words that also describe Shinzon, "between the watching and the mirror, the body idealized, projected, and bound within the circle of his own, projective desire." Shinzon overturns his own status as Picard's mirror, using the Picard original as *his* mirror. No less than Picard watching him, Shinzon watches Picard watch him as he dies striding Picard's long phallic lance, certainly a profound cinematic representation of Leo Bersani's theory of masochistic orgasmic *jouissance* as a "self-shattering."[26]

Butler's description of what Paul's death achieves can be applied to Shinzon's:

> Released from prohibitive scrutiny, the body frees itself only through its own dissolution. The final figure of Paul "dropped back into the immense design of things" confirms the ultimate force of the law, but this force unwittingly sustains the eroticism it seeks to foreclose: is this his death or his erotic release? "Paul dropped back": ambiguously dropped by another and by himself, his agency arrested and, perhaps, finally yielded.[27]

Shinzon's death is not a yielding of agency but a memorial to its own mysterious impetus, an inflicted wound upon the psychic life of the Symbolic, left to flash, in diabolical rather than Wordsworthian fashion, forever on Picard's inward eye. Picard, the ultimate force of the law, sustains the eroticism of Shinzon's death, his ultimate erotic release.

Shinzon's narcissism emerges less as a sustained mode of masculinity and more as a reflection of Picard's own narcissism. Shinzon resembles the masochist of Leo Bersani's formulation, the submissive passive partner who submits to his own dissolution. Yet if Shinzon is indeed this passive partner, he remains the decidedly unruly bottom. Shinzon's self-immolation is less about submission to Picard and to a Bersani politics of masochistic self-extinction than it is about resisting and thwarting Picard, refusing to yield to him. Shinzon is much closer to Milton's Satan than he is to Bersani's masochistic male, a figure who is a copy of a "higher power" who insists, murderously, upon not only his legitimacy but also his superiority. Shinzon insists that the copy is prior.

In *Paradise Lost*, Satan's need preeminently to reflect God quickly devolves into a need to reflect him*self*. This need begins to account for the deliberate and strategic anonymity Satan tries to impose on his evil angel apostles in Book V: Do you remember when you were not as you are now? Do you remember who made you? *When* you were made? The amnesia here only loosely masks the urgency behind Satan's wish to forget God's making of him. For only by killing off God can Satan be as original *as* God. But in *Nemesis*, Shinzon chooses death, an option that reflects an intransigent resistance to the Father's power to kill. Shinzon dies not for the sake of self-immolation but so that Picard can register his undying, intransigent hate and defiance. *From Hell's heart, I stab at thee*, as the Melvillean villain Khan said, and as the Miltonic Shinzon continues.

Like *Paradise Lost* and *Moby-Dick* both, *Nemesis* finally asks us to consider the *Father's* narcissism. If, as Michael Warner has argued, narcissism has been "primitively" used in psychoanalytic theory to calumniate queer sexuality as regressive and self-fixated, Picard in this film explodes any such primitive formulation.[28] Gazing transfixedly at dying Shinzon, Picard — who in this film represents the Law of the Father and the Name of the Father — is mesmerized by a copy of himself that is only ostensibly his inferior double. Picard is fascinated precisely by the copy's relationship to Picard's own originality, falling in love with the copy's love for *him*. In this way, Picard co-opts Shinzon's transgressive power, makes the copy's assault on hegemonic originality precisely an ode to this originality's inexhaustible, infinite appeal. But the film exposes Picard's patriarchal triumph as a self-exposure of a murderous patriarchal narcissism. What many critics and *Trek* fans have dismissed as a naïve and unsatisfying genre entry is one of the most challenging and daring critiques of normative masculinity in contemporary Hollywood films.

AFTERWORD
J. J. Abrams and the Fate of *Trek*

I write this Afterword in the wake of the premiere of the eleventh *Star Trek* film. Made by J. J. Abrams, the inventive creator of the notable television series *Alias*, *Lost*, and *Fringe*, this *Star Trek* is a reboot of the franchise, taking us back to the characters of the original series and showing us how they developed into these mythic characters. It could be titled *Star Trek: Origins*. We see how Kirk gets his first command, and, most significantly, how he and Spock, who in this version initially loathe each other, come to be friends. Of course, none of this really particularly matters if you're an avid fan of the original series, because — in a maneuver designed to appease hardcore traditionalists and newbies both — the film's plot diverges from the course of canonical Trekkian narrative, establishing an alternative timeline. In other words, nothing that happens in it — or in the subsequent films that given the new film's lavish success, will undoubtedly be made — will interfere with the established story or timeline.

This alternate timeline is quite a relief to me, since I have come away from the new film feeling dismayed on several levels. To say that this is not a good *film* is an understatement: it's poorly made, hazily plotted, so dramatically limp and emotionally vacant as to be indistinguishable from the inevitable video games it will spawn. But I also don't believe that it's a good fan film, a kind of experience that transcends cinema aesthetics because it's personally meaningful. Nevertheless, the ardently positive reviews the film has garnered, the strong box-office showing, and the relieved enthusiasm of traditional fans all attest to the film's timely and much-appreciated success. Obviously, any skeptical critique of such an attention-getting film runs the risk of seeming curmudgeonly and out of step with popular taste. With such hazards taken well into consideration, and with the themes of this book as a whole in mind, I will offer a brief discussion of the film that explores how it fits within the Trekkian oeuvre generally and its relevance to *Trek* in the post–9/11 era.

The film opens with a battle between the doomed USS *Kelvin* and a rogue

Romulan ship. During the course of this battle, Kirk's father assumes command and sacrifices himself to save his crew, fleeing the battle in shuttlepods. In one of the shuttlepods, Kirk's mother gives birth to him, talking to his father in his final few moments before the *Kelvin* crashes into the Romulan ship. The film establishes its oedipal themes right from the start: the father who is killed off early will continue to haunt the film, impelling the rebellious, ne'er-do-well young Kirk, at the instigation of Captain Pike (Bruce Greenwood), to join Starfleet.

Meanwhile, on his home planet, the young human–Vulcan Spock deftly fends off insults from Vulcan children. As ever, Spock must negotiate between two worlds, the Vulcan of his father, Sarek (Ben Cross), and the Earth of his mother, Amanda (Winona Ryder)—in other words, between logic and feeling. This version, however, eliminates the conflict between Sarek and Spock that characterized their relationship in the original series. If anything, the person who seems to be more troubling to this Spock, played by Zachary Quinto of the NBC television series *Heroes*, is his meddlesome mother, fussing over him with her emotional complications. As played briefly but indelibly by Winona Ryder, Amanda promises to be one of the most interesting of the newly incarnated characters. But in the one moment of the film that has any authentic emotional resonance, Amanda dies right before Spock's eyes, in only her second scene. To rescue his parents, Spock beams down to the imploding planet Vulcan, in the process of being destroyed by the Romulan villain. As the party is being beamed back to the *Enterprise*, the ground gives way beneath Amanda's feet, and she falls out of the transporter beam to her death; Spock reaches out to grab her but can't save her. It is interesting that the most powerful moment in the film is the one in which the mother is destroyed; it confirms the oedipal politics of a film obsessed with its own patriarchal logic.

Tellingly, though we learn that Kirk's father sacrifices himself to save his family, we never again hear anything about Kirk's mother. We see his adolescent rebellion, his later barroom brawls, but there's not a single scene between the young Kirk and his mother. What cures Kirk of his anarchic streak is the appeal Captain Pike (the captain in the first, failed *Trek* TV pilot "The Cage," here a benevolently authoritarian father-figure to Kirk) makes to Kirk's feelings for his father. Much like the last *Trek* series to appear before this film, *Enterprise*, Abrams' *Trek* is a world of the fathers in which mothers disappear after their reproductive function has been established or drop off, literally, from the face of the earth. In this regard, the film evinces Abrams's sensibility as much as it does post–9/11 Trekkian views. His television shows are so naked in their oedipal obsessions as to seem a child's cry of anguish. On *Alias*, the spy Sydney Bristow has an emotionally perilous relationship with her father, a fellow spy who ultimately emerges, despite his ample character flaws, as a refuge for Sydney from the machinations of her truly malevolent mother, a Russian double agent. *Alias* ends in Sydney's spectacular destruction of her mother and tearful exchange of loving messages with her dying father. On the hyper-oedipal *Lost*, each of the major male characters — Jack, Sawyer, Locke — is locked into an agonized relationship with father or a father figure. On *Fringe*, the male counterpart to the heroine works with his loony, formerly institutionalized father, with whom he forges a difficult new bond as they investigate horrific scientific anomalies. If *Voyager* attempted to make a break with the patriarchal tendencies of *Trek*, those tendencies have undergone a massive retrenchment between *Enterprise* and the Abrams version. Indeed, the reboot is a bland rip-off of one of *Voyager*'s greatest episodes, the two-parter "Year of Hell." In it, a time-traveling villain, Annorax, destroys entire timelines and worlds to restore the life of his wife, just as Eric Bana's grimacing and tepid villain does here (though it happens with much greater complexity and pathos in the *Voyager* version). There is a profoundly feminist moment in "Year of Hell" in which Janeway observes, as she thwarts Annorax's efforts to obliterate her ship and crew, "He's trying to erase us from history." This line has a multi-leveled resonance, especially for *Trek*, speaking for the erased peoples of the world, other races, women, sexual minorities. But no such line, and certainly no such resonance, resounds within the Abrams reboot.

At least three times, Kirk is shown hanging desperately above a precipice, like Nietzsche's image of man suspended over a vast abyss. The planet Vulcan imploding from within looks like aquarium sand falling into a sinkhole. The Romulan villain's ship suggests a huge, black, poisonous flower, a kind of menacing, maw-like plant, threatening to devour the hard, pristine, phallic *Enterprise*. When Amanda Spock dies, she falls into a great abyss, out of Spock's reach. A great deal of the film's symbolic design, in other words, resounds with yonic imagery. These images register a profound anxiety over female sexuality, the conventional markers of which — open spaces, flowers — are retooled as indicators of death. The oedipal politics of the film, then, are a massive defense against the feminine, a desperate cleaving to the protective Law of the Father.

Far from a break with the failed *Enterprise*, this film extends not only its misogynistic but also its racist sensibility. Notably, it shares that series' pronounced ambivalence towards the contact with alien races that had been at the core of *Trek* mythology. This ambivalence manifests itself in subtle ways: alien races barely register in this film, and when they do, they are almost always seen in rapidly edited shots that make them literally peripheral, like the huge-eyed alien woman whose function is to deliver the infant Kirk. Or they become silent, comedic foils like the strangely melancholy, diminutive gray alien with huge black eyes that follows around the engineer Scotty (Simon Pegg). (These enormous black optics and the silence of the figures suggest the utter unknowability of the Other.) The chief blank spot in the film's emotional logic is a deeply telling one for issues of race: at the mention of the genetic linkages between Romulans and Vulcans, Spock and the villain have nothing to say to each other. The issue is left completely unexplored. It's almost as if racial conflict is too 1960s to be mentioned, too passé even in light of the destruction of entire worlds.

The series *Enterprise* expressed a deep ambivalence over Vulcans by figuring this noble, rational race as cold, inhuman oppressors of human progress who have only their own interests in mind: they come across as Nazi-like, which is especially bizarre considering how often the Spock character and the Vulcan race have been interpreted as a Jewish metaphor. The Vulcan-Jews of *Enterprise* are not so much a contrast to as they are an amplification of the threat from the shape-shifting, Arab-terrorist Suliban. The newly articulated ambivalence towards Vulcans finds a devastating fulfillment in Abrams's film, in which the planet Vulcan *itself* is utterly destroyed, "imploding into gray dust, collapsing like a desiccated piece of fruit," as Manohla Dargis writes in her enthusiastic review of the film.[1] Now, only 10,000 Vulcans survive. The film retools this decimated race into a new Diaspora, simultaneously deepening the Vulcan-Jewish metaphor and relegating Vulcans to the dustbin of Trekkian history.

Race isn't the only thing that makes this new version of *Trek* squeamish. As I have argued throughout this book, one of the most affecting themes in *Trek* is the tender love between Kirk and Spock, which has over the decades lent itself to intense speculation, most notably in the form of slash fiction, in which voluminous versions of Kirk/Spock romances have appeared. Perhaps scores of slash stories will be spawned by this new film and its sequels as well; slash can flower abundantly from the most inhospitable narrative soil, after all. Yet the film's representation of Kirk and Spock as, initially and for most of the film, rivals who are deeply contemptuous of each other is revealing. Manohla Dargis reads the film's depiction of Kirk and Spock as antagonistic rivals positively: "In the tradition of many great romances, the two men take almost an instant dislike to each other, an antagonism that literalizes the Western divide between the mind (Spock) and body (Kirk) that gives the story emotional and dramatic force as well as some generous laughs."

Unlike Dargis, I do not see this film's antagonistic Kirk-Spock as participants in a great romance. Rather, I see the antagonism between them as another, and the most significant, betrayal of the original spirit of *Trek*, which valorized male-male love as ardently as did the *Iliad* in its depiction of the love between Achilles and Patroclus. Here, the war established between Kirk and Spock has, to my mind, a covert purpose: to obscure and transcend the established homoeroticism in this famous bond and to blunt, if not altogether obviate, the emotional power of male friendship. Or to put it another way: whereas the original series and its subsequent film versions established Kirk and Spock's friendship as a loving one, this film transmutes love and mutual respect between men into violence. As I have argued in this book and in my book *Manhood in Hollywood from Bush to Bush*, homoeroticism often finds vent in violence between men, as if the only way to register male-male desire for physical contact is through the impact of fists on flesh. While this can have a subversive edge, as it does in the seventh *Trek* film, *First Contact*, it can also have fascist connotations, as it does in David Fincher's undeniably, disquietingly popular film *Fight Club*. I would argue the Abrams *Trek* has much more in common with *Fight Club* than it does with *First Contact*, its rivalrous Kirk and Spock much more akin to bruising brutes than to Beatrice and Benedick.

On the original series, the sparring between Spock and Dr. McCoy gave vent to whatever kinds of anxieties were aroused by the Kirk-Spock relationship; rarely are these males ever locked in conflict themselves. Though notes of discord resound through their conflicting attitudes towards reconciliation with the Klingons in *The Undiscovered Country*, the last film with the complete original cast, Kirk and Spock generally treat each other with mutual admiration and quiet concern throughout the first series and the six feature films that followed. I can't think of an instance in which violence, contempt, or cruelty infused their rapport unless some alien influence was involved. In the Abrams film, however, the brash, goofy Kirk of Chris Pine's interpretation and the glowering, snide Spock of Zachary Quinto detest each other; the actors are skillful enough to convey the real depth of their characters' dislike of each other but very little of whatever tenderness lies beneath their hostility or may bloom later. It will be interesting indeed to see what the later sequels do with the relationship, given its homoerotic history. At this stage, the film successfully deflects the question by having the men detest each other, and even, at one point (in a ruse Kirk devises), physically battle each other.

The film is very much aware of its homoerotic potentiality, however, even as it mounts a considerable campaign against it. Quinto's Spock, with his gamine eyes and earnest-boy haircut, is an idealized exotic male figure; Pine's Kirk is a parodistic fantasy of an all–American jock, whose ironic disposition towards everything makes everything about him, including his cartoonishly exaggerated heterosexual rapacity, a kind of postmodern joke. Ironic distance and violence both camouflage the homoerotic secret of the film, one that threatens to explode, but they are also expressions of the very sexual energies they attempt to guard. More than ever, *Trek* plays out like Leslie Fiedler's version of American manhood: an adolescent male fantasy of escape from adulthood (marriage, family, responsibility) through the company of other men, especially the pairing of white and non-white men. But whereas Natty Bumppo and Chingachgook or Ishmael and Queequeg were stoic yet loving pairs, the reboot's Kirk and Spock are competitors, embodiments of the male enmity that is the logic of homosocial relations in American culture, the central theme in my 2005 book *Men Beyond Desire*.

This conventional male brutality and the anxieties that fuel it have, as ever, negative implications for the female characters. The Uhura of this film, though wonderfully played by the intelligent and sensual Zoë Saldana, is ultimately a more retrograde portrait of a woman professional than the original Uhura. Nichelle Nichols' considerable strengths and appeal as an actor transcended the limitations of role, but those limitations are starkly apparent. The new Uhura may be a fancier-sounding expert in xenolinguistics, but, unlike Nichols' original version, she is cast in the typical role of long-suffering girlfriend, this time to Spock. As, in my view, another effort to squelch the attendant homoeroticism of the Kirk-Spock relationship, this Uhura's passionate turbo-lift embrace of Spock communicates that a long-term sexual relationship exists between them. While his staunch resistance to her sultry, tender embrace establishes Spock's resolve against the allure of emotional, romantic, and sexual contact (suggesting that the Vulcan *pon-farr* is no longer an important issue), establishing his conflicts in this area, it also makes him a normatively heterosexual male figure by reassuring us of his interest in the opposite sex and, perhaps even more importantly, the opposite sex's interest in him.

Far from a rejection of *Enterprise*, which signaled the failure of second wave *Trek*, this reboot has a great deal in common with that unsuccessful series. Post–9/11 *Trek* has renounced the idealism of the monomyth, first with neoconservative politics, now with a general dumbing-down. I like Chris Pine, who gives an entertaining performance as Kirk. But William Shatner's Kirk, for all of his emotionalism, had gravitas and tact. In the early Original *Trek* episode "Where No Man Has Gone Before," Kirk's mind-zapped old friend from his Starfleet Academy days reveals that Kirk was both an avid reader and a stickler for discipline. It's impossible to imagine the sophomoric, leering Kirk of this film having either of those qualities. This Kirk doesn't have anything like the authentic daring or the sensitivity of the original Kirk.

Quinto's Spock replaces Nimoy's dignity and quiet emotional anguish with snideness and coiled rage. Both characters are unrecognizable in the new film.

Trek has joined the postmodern collage of American culture, become the stuff of citation and allusion — which is to say that at last, in cultural terms, it has arrived. The adulation that has met Abrams' *Trek* is, it would appear, a sigh of relief that *Trek* has been revivified; the last *Trek* film, *Nemesis,* is often cited in reviews as one of the chief indications of the franchise's failure before Abrams rescued it. As I argued in the last chapter, *Nemesis* is one of the most challenging of all science-fiction films, yet for many fans the film was an unparalleled disaster. What is interesting here is the way in which mainstream and fan cultures now intersect, merge into one. One of the most significant aspects of popular culture of the past decade has been the rise of the geeks. Fanboy culture, fueled by sites such as *Ain't It Cool News,* now wields considerable marketing power and with it the ability to dictate the directions of popular culture. The vast popular and critical success of the reboot indicates that the fringe has joined the mainstream, that *Trek* fans have been assimilated into American fan-culture. Blandness is the new black. But for better or worse (as ever, I hope for better), *Trek* seems here to stay, and the monomyth will endure as one of the most significant, affecting, and confounding achievements of American popular culture.

Chapter Notes

Introduction

1. See Northrop Frye, *Anatomy of Criticism* (Princeton, NJ: Princeton University Press, 2000). Frye believes that all of literature comprises one complete story called the monomyth. There are four separate phases, with each phase corresponding to a season of the year: the *romance phase* (summer story, wishes fulfilled, happiness achieved); the *anti-romance phase* (opposite of summer, bondage, imprisonment, frustration, and fear); the *spring phase* (comedy); and the *fall phase* (tragedy). Adapted from Charles E. Bressler, *Literary Criticism: An Introduction to Theory and Practice* (Upper Saddle River, NJ: Pearson Prentice Hall, 2007).

2. Robert B. Ray, *A Certain Tendency of the Hollywood Cinema, 1930–1980* (Princeton, NJ: Princeton University Press, 1985).

3. A. S. Byatt, *Passions of the Mind* (New York: Vintage, 1991), xvi.

4. Angus Fletcher, *Allegory: The Theory of a Symbolic Mode* (Ithaca, NY: Cornell University Press, 1964), 2–3.

5. *Ibid.*, 8.

6. Also important is John MacQueen's point that it "is quite wrong to think of allegory as necessarily verbal; throughout the Middle Ages and Renaissance the visual as well as the verbal arts became vehicles for allegory, both biblical and classical" (John MacQueen, *Allegory* [London: Methuen, 1970], 40).

7. Fletcher, *Allegory*, 8.

8. MacQueen, *Allegory*, 40.

9. Leslie Fiedler, *Love and Death in the American Novel* (1960; reprint, New York: Dell, 1966), 211.

10. For elaborations on slash fiction and the pairing of male characters on TV shows such as *Star Trek* in homoerotic situations (most famously Original *Trek*'s Kirk and Spock), see especially Constance Penley's *NASA/Trek: Popular Science and Sex in America* (New York: Verso, 1997) and Henry Jenkins's *Textual Poachers: Television Fans and Participatory Culture* (New York: Routledge, 1992).

11. See Eve Kosofsky Sedgwick, *Epistemology of the Closet* (Berkeley: University of California Press, 1990) and D.A. Miller, *The Novel and the Police* (Berkeley: University of California Press, 1988).

Chapter One

1. In terms of the representation of women, Original *Trek* and sixties television generally occupy the liminal space between fifties traditionalism and the feminism of the seventies. Certainly women characters on some other 1960s programs, such as the butt-kicking, leather-clad, witty Diana Rigg of *The Avengers*, had more flexible social roles than could be found in *Trek*. But, as one critic argues about the women of *The Avengers*, "while they have more agency than most do," they "still function as the fetishized objects of the male gaze that feminist theorists have argued determines the nature of gender" (James Chapman, "*The Avengers*: Television and Popular Culture in the 'High Sixties,'" in *Windows on the Sixties: Exploring Key Texts of Media and Culture*, ed. Anthony Aldgate et al. [London: I.B. Tauris, 2000], 57).

2. Joan Wallach Scott, *Gender and the Politics of History* (New York: Columbia University Press, 1999), 45.

3. If, as Paul Morrison has recently argued, "traditional narrative is both heterosexual and heterosexualizing," the *Star Trek* mega-text would appear to be a vast, diffuse narrative of heterosexualization. Yet, as I will show throughout this book, heterosexualization is as much refused as it is enforced by the mega-text. See Paul Morrison, *The Explanation for Everything: Essays on Sexual Subjectivity* (New York: New York University Press, 2001), 72.

4. Adrienne Rich, "Compulsory Heterosexuality and Lesbian Existence," *Signs* 5, no. 4 (1980): 631–60. Though I am drawing on Rich's argument broadly that heterosexuality is compulsory in our culture, it should be noted that Rich's argument unfortunately employs and mobilizes biased representations of gay male sexu-

ality to make her points about the appeal of the alternative of lesbianism.

5. Allegorical representation, ranging from *Pilgrim's Progress* to Nathaniel Hawthorne's fiction to the films of Guillermo Del Toro, generally features characters who represent concepts, ideas, and themes. In Bunyan's *Pilgrim's Progress*, the names reveal the functions of the characters: the earnest protagonist is named Christian, and one of the characters he meets (just for example) is Mr. Worldly-Wise Man, who represents the fallen logic of secular man. In Hawthorne's "Young Goodman Brown," the protagonist's wife—whose pink ribbons connote her innocence, and whom the protagonist leaves behind to venture into the dark nighttime forest of knowledge and evil—is named Faith. Names most obviously reveal allegorical intentions; allegorical designs can encompass a broad range of devices and desires.

6. Whatever one's opinions about Jungian theories, Jung's work on gendered and mythic archetypes has given us a particular language to discuss gendered and sexual essence. What I reject in Jung is any notion of some innate human knowledge of archetypal figures (the collective unconscious); rather, it is important to note that these figures are significant because they are culturally reproduced over time.

7. Steven Drukman, "The Gay Gaze, or Why I Want My MTV," in *A Queer Romance: Lesbians, Gay Men and Popular Culture*, ed. Paul Burston and Colin Richardson (New York: Routledge, 1995), 92.

8. Sigmund Freud, *Sexuality and the Psychology of Love*, ed. Philip Rieff (1922; reprint, New York: Macmillan, 1963), 193.

9. Judith Halberstam, *Skin Shows: Gothic Horror and the Technology of Monsters* (1995; reprint, Durham, NC: Duke University Press, 2000), 166.

10. Bernadette Casey et al., ed., *Television Studies: The Key Concepts* (New York: Routledge, 2002), 184–85.

11. For a discussion of the endurance generally of Original Hollywood filmmaking techniques well into the 1970s, see David Bordwell et al., *The Classical Hollywood Cinema: Film Style and Mode of Production to 1960* (New York: Columbia University Press, 1985), 365–78.

12. Richard Dyer, *The Matter of Images: Essays on Representations* (New York: Routledge, 1993), 161. An important aspect of Dyer's reading of this film and masculinity is the lewd comedy's grotesque depiction of the male protagonist's body and affect.

13. Laura Mulvey, "Visual Pleasure and Narrative Cinema," in *Feminist Film Theory: A Reader*, ed. Sue Thornham (New York: New York University Press, 1999), 63–64.

14. Ibid., 62–63.
15. Ibid., 65.
16. For Freud's discussion of scopophilia, see Sigmund Freud, *Three Essays on the Theory of Sexuality*, ed. James Strachey (NewYork: Basic Books, 1962), 58–59.

17. It should be noted that "Visual Pleasure and Narrative Cinema" was a very early Mulvey article, and her own views have evolved over time, though this evolution has not resolved their controversial nature. Mulvey's essay on the 1941 *Citizen Kane* for the BFI Film Originals series (London: BFI, 1992) bespeaks considerable development in her views of the male gaze: "[Orson] Welles's own towering presence on the screen provides a magnetic draw for the spectator's eye and leaves little space for sexualised voyeurism" (17). This interpretation of the figure of Kane defies Mulvey's own definitive 1975 remarks on Hollywood cinema and the patriarchal gaze that objectifies women, always presented as spectacular objects. In her recent arguments in such works as *Fetishism and Curiosity* (1996) and *Death 24x a Second* (2006), which brim with brilliant insights, Mulvey has offered new positions to choose from; particularly valuable are her developments of the idea of the "curious" spectator (1996) and the "possessive spectator" (2006).

18. Gaylyn Studlar, *In the Realm of Pleasure: Von Sternberg, Dietrich, and the Masochistic Aesthetic* (New York: Columbia University Press, 1993). In my view, the narcissistic male sexuality repudiated by Mulvey can be just as positively recuperated as masochism and, given its considerable queer potentialities, may be preferable to masochism as a resistant sexual mode. Studlar's work is provocative but substitutes an orthodoxy of male passivity for Mulvey's critique of male aggressivity. I offer a reading of Kirk's sexuality as masochistic provisionally because, as I argue elsewhere, masochism seems increasingly unlike the radical departure from masculine hegemony that several film and psychoanalytic theory accounts describe; rather, it now seems a normative model of masculine behavior that repudiates narcissistic male sexuality, which deserves recuperation as a mode of male sexuality with considerable potentialities for queer theory. See Chapter One of my book *Manhood in Hollywood from Bush to Bush* (Austin: University of Texas Press, 2009) for a sustained discussion of masochism and narcissism in theory and contemporary film.

19. Leo Bersani, "Representation and Its Discontents," in *Allegory and Representation*, ed. Stephen Greenblatt (Baltimore: Johns Hopkins University Press, 1981), 158. This essay remains relevant because it reflects concerns that inform Bersani's most recent work.

20. For a highly interesting discussion of masochism and the dephallicization of the male, as embodied by the career of Montgomery Clift, see Brett Farmer's study of Hollywood and queer cinephilia, *Spectacular Passions: Cinema, Fantasy, Gay Male Spectatorships* (Durham, NC: Duke University Press, 2000), 224–47.

21. In Freud's 1927 essay "Fetishism," he explains why "some men" develop fetishes. The fetishist — who privileges, as the site of his sexual desire, a foot, a shoe, a nose, even the shine on a nose rather than the woman herself — has, through his fetish and his act of fetishizing, discovered an ingenious strategy for defending against and coping with a profound childhood psychic trauma with which every man must grapple all his life: the discovery that his mother, who seemed the embodiment of fullness, presence, oneness, totality, does not have a phallus. The fetishist devises a peculiar, specific strategy for coping with the trauma of this discovery, but in enduring the trauma he joins the ranks of all men, who may be divided into three categories, the fetishist, the homosexual, and the normal heterosexual male. Why some men become fetishists, others homosexuals, and most normal heterosexuals cannot be easily explained, if at all, but all men must cope with the trauma, and these three sexual categories represent the available coping strategies.

If Freud's accounts of female sexuality remain deeply unsatisfying, he nevertheless offers a profound and profoundly consistent view of male subjectivity and sexuality as tormented almost from its inception. Male identity in Freud emerges as a desperate series of psychic defenses, strategies for overcoming, forgetting, and shielding against trauma, all of which fail and, despite their inherent futility, need to be perpetually renewed, taken up again as if for the first time. As Freud puts it: "The boy cannot accept the mother's lack of a penis. No, that cannot be true, for if a woman can be castrated than his own penis is in danger; and against that there rebels part of his narcissism which Nature has providentially attached to this particular organ. In later life, grown men may experience a similar panic, perhaps when the cry goes up that throne and altar are in danger, and similar illogical consequences will also follow them" (Sigmund Freud, "Fetishism," in Sigmund Freud, *Sexuality and the Psychology of Love*, ed. Philip Rieff [1922; reprint, New York: Macmillan, 1963], 215. All references from this work are noted parenthetically in the text.)

22. As Marcia Ian, in her excellent study *Remembering the Phallic Mother*, writes, "the image of the phallic mother [is not] about women; it does not refer to women or to mothers. It does not refer at all, except to the possible collapse of sign and referent — a collapse represented as and replaced by the fetishization of their phantom connection to the mother." What the phallic mother represents, ultimately, is the "end of contradiction and the end of ambivalence," since she is not two, but one, the mother who "inseminates and lactates." The phallic mother is "neither hermaphrodite nor androgyne, human nor monster, because she is emphatically Mother" (Marcia Ian, *Remembering the Phallic Mother: Psychoanalysis, Modernism and the Fetish* [Ithaca, NY: Cornell University Press, 1996], 8–9).

23. My argument extends to classical Hollywood techniques as well, and I contend that, to whatever extent the paradigms of Mulvey's influential 1975 essay continue to inform theories of the film and television gaze, the theories need a profound overhaul in terms of this sense of the gaze as the site of the un-seeable rather than as the endless (masculinist) access to visual power.

24. Todd McGowan, *The Real Gaze: Film Theory After Lacan* (Albany, NY: State University of New York Press, 2008), 5–6. See also Jacques Lacan, *The Four Fundamental Concepts of Psycho-Analysis*, trans. Alan Sheridan (New York: Norton, 1978).

25. See Freud, *Three Essays*, 58–59.

26. Review by Jamahl Epsicokhan can be found online at the website *Jammer's Reviews* under "Requiem for Methuselah," http://www.st-hypertext.com/tos/tos-3rev.html#requiem (accessed 1 February 2009).

27. In "Space Seed," Marla McGivers is so drawn to Khan erotically that she betrays Kirk and assists Khan in overtaking the ship. Marla McGivers's desire for Khan brings up an interesting question, the inextricability of sexuality and race. *Trek* makes the allure of racial otherness palpable as it marshals its forces against this very allure. The Other is a prohibited site of desire; to desire the Other is to desire transgressively. Khan represents the threatening appeal of race and the attempt to eradicate race. In *Trek*, the Other represents both prohibited object and prohibition itself. The theme of impossible desire, the allure and the prohibition against interracial sex, intersects with race in *Trek*, and as such an intersected theme, it recurs throughout the monomyth: Kirk-Spock, Decker-Ilia (*Star Trek: The Motion Picture*), Worf-Troi (*TNG*), Odo-Kira (*DS9*), Janeway-Chakotay (*VOY*), Tom Paris-B'Elanna (*VOY*).

28. Harold Bloom, *Shakespeare: The Invention of the Human* (New York: Riverhead, 1999).

29. For elaborations on slash fiction and the pairing of male characters on TV shows such as *Star Trek* in homoerotic situations (most famously Original *Trek*'s Kirk and Spock), see especially Constance Penley's *NASA*/Trek: *Popular*

Science and Sex in America (New York: Verso, 1997) and Henry Jenkins's *Textual Poachers: Television Fans and Participatory Culture* (New York: Routledge, 1992).

Chapter Two

1. "Demon" fulfils the promise of queer energies that bubbled throughout the Paris-Kim relationship. Season Three's episode "The Chute," written by Kenneth Biller, is a prime example of the queer dimensions of their relationship, and an original example of "hurt/comfort" scenarios in slash fiction. The Web teems with "P/K" slash-rings.
2. Judith Butler, "Imitation and Gender Insubordination," in *Inside/Out: Lesbian Theories, Gay Theories*, ed. Diana Fuss (New York: Routledge, 1991), 20–21.
3. Review accessed at http://www.jammersreviews.com/st-voy/s5/oblivion.php (3 January 2009). Reviews by Jamahl Episcokhan on *Jammer's Reviews*.
4. Robin Roberts, *Sexual Generations:* Star Trek: The Next Generation *and Gender* (Urbana: University of Illinois Press, 1999), 118.
5. Ibid., 121.
6. StarTrek.com, "Stigma," *Star Trek Enterprise*, 2007, http://www.startrek.com/startrek/view/series/ENT/episode/127400.html (accessed 5 January 2009).

Chapter Three

1. Sigmund Freud, *Leonardo da Vinci and a Memory of His Childhood*, trans. Alan Tyson (1910; reprint, New York: Norton, 1989). Page numbers for quotes from this work are noted parenthetically in the text.
2. Though this passage lends itself to one of the eeriest and most beautiful readings of the Freudian canon, it is also the chief site of the controversy surrounding Freud's *Leonardo*, since he relies upon a German mistranslation of the Italian word *nibio*, which means "kite" (another type of bird) not "vulture." Kites are, on occasion, like vultures, carrion birds, and the fuss over this mistranslation strikes me as inordinate, but many critics have seen it as extremely problematic. The mistranslation also excludes a word: *dentro*, meaning "within," as James Strachey, the editor of the Standard Edition translations of Freud, points out.
3. Sigmund Freud, *Sexuality and the Psychology of Love*, ed. Philip Rieff (1922; reprint, New York: Macmillan, 1963), 216.

4. See the following by Laura Mulvey: "Visual Pleasure and Narrative Cinema," *Screen* 16, no. 3 (1975): 6–18; reprint in *Visual and Other Pleasures* (Bloomington: Indiana University Press, 1989), 14–27; "Afterthoughts on 'Visual Pleasure and Narrative Cinema' Inspired by King Vidor's *Duel in the Sun*," *Framework* 15/16/17 (1981): 12–15; reprint in *Visual and Other Pleasures* (Bloomington: Indiana University Press), 29–38. I do not mean to denigrate Mulvey's bold and revolutionary work; as much as anything, I am critiquing its continued hold on critical accounts of the gaze. "Visual Pleasure and Narrative Cinema" was a very early Mulvey article; see Chapter One, note 17, for comments on how Mulvey's views have evolved over time.
5. See Brett Farmer, *Spectacular Passions: Cinema, Fantasy, Gay Male Spectatorships* (Durham, NC: Duke University Press, 2000), 192, 195. For further discussions of a politically useful and disruptive disorganization of normative manhood, see Kaja Silverman, *Male Subjectivity at the Margins* (New York: Routledge, 1992) and Leo Bersani's *Homos* (Cambridge, MA: Harvard University Press, 1995).
6. Farmer, *Spectacular Passions*, 197.
7. For Lacan, the Imaginary realm is the world before language, the pre-oedipal time of connection to the mother; the Symbolic realm is the world of the Name and the Law of the Father, of language and the constitution of the subject within patriarchy.
8. In his well-known essay on the gay male idealization of Judy Garland, Richard Dyer writes: "There is nothing arbitrary about the gay reading of Garland; it is a product of the way homosexuality is socially constructed, without and within the gay subculture itself. It does not tell us what gay men are inevitably and naturally drawn to from some built-in disposition granted by their sexuality, but it does tell us of the way that a social-sexual identity has been understood and felt at a certain period of time... [Garland's qualities] mean a lot because they are made expressive of what it has been to be gay in the past half century" (Richard Dyer, *Heavenly Bodies: Film Stars and Society* (London: BFI, 1986), 194).
Certainly Dyer has a point. But what, then, beyond simple and overwhelming nostalgia, accounts for the queer re-energization of gay singer-songwriter Rufus Wainwright's recent recreation of a famous Judy Garland concert? Is it possible that gay identity isn't fixed in the amber of time but endures as a coherent sensibility, however shaped by culture into distinct patterns, across time?
9. Thomas Waugh, "The Third Body: Patterns in the Construction of the Subject in Gay Male Narrative Film," in *Queer Looks: Perspec-*

tives on Lesbian and Gay Film and Video, ed. Martha Gever, Pratibha Parmar, and John Greyson (New York: Routledge, 1993), 141–45.

10. David Greven, "The Fantastic Powers of the Other Sex: Male Mothers from Classical to Contemporary Culture," *The Journal of the Fantastic in the Arts* 14 (Fall 2003). This essay is the basis for Chapter Four of this book.

11. British mathematician Alan Turing committed suicide in 1954 by biting into a cyanide-infused apple. (Leavitt reopens the debate over whether this was a suicide or a murder.) Turing famously broke the German Enigma Code during World War II. In his famous 1937 paper "On Computable Numbers," Turing argued for the inevitable sentience of machines. Sadly, despite his contributions (some of which, like his breaking the Enigma Code, had to remain a secret), he was persecuted for his homosexuality, arrested in 1952 and charged with committing acts of gross indecency with another man.

12. Judith Butler, *Bodies That Matter: On the Discursive Limits of "Sex"* (New York: Routledge, 1993), 152–54.

13. Stanley Siegel and Ed Lowe, *Uncharted Lives: Understanding the Life Passages of Gay Men* (1994; reprint, New York: Plume, 1995), 38.

14. I am late to the Buffy orgy of worldwide fan and critical love, and one of the major reasons why I avoided the show in its original run was a hostility to what I perceived to be its self-conscious meta-textuality and relentless jokiness, if not snarkiness. Having now watched a great deal of the show, I have come to appreciate its wit and inventiveness and, much to my surprise, heart. There are numerous qualities to admire about the show, even as numerous ones continue to exasperate. (The endless jokiness does wear on the nerves.)

15. Walter Benjamin, *Illuminations: Essays and Reflections* (New York: Schocken, 1969), 94.

16. Anne Billson, *Buffy, the Vampire Slayer: A Critical Reading of the Series* (London: BFI, 2005), 118.

17. Ibid., 119.

18. Ibid., 118.

19. René Girard, *Violence and the Sacred* (1972; reprint, Baltimore: Johns Hopkins University Press, 1977), 77.

20. Jerry Tartaglia, "Ecce Homo: On Making Personal Gay Cinema," in *Queer Looks: Perspectives on Lesbian and Gay Film and Video*, ed. Martha Gever, Pratibha Parmar, and John Greyson (New York: Routledge, 1993), 206.

21. Michel de Certeau, *The Practice of Everyday Life*, trans. Steven Rendall (Berkeley: California University Press, 1984), xxi.

22. Alan Sinfield, *The Wilde Century: Effeminacy, Oscar Wilde, and the Queer Moment* (New York: Columbia University Press, 1994), 26.

23. Sylvester Graham, *A Lecture to Young Men on Chastity* (1834; reprint, New York: Arno, 1974), 43.

24. "Inside the Buffy-mentary." http://actionadventure.about.com/library/weekly/aa0216 03.htm.

Chapter Four

1. Bruno Bettelheim, *Symbolic Wounds: Puberty Rites and the Envious Male* (New York: Collier, 1962). Page numbers for quotes from this work are noted parenthetically in the text.

2. Eva Feder Kittay, "Mastering Envy: From Freud's Narcissistic Wounds to Bettelheim's Symbolic Wounds to a Vision of Healing," in *Gender and Envy*, ed. Nancy Burke (New York: Routledge, 1998), 178.

3. Robert D. Stevick, ed., *One Hundred Middle English Lyrics*, rev. ed. (Urbana: University of Illinois Press, 1994), 90.

4. Marjorie Garber, *Shakespeare's Ghost Writers: Literature as Uncanny Causality* (New York: Methuen, 1987), 101–03.

5. Robin Wood, *Hollywood from Vietnam to Reagan* (New York: Columbia University Press, 1986), 174.

6. Barbara Creed, *The Monstrous-Feminine: Film, Feminism, Psychoanalysis* (New York: Routledge, 1993), 54.

7. Suzanne Pharr, "Homophobia as a Weapon of Sexism," in *Race, Class, and Gender in the United States*, ed. Paula S. Rothenberg, 5th ed. (New York: Worth, 2001), 146.

8. Sigmund Freud, "Medusa's Head," *Writings on Art and Literature*, ed. James Strachey (Stanford: Meridian, 1997), 264–5.

9. C. G. Jung, *Aspects of the Feminine*, trans. R.F.C. Hull (Princeton: Princeton University Press, 1982), 110.

10. Kittay, "Mastering Envy," 186.

11. Wood, *Hollywood*, 48.

12. Andrew Sullivan, *Virtually Normal: An Argument About Homosexuality* (New York: Knopf, 1995), 20–21.

Chapter Five

1. James Snead, *White Screens, Black Images: Hollywood from the Dark Side* (New York: Routledge, 1994), 139–47.

2. The issue of racism in *Trek* has occupied many scholars; it is the focus of Daniel Bernardi in *Star Trek and History*, in which he argues that *Trek* mounts an ideal of whiteness that has broad political and cultural implications — that the

Trekkian vision is one in which non-white races conform to a white ideal. Primarily Bernardi examines *TNG*, which he treats as neo-conservative in ideological character. Leah R. Vande Berg, along similar lines, writes that "*TNG* would have viewers believe that in the twenty-fourth-century Federation world there is no 'racism' or 'race consciousness.' However, as a closer analysis of the series's episodes indicates, racial tensions, differences, and issues have not disappeared; they have merely been transformed into species differences. In *TNG*, species has become a metaphor for race" (Leah R. Vande Berg, "Worf as Metonymic Signifier of Racial, Cultural, and National Differences," in *Enterprise Zones: Critical Positions on* Star Trek, ed. Taylor Harrison et al. [Boulder, CO: Westview, 1996], 55). In contrast to this view and to Bernardi's, Michele Barrett and her son Duncan Barrett argue that "to conflate *Star Trek*'s undoubted preference for human beings over non-humans with racism is wrong." Arguing that Bernardi's views are often "illogical," they make the case that underlying these disputes over the series' racism is "a thoroughgoing refusal to credit the fact that people are actually interested in how to think about 'human nature.' ... The problem is that the theoretical anti-humanism underscoring these critical positions is simply not shared by either the makers or the audiences of *Star Trek*: they are fascinated by human nature and they incline towards 'humanist' values" (Michele Barrett and Duncan Barrett, Star Trek*: The Human Frontier* [New York: Routledge, 2001], 90–91). As I will suggest in this chapter, the problem with *Star Trek* is that it is both racist and anti-racist at once; the challenge for the critic is to decide on which tendency prevails in the *Star Trek* mega-text.

3. Richard Dyer, *White* (New York: Routledge, 1997), 89.

4. For a discussion of the black male intellectual's challenge to Establishment whiteness, see W. D. Wright, *Black Intellectuals, Black Cognition, and a Black Aesthetic* (New York: Praeger, 1997).

5. Kobena Mercer, *Welcome to the Jungle* (New York: Routledge, 1994), 133.

6. See Frantz Fanon's famous *Black Skin, White Masks*, trans. Richard Philcox (New York: Grove, 1967).

7. The figure of the black woman is an unlikely choice as the conduit for the restoration of white masculine order, but it is a trope that runs throughout several *Trek* series. In *The Animated Series* (*TAS*), a children's program that aired from 1973 to 1974, Uhura has a slightly expanded role. Her role on Original *Trek* infamously consisted mainly of announcing, "Hailing frequencies open, Captain," although the warmth, beauty, sensitivity, and intelligence of Nichelle Nichols's characterization made Uhura deeply beloved by legions of *Trek* fans (myself more than included). In Uhura's greatest showcase on *TAS*, "The Lorelai Signal," she and Nurse Chapel rescue Kirk, McCoy, Spock, and others from the clutches of mournful, predatory women who lure men down to their planet so they can deplete them of their masculine lifeforce, which these siren-women need to survive. Thrillingly, Uhura takes command of the *Enterprise*. Nurse Chapel—ever a bit of a pill—exclaims, "What are you doing?" Uhura triumphantly answers, "Taking command of this ship! No one is to beam down unless it's on my order!" Uhura takes an armed Away team of female crew members to the planet (where the grotesquely super-aged, depleted, dying Kirk, Spock, and McCoy gasp their last), since the females (in typical Trekkian heterosexism) are immune to siren-song power. Uhura and the female Away team stun the siren-women, taking charge of the situation and rescuing the men. This is Uhura's—and Uhura fans'—big moment, the moment in which she blazingly comes alive as a heroic member of the Trekverse. Sadly, Uhura's big moment comes at the expense of feminism. She can triumph only by vanquishing other women, and her near-annihilation of the siren-women enables the restoration of the male order of Kirk and Co.

The episode ends, along these lines, ambiguously. It turns out that *Enterprise* can help the siren-women. Elatedly, Uhura tells the siren-chief that now she and her race of sad sirens can leave this planet, meet men and have children. "Children?" says the chief-siren, overcome with joy at this heretofore unthinkable possibility. Uhura and the sirens have an opportunity to bond; the sirens are not simply vanquished and discarded. Yet the bond between Uhura and the pointedly white-raced sirens emerges through an affirmation of conventional family values, of anatomy-is-destiny, of the proper restoration of domestic and marital roles to this race of women whose sexual desires, untethered to marriage and family, and power over men make them dangerous enemies of civilization. Again, Uhura is the conduit for the restoration of white male rule.

The problem of Pop: I still love this episode and the adrenalizing kick it gives me to see Uhura in a position of heroic power, after having been so long relegated to the sidelines. (There was a marvelous Uhura story in one of the volumes of *Strange New Worlds*, a series of *Trek* stories written by *Trek* fans, in which two women writers imagine Uhura in Shakespeare's England as the inspiration for the famous sonnet "My mistress' eyes are nothing like the sun.") So, though I recognize the expensive maneuver of making her a hero in "The Lorelai Signal"— the misogyny bartered for the heroism — I still revel in her heroism granted.

8. A very similar phenomenon occurs in the sixth-season *Voyager* episode "Ashes to Ashes," when Ensign Lindsay Ballard, having been reanimated and given a new identity by a species that transforms corpses into new, living members of their own race, returns from the seeming dead. When explaining a solution to a problem to Chief Engineer B'Elanna Torres, Lindsay breaks out into the distinct metaphors of her newly acquired race's language; as she linguistically code-switches, the other personnel in Engineering give her cold, mystified, critical stares. Very often, *Trek* suggests that its futuristic humans haven't put aside as many of their prejudices and limitations as they believe.

9. Rhonda V. Wilcox, in her essay "Dating Data," argues that Lal should be seen as an allegory of the mulatto figure. "Though Lal displays many characteristics of the mulatto, she is made less threatening not only by being made female but also by being born asexually." See Rhonda V. Wilcox, "Dating Data: Miscegenation in *Star Trek: The Next Generation*," in *Enterprise Zones: Critical Positions on Star Trek*, ed. Taylor Harrison et al. (Boulder, CO: Westview, 1996), 81.

Chapter Six

1. J. Hoberman, *The Dream Life: Movies, Media, and the Mythology of the Sixties* (New York: New Press, 2003), 265.

2. Robin Wood, *Hollywood from Vietnam to Reagan* (New York: Columbia University Press, 1986), 62.

3. *Ibid.*, a general point in the work.

4. These lines are quoted from a fine essay by Robert Asa, which continues: "Not yet embracing science fiction films as an art form or as a medium for social comment, American society yawned at *Star Trek*. In retrospect, *Star Trek*'s creator and contributors appear in many respects to have been unsung heroes, bravely saying through poetry what few others were saying in prose.... [But for *Star Trek*'s fans,] *Star Trek* was real. *Star Trek* meant something. *Star Trek* spoke the truth. Kirk, Spock, and McCoy were ... flesh and blood people who could serve as role models.... [The show's intergalactic conflicts were] fights for human rights, human freedom, and human destiny" (Robert Asa, "Original *Star Trek* and the Death of God: A Case Study of 'Who Mourns for Adonais?'" in Star Trek *and Sacred Ground: Explorations of* Star Trek, *Religion, and American Culture,* ed. Jennifer E. Porter and Darcee L. McLaren [Albany: State University of New York Press, 1999], 34).

5. See Daniel Bernardi, Star Trek *and History: Race-Ing Toward a White Future* (Piscataway, NJ: Rutgers University Press, 1998), especially Chapter Four.

6. Even more decisively than Bernardi, Kent A. Ono finds in *Trek* the master narratives of colonialism and empire. He argues that *TNG* "produces a unique space wherein viewers may imagine the continuous recreation of empire through the simultaneous articulation and elimination of difference" (Kent A. Ono, "Domesticating Terrorism: A Neocolonial Economy of *Différance*," in *Enterprise Zones: Critical Positions on* Star Trek, ed. Taylor Harrison et al. [Boulder, CO: Westview, 1996], 157). For an opposing perspective to both Bernardi and Ono, see Michele Barrett and Duncan Barrett, Star Trek: *The Human Frontier* (New York: Routledge, 2001), who argue that all the *Trek* series and films productively and daringly explore the nature and mysteries of "the human."

7. James Mann, *Rise of the Vulcans: The History of Bush's War Cabinet* (New York: Penguin, 2004), 90–91.

8. Richard Chase, *Herman Melville* (New York: Macmillan, 1949), vii.

9. Thomas Schaub, *American Fiction in the Cold War* (Madison: University of Wisconsin Press, 1991), 7–11.

10. D. H. Lawrence, *Studies in Classic American Literature* (1923; reprint, New York: Doubleday, 1951), 63.

11. To be fair, Manny Coto, who oversaw the show's final season, seemed determined to right some of the series' multivalent wrongs, and he gave Hoshi some of her best moments, albeit in the penultimate episode of the series, "Terra Prime," in which Hoshi unflinchingly takes command. Sadly, the other great Hoshi moments occur for a different character: in "In a Mirror Darkly, Part II," evil Mirror-Hoshi takes command in the end. This two-parter's use of Hoshi unfortunately conforms to dragon-lady Asian-woman stereotypes, thereby undermining the effort to enlarge Hoshi's role.

12. See Barbara Creed, *The Monstrous-Feminine: Film, Feminism, Psychoanalysis* (New York: Routledge, 1993).

13. Cited in Jonathan Culler's *On Deconstruction* (1982; reprint, Ithaca, NY: Cornell University Press, 1994), 51–52. See also Judith Fetterley's *The Resisting Reader: A Feminist Approach to American Fiction* (Bloomington: Indiana University Press, 1978).

14. "I have mixed feelings about all that. It was very difficult for me to justify. Why would T'Pol want to do this to herself? Why are emotions so important to her? I felt that she lost her-

self there. She lost her culture, she lost her person — she lost T'Pol. She even lost her reputation!" "T'Pol to Evolve in Season Four, Says Actress," http://scifipulse.net/Trek%20Archive/September2004/JoleneBlalock.html.

15. See Bernardi, Star Trek and History, 140–42.

16. For a visual comparison, see pictures of Surak then and now at StarTrek.com, "Surak," StarTrek.com, 2006, http://www.startrek.com/startrek/view/library/character/bio/1115257.html.

17. The crew is also besieged by siren-like women in "The Lorelai Signal," an episode of *The Animated Series* (*TAS*), which aired in the early 1970s on Saturday mornings for a children's audience. Written by Margaret Armen, the episode sees the male principals — Kirk, Spock, McCoy — all entrapped by siren-women, who deplete them of energy. Uhura and Nurse Chapel beam down to the siren-planet and save the crew, an especially thrilling resolution given the paucity of opportunities for the female characters and the women who played them on Original *Trek*. While one can easily grimace at seeing women sicced on other women — underrepresented Uhura and Chapel come into their own by attacking predatory women — the radicalism of their swing into action provides partial compensation. See Chapter Five, note 7, for more on "The Lorelai Signal."

18. These creatures from Greek mythology draw sailors irresistibly to their beautiful singing, but ships that approach their island are doomed to destruction on the rocks (Virgil V, 846; Ovid XIV, 88). Heroes of Greek epics avoid their charm by extraordinary means. For example, when the Argonauts pass their island, Orpheus saves the ship by singing so loudly that he drowns out the Siren song. Odysseus saves his men by having them plug their ears with wax; he does not plug his own ears, however, but has himself tied to the mast so that he can hear their beautiful voices without endangering himself or his ship. (Micha F. Lindemans, "'Sirens,'" Encyclopedia Mythica 2006, http://www.pantheon.org/articles/s/sirens.html (accessed 17 February 2009). Special thanks to G'inny for her observation of the bird-like movements of dancing Orion slave women.

Chapter Seven

1. Kwame Anthony Appiah, "Race," in *Critical Terms for Literary Study*, ed. Frank Lentricchia and Thomas McLaughlin (Chicago: Chicago University Press, 1995), 276.

2. Joseph D. Adriano, *Immortal Monster: The Mythological Evolution of the Fantastic Beast in Modern Fiction and Film* (Westport, CT: Greenwood, 1999), 3.

3. Toni Morrison, *Playing in the Dark: Whiteness and the Literary Imagination* (New York: Vintage, 1992), 52.

4. See Harold Bloom, *The Anxiety of Influence: A Theory of Poetry* (1973; reprint, New York: Oxford University Press, 1997), passim.

5. This is D. H. Lawrence's famous description of the now-mythic character of Natty Bumppo in James Fenimore Cooper's Leatherstocking Tales, the series of novels that features *The Last of the Mohicans* (D. H. Lawrence, *Studies in Classic American Literature* [1923; reprint, New York: Doubleday, 1951], 63).

6. Lee Edelman, *No Future: Queer Theory and the Death Drive* (Durham, NC: Duke University Press, 2005). This is the thesis of Edelman's book generally.

7. Stephen Farber, "Violence and the Bitch Goddess," in *Film Noir Reader 2*, ed. Alain Silver and James Ursini (New York: Limelight, 1999), 45–56.

8. Another example of this occurs in the 2005 film *Casanova*. Though a film about a famed seducer, *Casanova* exhibits more interest in depicting the title character (played by Heath Ledger) as the object of the gaze and the unwilling recipient of sexual pleasure, as evinced by Casanova's profound discomfort during fellatio (from a woman hiding beneath a table) that he is forced to experience. See my book *Manhood in Hollywood from Bush to Bush* (Austin: University of Texas Press, 2009) for a discussion of these trends in Hollywood masculinity of the past two decades. My thesis is that Hollywood masculinity of this period can be defined as a struggle between narcissistic and masochistic modes of manhood.

9. Ann Pellegrini, *Performance Anxieties: Staging Psychoanalysis, Staging Race* (New York: Routledge, 1997), 163.

10. Ibid. (emphasis original), 163.

11. Barbara Creed, *The Monstrous-Feminine: Film, Feminism, Psychoanalysis* (New York: Routledge, 1993).

12. Anne Cranny-Francis, "The Erotics of the (cy)Borg," in *Future Females, the Next Generation*, ed. Marleen S. Barr (New York: Rowman and Littlefield, 2000), 156.

13. Mark Dery, "Slashing the Borg: Resistance Is Fertile," 1996, http://www.markdery.com/articles.html (accessed 12 February, 2009).

14. For elaborations on slash fiction, see especially Constance Penley's *NASA/Trek: Popular Science and Sex in America* (New York: Verso, 1997) and Henry Jenkins's *Textual Poachers: Television Fans and Participatory Culture* (New York: Routledge, 1992).

15. Sigmund Freud, *Totem and Taboo*, trans. and ed. James Strachey (1913; reprint, New York: Norton, 1989).

16. Brett Farmer, *Spectacular Passions: Cinema, Fantasy, Gay Male Spectatorships* (Durham, NC: Duke University Press, 2000), 197.
17. There have been numerous discussions in the past decade of the previously overlooked valences between queerness and race. See for example Ian Barnard's *Queer Race: Cultural Interventions in the Racial Politics of Queer Theory* (New York: Peter Lang, 2004); Jose Esteban Munoz's *Disidentifications: Queers of Color and the Performance of Politics* (Minneapolis: University of Minnesota Press, 1999); and Siobhan Somerville's *Queering the Color Line: Race and the Invention of Homosexuality in American Culture* (Durham, NC: Duke University Press, 2000).
18. T. L. Mancour, *Star Trek: The Next Generation: Spartacus* (New York: Simon and Schuster, 1992), 221; 231.
19. Robin A. Roberts, "Science, Race, and Gender in *Star Trek: Voyager*," in *Fantasy Girls: Gender in the New Universe of Science Fiction and Fantasy Television*, ed. Elyce Rae Helford (Lanham, MD: Rowman and Littlefield, 2000), 207.
20. See Wikia Entertainment, "Hawk (Lieutenant)," Memory Alpha, the *Star Trek* Wiki, http://memory-alpha.org/en/wiki/Hawk_(Lieutenant) (30 December 2008).
21. Kobena Mercer, *Welcome to the Jungle* (New York: Routledge, 1994), 133.

Chapter Eight

1. Georg Lukács, *The Theory of the Novel*, trans. Anna Bostock (1920; reprint, Cambridge, MA: MIT Press, 1996).
2. This is not meant to be taken as an endorsement of the Lukács view or as an attempt to perpetuate the cultural uses of the classical past, most of which have been in service to the myth of Western supremacy. Nevertheless, the importance of classical antiquity to Western concepts of self, art, and culture cannot be denied.
3. Carolyn G. Heilbrun, *Writing a Woman's Life* (1986; reprint, New York: Ballantine, 1989), passim.
4. Sigmund Freud, "Some Psychological Consequences of Anatomical Distinction between the Sexes," in Sigmund Freud, *Sexuality and the Psychology of Love*, ed. Philip Rieff (1922; reprint, New York: Macmillan, 1963), 189–91.
5. Slavoj Žižek, parsing Lacan, describes the "Father-of-Enjoyment" as an "obscene and revengeful figure ... split between cruel revenge and crazy laughter" (Slavoj Žižek, *Looking Awry: An Introduction to Jacques Lacan through Popular Culture* [Cambridge, MA: MIT Press, 1991], 23.

6. In making a case for reading reparatively, I am following the lead of Eve Kosofsky Sedgwick's most recent work. Sedgwick, reworking Melanie Klein, argues for reparative criticism, which holds the promise of finding value in politically troublesome and irksome work — which Freud's certainly is for many.
7. Robert B. Ray, *A Certain Tendency of the Hollywood Cinema, 1930–1980* (Princeton, NJ: Princeton University Press, 1985).
8. Melissa M. M. Hidalgo, "'Going Native on Wonder Woman's Island': The Exoticization of Lesbian Sexuality," in *Sex and the City Televising Queer Women: A Reader*, ed. Rebecca Beirne (New York: Palgrave Macmillan, 2007), 132.
9. Sigmund Freud, *Leonardo da Vinci and a Memory of His Childhood*, trans. Alan Tyson (1910; reprint, New York: Norton, 1989), 47.
10. Ibid., 40–41.
11. Judith Halberstam, *Female Masculinity* (Durham, NC: Duke University Press, 1998).
12. Michelle Erica Green, "'Dark Frontier' Plot Summary," Dark Frontier, http://www.littlereview.com/getcritical/voyreviews/darkfron.htm (accessed 23 December 2008).
13. *Ibid*.
14. We have a word for male sexuality that is separate and distant from biological sexuality — "phallus," as opposed to "penis." This yields the useful adjective "phallic." Yet no such word exists in current usage for female sexuality, and I therefore propose the adjective "yonic," taken from "yoni," which the *Oxford English Dictionary* defines as " figure or symbol of the female organ of generation as an object of veneration among the Hindus and others."
15. Judith Butler, *Bodies That Matter: On the Discursive Limits of "Sex"* (New York: Routledge, 1993), 91.

Chapter Nine

1. *Nemesis* was the tenth *Star Trek* film. As it came on the heels of the financially disappointing *Star Trek: Insurrection* (1998) and was written by Joshua Logan, screenwriter of the eminently successful *Gladiator* (2000), there were exceedingly high hopes for and expectations of *Nemesis*. The film went on to make the least amount of money of any *Trek* film and was roundly drubbed by fans and critics. The failure of *Nemesis* was a big disappointment in myriad ways. *Nemesis* was perhaps the only *Trek* film since the very first to be a truly philosophical meditation on the nature of human identity. And it's the only *Star Trek* film to be a meditation on sexuality, race, and gender that eschews

phobia and promotes difference. No wonder this film was a flop.

2. My book *Manhood in Hollywood from Bush to Bush* (Austin: University of Texas Press, 2009) examines the rise of queer visibility in Hollywood from 1989 to the present and its impact on the representation of masculinity in both queer and straight contexts.

3. See K. J. Dover, *Greek Homosexuality* (New York: Vintage, 1978), 70. The sexual practice of intercrural intercourse — whereby the erastes, the older man, slid his penis between the thighs of the eromenos, the young male object of desire, in contact with his scrotum and perineum — was strictly limited in Ancient Greece to pederastic relationships, which were the legally and socially sanctioned form of homosexual sex in Hellenic culture.

4. Sigmund Freud, "Certain Neurotic Mechanisms in Jealousy, Paranoia and Homosexuality," in *Sexuality and the Psychology of Love* (New York: Macmillan, 1963), 160.

5. See Jacques Lacan, *The Four Fundamental Concepts of Psycho-Analysis*, trans. Alan Sheridan (New York: Norton, 1978). Lacan is quoted in Mark Pizzato's chapter, "Jeffrey Dahmer and Media Cannibalism: The Lure and Failure of Sacrifice," in *Mythologies of Violence in Postmodern Media*, ed. Christopher Sharrett (Detroit: Wayne State University Press, 1999), 95.

6. Here is Butler's language in fuller detail: "Drag is not the putting on of a gender that belongs properly to some other group, i.e. an act of expropriation or *ap*propriation that assumes that gender is the rightful property of sex, that 'masculine' belongs to 'male and 'feminine' belongs to 'female.' There is no 'proper' gender, a gender proper to one sex rather than another, which is in some sense that sex's cultural property. Where that notion of the 'proper' operates, it is always and only *improperly* installed as the effect of a compulsory system. Drag ... implies that all gendering is a kind of impersonation and approximation. If this is true, it seems, there is no original or primary gender that drag imitates, but *gender is a kind of imitation for which there is no original*" (emphasis original; Judith Butler, "Imitation and Gender Insubordination," in *Inside/Out: Lesbian Theories, Gay Theories*, edited by Diana Fuss [New York: Routledge, 1991], 20–21).

7. Freud's 1914 essay "On Narcissism" is collected in Sigmund Freud, *General Psychological Theory*, 56–83.

8. *Ibid.*, 313.

9. Leo Bersani, *The Freudian Body* (New York: Columbia University Press, 1986), 22.

10. Fanboy culture has many things to recommend it, but reliable critical perspectives are not among them. The loathing towards this film expressed in online *Trek* discussion groups is indicative of the increasing intolerance of fan culture.

11. What reaffirms the Exaltation speech as God's cruelly knowing taunting of Satan is the manner with which he and the Son confer over the brewing rebellion:
And smiling to his only Son thus said,

"Son, thou in whom my glory I behold,
In full resplendence....
Let us advise, and to this hazard draw
With speech what force is left...."
The Son, "Light'ning Divine," accurately
   responds to God's chortling demeanor:
"Mighty Father, thou thy foes
Justly hast in derision, and secure
Laugh'st at their vain designs..." [V 735 ff].

I've a hard time believing that Milton himself did not find this an astonishingly frightening scene. God's prized creations, the angels, display for the first time a propensity for rebellion and evil; the once-seraphic Satan has betrayed his Maker; the Son must wage war: and yet God smiles; and yet God laughs, an icily smug reaction to the surrounding chaos. Satan, to his discredit, has taken God's bait, and unfolded Hell's gates. But where is God's grief, God's sense of pathos? If God can laugh, he can cry.

12. The dandy figure did not come to be associated with homosexuality until the later, Oscar Wilde figure. The "diabolical" dandy was just as much a problematic figure because of his rapacious lust. Though generally conceived as heterosexual, the dandy's "cross-sex philandering" exposes him as effeminate, unmanly in his lack of normative self-control and properly marital sexuality, even if women are the object of his rapacious sexual aims. See Alan Sinfield, *The Wilde Century: Effeminacy, Oscar Wilde, and the Queer Moment* (New York: Columbia University Press, 1994), 27; 70–71.

13. Robert Graves, *The Greek Myths: I* (New York: Penguin, 1985), 287.

14. See Hélène Cixous, "Castration or Decapitation?," in *Contemporary Literary Criticism*, ed. Robert Con Davis and Robert Scheifler (1976; reprint, New York: Longman, 1989), 488–90.

15. Kaja Silverman, *The Acoustic Mirror: The Female Voice in Psychoanalysis and the Cinema* (Bloomington: Indiana University Press, 1988), 31. Though I'm not entirely in agreement with Silverman's views of voices and gendered identity in original Hollywood cinema, a more contested battleground than she allows, I take her lucid, eloquent points very seriously.

16. Butler, "Imitation," 21.

17. Judith Butler, *Bodies That Matter: On the Discursive Limits of "Sex"* (New York: Routledge, 1993), xi.

18. *Ibid.*, 2.
19. *Ibid.*, 5.
20. *Ibid.*, 9.
21. In Guy Hocquenghem's revolutionary 1972 study *Homosexual Desire* (Durham, NC: Duke University Press, 1993), he discusses homosexual desire as "an arbitrarily frozen frame in an unbroken and polyvocal flux" (50). Hocquenghem's refuses to distinguish homosexual from any other form of desire — which is to say, desire has multiple forms, and cannot be subdivided into homosexuality or heterosexuality, i.e., imitative and prior forms. Hocquenghem writes, "Homosexuality exists and does not exist, at one and the same time: indeed, its very mode of existence questions again and again the certainty of existence" (53).
22. Dollimore reclaims Freudian perversity as a vital social and creative energy. The perverse dynamic, Dollimore says, "signifies that fearful interconnectedness whereby the antithetical inheres within, and is partly produced by, what it opposes." In further explicating his concept of the perverse dynamic, Dollimore finds that "within metaphysical constructions of the Other what is typically occluded is the significance of the proximate — i.e., that which is (1) adjacent ... or (2) that which is approaching (again either temporally or spatially), hence the verb 'to approach or draw neere,' (1623, OED), and thus (3) the opposite of remote or ultimate" (Jonathan Dollimore, *Sexual Dissidence* [New York: Oxford University Press, 1991], 33).
23. Paul Morrison, *The Explanation for Everything: Essays on Sexual Subjectivity* (New York: New York University Press, 2001), 54. In the context of Morrison's argument here, he discusses the media representation of Rock Hudson after the disclosure of Hudson's full-blown AIDS, constructed by the media as the "truth" of Hudson's life and star identity.
24. In the final episodes of *Buffy the Vampire Slayer*'s sixth season, when good witch Willow transforms into a hell-fired fury avenging the death of her beloved girlfriend, Tara, Willow sports similar dark veins and mood clothing. The queer figure wears her queerness on flesh and garment.
25. Butler, *Bodies*, 163.

26. Bersani brilliantly argues that "masochistic jouissance" is a "self-shattering" that "disrupts the ego's coherence and dissolves it boundaries," and that this "self-shattering is intrinsic to the homo-ness in homosexuality. Homo-ness is an anti-identitarian identity." (101). This point is crucial not only to Bersani's reconceptualization of masochism as a strategy for making "the subject unfindable as an object of discipline" but also to his framing of psychoanalysis as, *pace* Foucauldian orthodoxy, potentially challenging and radical in its proposition that we imagine "*a nonsuicidal disappearance of the subject*— or, in other terms, to dissociate masochism from the death drive." See Bersani, *Homos* (Cambridge, MA: Harvard University Press, 1995), 99–101. If Shinzon is a masochist, does his self-impalement signify the fulfillment of his death-drive? Or is his death not the result of the death-drive but, instead, the self-shattering Bersani posits as masochistic jouissance? I would argue that *Nemesis* confuses the question — it makes the masochistic death-drive, in its status as powerful revolt against the masculinist Symbolic, and in Shinzon's case a feverishly pleasurable revolt, itself the source of self-shattering jouissance. Lee Edelman takes such a view much further in his *No Future*, in which he argues that queers should embrace their social function as the embodiment of the death-drive, in perpetual enmity against the Symbolic order. This is an arresting argument, to be sure, but there is something ultimately facile about its nihilism, in my view. I would not argue that the Shinzon-Edelman approach is the only way to challenge the Symbolic order, despite my appreciation for their respective flamboyances.
27. Butler, *Bodies*, 166.
28. See Michael Warner, "Homo-Narcissism; or, Heterosexuality," in *Engendering Men*, ed. Joseph A. Boone and Michael Cadden (New York: Routledge, 1990), 190–207.

Afterword

1. Manohla Dargis, "A Franchise Goes Boldly Backward," *The New York Times*, May 8, 2009.

BIBLIOGRAPHY

Adriano, Joseph D. *Immortal Monster: The Mythological Evolution of the Fantastic Beast in Modern Fiction and Film.* Westport, CT: Greenwood, 1999.

Appiah, Kwame Anthony. "Race." In *Critical Terms for Literary Study,* edited by Frank Lentricchia and Thomas McLaughlin, 274–87. Chicago: Chicago University Press, 1995.

Asa, Robert. "Classic *Star Trek* and the Death of God: A Case Study of 'Who Mourns for Adonais?'" In Star Trek *and Sacred Ground: Explorations of* Star Trek, *Religion, and American Culture,* edited by Jennifer E. Porter and Darcee L. McLaren, 33–60. Albany: State University of New York Press, 1999.

Barnard, Ian. *Queer Race: Cultural Interventions in the Racial Politics of Queer Theory.* New York: Peter Lang, 2004.

Barrett, Michele, and Duncan Barrett. Star Trek: *The Human Frontier.* New York: Routledge, 2001.

Benjamin, Walter. *Illuminations: Essays and Reflections.* New York: Schocken, 1969.

Bernardi, Daniel J. Star Trek *and History: Race-Ing Toward a White Future.* Piscataway, NJ: Rutgers University Press, 1998.

Bersani, Leo. *The Freudian Body.* New York: Columbia University Press, 1986.

———. *Homos.* Cambridge, MA: Harvard University Press, 1995.

———. "Representation and Its Discontents." In *Allegory and Representation,* edited by Stephen Greenblatt, 145–163. Baltimore: Johns Hopkins University Press, 1981.

Bettelheim, Bruno. *Symbolic Wounds: Puberty Rites and the Envious Male.* New York: Collier, 1962.

Billson, Anne. Buffy the Vampire Slayer: *A Critical Reading of the Series.* London: BFI, 2005.

Bloom, Harold. *The Anxiety of Influence: A Theory of Poetry.* 1973. Reprint, New York: Oxford University Press, 1997.

Bordwell, David, Janet Staiger, and Kristin Thompson. *The Classical Hollywood Cinema: Film Style and Mode of Production to 1960.* New York: Columbia University Press, 1985.

Bressler, Charles E. *Literary Criticism: An Introduction to Theory and Practice.* Upper Saddle River, NJ: Pearson Prentice Hall, 2007.

Butler, Judith. *Bodies That Matter: On the Discursive Limits of "Sex."* New York: Routledge, 1993.

———. "Imitation and Gender Insubordination." In *Inside/Out: Lesbian Theories, Gay Theories,* edited by Diana Fuss, 13–31. New York: Routledge, 1991.

Byatt, A. S. *Passions of the Mind.* New York: Vintage, 1991.

Casey, Bernadette, Neil Casey, Ben Calvert, Liam French, and Justin Lewis, eds. *Television Studies: The Key Concepts.* New York: Routledge, 2002.

Chapman, James. "*The Avengers*: Television and Popular Culture in the 'High Sixties.'" In *Windows on the Sixties: Exploring Key Texts of Media and Culture,* edited by Anthony Aldgate, James Chapman, and Arthur Marwick, 37–69. London: I.B. Tauris, 2000.

Chase, Richard. *Herman Melville.* New York: Macmillan, 1949.

Cixous, Hélène. "Castration or Decapitation?" In *Contemporary Literary Criticism,* edited by Robert Con Davis and Robert Scheifler. 1976. Reprint, New York: Longman, 1989.

Cranny-Francis, Anne. "The Erotics of the (cy)Borg: Authority and Gender in the Sociocultural Imaginary." In *Future Females, the Next Generation*, edited by Marleen S. Barr, 145–165. New York: Rowman and Littlefield, 2000.

Creed, Barbara. *The Monstrous-Feminine: Film, Feminism, Psychoanalysis.* New York: Routledge, 1993.

Culler, Jonathan. *On Deconstruction.* 1982. Reprint, Ithaca, NY: Cornell University Press, 1994.

De Certeau, Michel. *The Practice of Everyday Life.* Translated by Steven Rendall. Berkeley: University of California Press, 1984.

Dollimore, Jonathan. *Sexual Dissidence.* New York: Oxford University Press, 1991.

Dover, K. J. *Greek Homosexuality.* New York: Vintage, 1978.

Drukman, Steven. "The Gay Gaze, or Why I Want My MTV." In *A Queer Romance: Lesbians, Gay Men and Popular Culture*, edited by Paul Burston and Colin Richardson, 89–105. New York: Routledge, 1995.

Dyer, Richard. *Heavenly Bodies: Film Stars and Society.* London: BFI, 1986.

———. *The Matter of Images: Essays on Representations.* New York: Routledge, 1993.

———. *White.* New York: Routledge, 1997.

Edelman, Lee. *No Future: Queer Theory and the Death Drive.* Durham, NC: Duke University Press, 2005.

Epsicokhan, Jamahl. "Requiem for Methuselah." *Jammer's Reviews*, 2009. http://www.st-hypertext.com/tos/tos-3rev.html#requiem.

Fanon, Frantz. *Black Skin, White Masks.* Translated by Richard Philcox. New York: Grove, 1967.

Farber, Stephen. "Violence and the Bitch Goddess." In *Film Noir Reader 2*, edited by Alain Silver and James Ursini, 45–56. New York: Limelight, 1999.

Farmer, Brett. *Spectacular Passions: Cinema, Fantasy, Gay Male Spectatorships.* Durham, NC: Duke University Press, 2000.

Fetterley, Judith. *The Resisting Reader: A Feminist Approach to American Fiction.* Bloomington: Indiana University Press, 1978.

Fiedler, Leslie. *Love and Death in the American Novel.* 1960. Reprint, New York: Dell, 1966.

Fletcher, Angus. *Allegory: The Theory of a Symbolic Mode.* Ithaca, NY: Cornell University Press, 1964.

Freud, Sigmund. "Certain Neurotic Mechanisms in Jealousy, Paranoia and Homosexuality." In Sigmund Freud, *Sexuality and the Psychology of Love*, edited by Philip Rieff. 1922. Reprint, New York: Macmillan, 1963.

———. "Fetishism." In Sigmund Freud, *Sexuality and the Psychology of Love*, edited by Philip Rieff. 1922. Reprint, New York: Macmillan, 1963.

———. *Leonardo da Vinci and a Memory of His Childhood.* Translated by Alan Tyson. 1910. Reprint, New York: Norton, 1989.

———. "Medusa's Head." In Sigmund Freud, *Writings on Art and Literature*, ed. James Strachey. Stanford, CA: Stanford University Press, 1997.

———. "On Narcissism: An Introduction." In Sigmund Freud, *General Psychological Theory*, ed. Philip Rieff, 56–83. New York: Touchstone, 1997.

———. *Sexuality and the Psychology of Love*, edited by Philip Rieff. 1922. Reprint, New York: Macmillan, 1963.

———. "Some Psychological Consequences of Anatomical Distinction Between the Sexes." In Sigmund Freud, *Sexuality and the Psychology of Love*, edited by Philip Rieff, 183–94. 1922. Reprint, New York: Macmillan, 1963.

———. *Three Essays on the Theory of Sexuality.* Edited by James Strachey. New York: Basic Books, 1962.

———. *Totem and Taboo.* Translated and edited by James Strachey. 1913. Reprint, New York: Norton, 1989.

Frye, Northrop. *Anatomy of Criticism.* Princeton, NJ: Princeton University Press, 2000.

Garber, Marjorie. *Shakespeare's Ghost Writers: Literature as Uncanny Causality.* New York: Methuen, 1987.

Girard, René. *Violence and the Sacred.* 1972. Reprint, Baltimore: Johns Hopkins University Press, 1977.

Graham, Sylvester. *A Lecture to Young Men on Chastity*. 1834. Reprint, New York: Arno, 1974.

Graves, Robert. *The Greek Myths: I*. New York: Penguin, 1985.

Greene, Michelle Erica. "Parturition." *Get Critical*. http://www.littlereview.com/getcritical/voyreviews/parturit.htm.

Greven, David. "The Fantastic Powers of the Other Sex: Male Mothers from Classical to Contemporary Culture." *The Journal of the Fantastic in the Arts* 14 (Fall 2003).

_____. *Manhood in Hollywood from Bush to Bush* (Austin: University of Texas Press, in press).

_____. *Men Beyond Desire: Manhood, Sex and Violation in American Literature* (New York: Palgrave Macmillan, 2005).

Halberstam, Judith. *Female Masculinity*. Durham, NC: Duke University Press, 1998.

_____. *Skin Shows: Gothic Horror and the Technology of Monsters*. 1995. Reprint, Durham, NC: Duke University Press, 2000.

Heilbrun, Carolyn G. *Writing a Woman's Life*. 1986. Reprint, New York: Ballantine, 1989.

Hidalgo, Melissa M. M. "'Going Native on Wonder Woman's Island': The Exoticization of Lesbian Sexuality in *Sex and the City*." In *Televising Queer Women: A Reader*, edited by Rebecca Beirne, 121–35. New York: Palgrave Macmillan, 2007.

Hoberman, J. *The Dream Life: Movies, Media, and the Mythology of the Sixties*. New York: New Press, 2003.

Hocquenghem, Guy. *Homosexual Desire*. Durham, NC: Duke University Press, 1993.

Ian, Marcia. *Remembering the Phallic Mother: Psychoanalysis, Modernism and the Fetish*. Ithaca, NY: Cornell University Press, 1996.

Jenkins, Henry. *Textual Poachers: Television Fans and Participatory Culture*. New York: Routledge, 1992.

Jung, C. G. *Aspects of the Feminine*. Translated by R.F.C. Hull. Princeton: Princeton University Press, 1982.

Kittay, Eva Feder. "Mastering Envy: From Freud's Narcissistic Wounds to Bettelheim's Symbolic Wounds to a Vision of Healing." In *Gender and Envy*, edited by Nancy Burke, 171–97. New York: Routledge, 1998..

Lacan, Jacques. *The Four Fundamental Concepts of Psycho-Analysis*. Translated by Alan Sheridan. New York: Norton, 1978.

Lawrence, D. H. *Studies in Classic American Literature*. 1923. Reprint, New York: Doubleday, 1951.

Lindemans, Micha F. "'Sirens.'" *Encyclopedia Mythica*, 2006. http://www.pantheon.org/articles/s/sirens.html.

Long, Thomas L. "Julian of Norwich's 'Christ as Mother' and Medieval Constructions of Gender." http://community.tncc.edu/faculty/longt/papers/Julian_Xt_as_Mother.html.

Lukács, Georg. *The Theory of the Novel*. Translated by Anna Bostock. 1920. Reprint, Cambridge, MA: MIT Press, 1996.

MacQueen, John. *Allegory*. London: Methuen, 1970.

Mancour, T. L. *Star Trek: The Next Generation: Spartacus*. New York: Simon and Schuster, 1992.

Mann, James. *Rise of the Vulcans: The History of Bush's War Cabinet*. New York: Penguin, 2004.

McGowan, Todd. *The Real Gaze: Film Theory After Lacan*. Albany, NY: State University of New York Press, 2008.

Mercer, Kobena. *Welcome to the Jungle*. New York: Routledge, 1994.

Miller, D.A. *The Novel and the Police*. Berkeley: University of California Pres, 1988.

Morrison, Paul. *The Explanation for Everything: Essays on Sexual Subjectivity*. New York: New York University Press, 2001.

Morrison, Toni. *Playing in the Dark: Whiteness and the Literary Imagination*. New York: Vintage, 1992.

Mulvey, Laura. "Afterthoughts on 'Visual Pleasure and Narrative Cinema' Inspired by King Vidor's *Duel in the Sun*." *Framework* 15/16/17 (1981): 12–15.

_____. *Visual and Other Pleasures* (Bloomington: Indiana University Press, 1989).

_____. "Visual Pleasure and Narrative Cinema." In *Feminist Film Theory: A Reader*, edited by Sue Thornham, 58–69. New York: New York University Press, 1999.

———. "Visual Pleasure and Narrative Cinema." *Screen* 16, no. 3 (1975): 6–18.

Munoz, Jose Esteban. *Disidentifications: Queers of Color and the Performance of Politics*. Minneapolis: University of Minnesota Press, 1999.

Ono, Kent A. "Domesticating Terrorism: A Neocolonial Economy of *Différance*." In *Enterprise Zones: Critical Positions on Star Trek*, edited by Taylor Harrison, Sarah Projansky, Kent A. Ono, and Elyce Rae Helford, 157–86. Boulder, CO: Westview, 1996.

Paglia, Camille. "Ask Camille: Harvard's Date-Rape Idiocy." Salon.com, March 17, 1999. http://www.salon.com/col/pagl/1999/03/nc_17pagl.html. Accessed August 10, 2009.

Pellegrini, Ann. *Performance Anxieties: Staging Psychoanalysis, Staging Race*. New York: Routledge, 1997.

Penley, Constance. *NASA/Trek: Popular Science and Sex in America*. New York: Verso, 1997.

Peretz, Eyal. *Becoming Visionary: Brian De Palma's Cinematic Education of the Senses*. Stanford, CA: Stanford University Press, 2008.

Pizzato, Mark. "Jeffrey Dahmer and Media Cannibalism: The Lure and Failure of Sacrifice." In *Mythologies of Violence in Postmodern Media*, edited by Christopher Sharrett. Detroit: Wayne State University Press, 1999.

Ray, Robert B. *A Certain Tendency of the Hollywood Cinema, 1930–1980*. Princeton, NJ: Princeton University Press, 1985.

Rich, Adrienne. "Compulsory Heterosexuality and Lesbian Existence." *Signs* 5, no. 4 (1980): 631–60.

Roberts, Robin. *Sexual Generations:* Star Trek: The Next Generation *and Gender*. Urbana: University of Illinois Press, 1999.

Roberts, Robin A. "Science, Race, and Gender in *Star Trek: Voyager*." In *Fantasy Girls: Gender in the New Universe of Science Fiction and Fantasy Television*, edited by Elyce Rae Helford, 203–23. Lanham, MD: Rowman and Littlefield, 2000.

Schaub, Thomas. *American Fiction in the Cold War*. Madison: University of Wisconsin Press, 1991.

Sedgwick, Eve Kosofsky. *Between Men: English Literature and Male Homosocial Desire*. New York: Columbia University Press, 1985.

———. *Epistemology of the Closet*. Berkeley: University of California Press, 1990.

Siegel, Stanley, and Ed Lowe. *Uncharted Lives: Understanding the Life Passages of Gay Men*. 1994. Reprint, New York: Plume, 1995.

Silverman, Kaja. *The Acoustic Mirror: The Female Voice in Psychoanalysis and the Cinema*. Bloomington: Indiana University Press, 1988.

———. *Male Subjectivity at the Margins*. New York: Routledge, 1992.

Sinfield, Alan. *The Wilde Century: Effeminacy, Oscar Wilde, and the Queer Moment*. New York: Columbia University Press, 1994.

Snead, James. *White Screens, Black Images: Hollywood from the Dark Side*. New York: Routledge, 1994.

Somerville, Siobhan. *Queering the Color Line: Race and the Invention of Homosexuality in American Culture*. Durham, NC: Duke University Press, 2000.

StarTrek.com. "Stigma." *Star Trek Enterprise*, 2007. http://www.startrek.com/startrek/view/series/ENT/episode/127400.html.

Stevick, Robert D., ed. *One Hundred Middle English Lyrics*. Rev. ed. Urbana: University of Illinois Press, 1994.

Studlar, Gaylyn. *In the Realm of Pleasure: Von Sternberg, Dietrich, and the Masochistic Aesthetic*. New York: Columbia University Press, 1993.

Sullivan, Andrew. *Virtually Normal: An Argument About Homosexuality*. New York: Knopf, 1995.

Tartaglia, Jerry. "*Ecce Homo*: On Making Personal Gay Cinema." In *Queer Looks: Perspectives on Lesbian and Gay Film and Video*, edited by Martha Gever, Pratibha Parmar, and John Greyson, 204–08. New York: Routledge, 1993.

Vande Berg, Leah R. "Worf as Metonymic Signifier of Racial, Cultural, and National Differences." In *Enterprise Zones: Critical Positions on* Star Trek, edited by Taylor Harrison, Sarah Projansky, Kent A. Ono, and Elyce Rae Helford, 51–68. Boulder, CO: Westview, 1996.

Warner, Michael. "Homo-Narcissism; or, Heterosexuality." In *Engendering Men*, edited by Joseph A. Boone and Michael Cadden, 190–207. New York: Routledge, 1990.

Waugh, Thomas. "The Third Body: Patterns in the Construction of the Subject in Gay Male Narrative Film." In *Queer Looks: Perspectives on Lesbian and Gay Film and Video*, edited by Martha Gever, Pratibha Parmar, and John Greyson, 141–61. New York: Routledge, 1993.

Wikia Entertainment. "Hawk (Lieutenant)." *Memory Alpha, the* Star Trek *Wiki*. http://memory-alpha.org/en/wiki/Hawk_(Lieutenant).

Wilcox, Rhonda V. "Dating Data: Miscegenation in *Star Trek: The Next Generation*." In *Enterprise Zones: Critical Positions on* Star Trek, edited by Taylor Harrison, Sarah Projansky, Kent A. Ono, and Elyce Rae Helford, 69–92. Boulder, CO: Westview, 1996.

Wood, Robin. *Hollywood from Vietnam to Reagan*. New York: Columbia University Press, 1986.

Wright, W. D. *Black Intellectuals, Black Cognition, and a Black Aesthetic*. New York: Praeger, 1997.

Žižek, Slavoj. *Looking Awry: An Introduction to Jacques Lacan through Popular Culture*. Cambridge, MA: MIT Press, 1991.

INDEX

Abrams, J. J. 203–9
"The Aenar" (*Enterprise* episode) 112
"Affliction" (*Enterprise* episode) 112
AIDS 45, 92, 150, 200
Ain't It Cool News 209
Aldrich, Robert 41
Alias 204–5
Alice 28
Alice Adams 167
alien, phallic woman 152–3
"All Our Yesterdays" (*Star Trek* episode) 24
allegory: defined 3–5; direct explication vs. 105; ironic vs. non-ironic audience 175; race 98; ruptured 164; gender and queer sexuality 11–15; *see also* heterosexuality; homosexuality; gaze; race
Alley, Kirstie 147
"Alliances" (*Voyager* episode) 170
Altman, Robert 28
American Adam and innocence 142
androgyny 113, 123
androids 113–117; human love 116
Angels in America 110
Appiah, Kwame Anthony 139
"Ashes to Ashes" (*Voyager* episode) 217n8
Asian stereotypes 100, 115, 123, 217n11
"Author, Author" (*Voyager* episode) 59–62

Baird, Stuart 197
Bakhtin, Mikhail 31
"Bartleby, the Scrivener" 30
"Basics, Part II" (*Voyager* episode) 55
Battlestar Galactica (new version) 118, 129–30
Benjamin, Walter 63
Berry, Halle 101
Bersani, Leo 22, 193–5
"The Best of Both Worlds" (*Star Trek: The Next Generation* episode) 157
Bettelheim, Bruno 74
Biggs-Dawson, Roxann 182
Bionic Woman 49
The Bionic Woman (70s version) 28
black femininity 109–10, 136–8

black male: intellectual 102–5; scientist 104, 108
black masculinity 97–117, 142; bodies 100, 103, 105, 106, 108; gaze 100; ghostly 108–9; technology 108
Blacula 102
"Blink of an Eye" (*Voyager* episode) 57
The Blithedale Romance 25
Bloom, Harold 28, 142–3
the Borg 110, 112; as queer race 157–60; race 184; sexual metaphor 163
Borg Queen 47, 152, 178; *see also* alien, phallic woman; masochism; pedophilia; phallic mother; "Dark Frontier"; *Star Trek: First Contact*
Braga, Brannon 105, 128–9, 155, 176
Buffy the Vampire Slayer 62–73, 130, 174
Bush, George W. 125
Butler, Judith 36, 185, 192, 199–202
Byatt, A.S. 2

"The Cage" (*Star Trek* episode) 32, 122, 204
La Cage Aux Folles 192
cannibalism 144
Captain Kathryn Janeway 123; fan criticism of 82; woman's film 166–7; transformations 167–171; mother 174–6; queer figure 176–8
"Caretaker" (*Voyager* episode) 92
Cather, Willa 201
"The Changeling" (*Star Trek* episode) 138
"Charlie X" (*Star Trek* episode) 9
Charlie's Angels 28
"Chimera" (*Deep Space Nine* episode) 139
Cixous, Hélène 198
classical antiquity 189
Clinton, Bill 123
Close, Glenn 32
"The Cloud Minders" (*Star Trek* episode) 24
"Cogenitor" (*Enterprise* episode) 43–6
"Cold Fire" (*Voyager* episode) 105
Cold War 98, 121
colonial subject 140

coming out scene 149
Coto, Manny 131
"Course: Oblivion" (*Voyager* episode) 36–9
Culea, Melinda 39

"Daedalus" (*Enterprise* episode) 104, 108
Daly, Tyne 28
Dargis, Manohla 206
"Dark Frontier, Parts I and II" (*Voyager* episode) 172–186
David Marcus as gay character 147–50
"Deadlock" (*Voyager* episode) 86, 170
Deadwood 119, 129–30
death drive 150–1
De Certeau, Michel 67
Deleuze, Gilles 20
Demeter-Persephone myth 172, 176
"Demon" (*Voyager* episode) 35–6
De Palma, Brian 28
Dery, Mark 158
desire: loss 10–11
"The Devil in the Dark" (*Star Trek* episode) 38
diabolical dandy 196
Diesel, Vin 101
"The Disease" (*Voyager* episode) 174
"Distant Origin" (*Voyager* episode) 89, 174
diva *see* gay males
"Divergence" (*Enterprise* episode) 112
Dollimore, Jonathan 200
Dorn, Michael 160, 161
"Drive" (*Voyager* episode) 83
"Drone" (*Voyager* episode) 87, 93, 111
Dyer, Richard 18

Earhart, Amelia 168
Eastwood, Clint 28
Echo 197–8
Edelman, Lee 37, 39, 47, 151
Edward Scissorhands 112
Eliot, George 2
Eliot, T.S. 78
"Elogium" (*Voyager* episode) 84
"The Empath" (*Star Trek* episode) 24
"Endgame" (*Voyager* episode) 54, 62, 93, 170, 172
The Enforcer 28
Enterprise 43–6, 110–111, 118–134, 205; *see also individual episodes*
"The Enterprise Incident" (*Star Trek* episode) 24
epic 166
Epsicokhan, Jamahl 25, 36
Eurydice 178
"The Expanse" (*Enterprise* episode) 125

"Fair Trade" (*Voyager* episode) 87
Family (ABC series) 149
family, ideology of 173–4; *see also* kinship
fanboy conservatism 209
Fanon, Frantz 107
Farmer, Brett 159
Fatal Attraction 32
"Father-of-Enjoyment" 173
"Favorite Son" (*Voyager* episode) 174
female guest star of TOS 12–15
feminism 123, 138, 196–7; queer 198; tragic 28
femme fatale 152
fetishism 19–20, 22, 49–51, 153–5, 213n21
Fiedler, Leslie 5, 208
Fight Club 207
"Flesh and Blood" (*Voyager* episode) 58–9
Fletcher, Angus 3
Foucault, Michel 72, 200
Frakes, Jonathan 40, 155, 161
Frankenstein's Monster 87, 106
Freud, Sigmund 7, 16, 22, 49–51, 85, 111, 147, 155, 159, 178, 181, 191
Fringe 49, 205
Frye, Northrop 1, 3
Fuller, Bryan 38
The Fury 28
"Fury" (*Voyager* episode) 90
"Fusion" (*Enterprise* episode) 45
"Future's End" (*Voyager* episode) 57

Garland, Judy 214n8
gay bears 79
gay cruising 107
gay male artist: gay narrative cinema 53; *Voyager* 65–70
gay male couples 35, 85, 90, 91, 106–7
gay men: as artist figures 49–51; relationship with the diva 49–53, 214n8
gaze 17–23, 145, 153; black male 100; female 197; queer 15
gender ambiguity 148, 161, 168–9, 181, 182
Genesis (biblical) 146, 152
"Genesis Device" 146, 150
genre and conservatism 95
ghostly masculinity 108–110
Girard, René 26, 65
Good Mother vs. Terrible Mother 89
Graves, Robert 197
Green, Michelle Erica 91, 182–3
Greenblatt, Stephen 22
Grey, Zane 4

hair as sexual metaphor 85–6
Halberstam, Judith 16, 17, 183
Halperin, David 39

Index

Hamlet 146
Hardy, Tom 189, 192
Harry Potter and the Sorcerer's Stone 81
"Haunting of Deck Twelve" (*Voyager* episode) 89
Hawthorne, Nathaniel 25, 27
Heilbrun, Carolyn 166
The Heiress 168
Heroes 204
heterosexuality 12; allegorical ritual 13; ambivalence 21; uncanny 16; in relation to queer sexuality 38–9
Hitchcock, Alfred 19, 181
Hoberman, J. 119
Hocquenghem, Guy 200
Hollywood, early 90s and queer sexuality 114; 1970s 119
holograms: emotions of 58–9; fan reaction to 55
"Homestead" (*Voyager* episode) 87
homosexuality: abjection 200; AIDS 200; denatured white body 112; father-son relationship 148–50; interracial 136–7, 144–6; male mother 92–6; narcissism 193; spectacle 160; violence 162
"The Host" (*Star Trek: The Next Generation* episode) 39
The House of Yes 85
hurt/comfort slash fiction 92

"I, Borg" (*Star Trek: The Next Generation* episode) 111, 112
The Iliad 166, 207
"Imperfection" (*Voyager* episode) 170
"In a Mirror, Darkly" (*Enterprise* episode) 108
"In Theory" (*Star Trek: The Next Generation* episode) 190
"Investigations" (*Voyager* episode) 87
"Is There In Truth No Beauty?" (*Star Trek* episode) 24–5

James, Henry 168
Jane Eyre 168
Janeway, Captain Kathryn *see* Captain Kathryn Janeway
Jenkins, Henry 5
Jesus Christ as male mother 77–8
Jewish-Arab conflicts 99, 131, 206
Julian of Norwich 78
Jung, Carl 89

Kelly, Grace 181
Khan Noonien Singh 26; race origins of 140
The Killing of Sister George 41
King Lear 146

kinship: nonhuman 114; non-biological 174, 179, 190
Kirk-Spock relationship 5–7, 28–30, 139, 144
Klingons: race 112
Krige, Alice 110, 152

Lacan, Jacques 22–3, 171, 192
The Last of the Mohicans 122
"Latent Image" (*Voyager* episode) 56
Lawrence, D.H. 122
Leaves of Grass 10
Leavitt, David 150
Leonardo da Vinci 181
lesbian sexuality 69–70, 170–1, 175, 176, 181–3, 185
"Let That Be Your Last Battlefield" (*Star Trek* episode) 4
Lieutenant Hawk as gay character 160, 162–3
Lieutenant Saavik and gender ambiguity 148
"Lifesigns" (*Voyager* episode) 57
Longtime Companion 92
"The Lorelai Signal" (*Star Trek: The Animated Series* episode) 216n7, 218n17
Lost 205
The Lost Language of Cranes 150
Lukács, Georg 166

male: inviolate 193; sexual objectification of 185
Male Medusa 78–9, 85
"The Man Trap" (*Star Trek* episode) 126
Mapplethorpe, Robert 107
marriage plot 166
masochism, male: 17, 20–21, 152–3, 201
maternal superego 173
McDonough, Neal 160
McGowan, Todd 23
"The Measure of a Man" (*Star Trek: The Next Generation* episode) 116
Medusa 85, 178, 197
"Meld" (*Voyager* episode) 91, 104, 106–7
Melville, Herman 30, 121, 141, 202
Memento 126
Menosky, Joe 176
Mercer, Kobena 160
Merrit Butrick 147
"Metamorphosis" (*Star Trek* episode) 33
Middlemarch 2–3
misogyny 124, 125, 129; spatialized woman 154
Moby-Dick 137, 141–6, 151, 202
monomyth 1
Monroe, Marilyn 18, 181
"The Monster" (Stephen Crane story) 106

Montalban, Ricardo 26, 140, 141, 145, 151
Moore, Ronald D. 155
Morrison, Paul 200
Morrison, Toni 142
mother-daughter relationship 171, 174
Muldaur, Diana 14, 15, 24
Mulgrew, Kate 176, 182
Mulvey, Laura 15, 17, 19, 51, 153
Mut 181
My Best Friend's Wedding 32

"Naked Now" (*Star Trek: The Next Generation* episode) 190
"The Naked Time" (*Star Trek* episode) 10
narcissism 104, 193, 196; The Father's 202
Nazism 140
neoconservatism 120
New Woman 168
Nichols, Nichelle 208
"Nightingale" (*Voyager* episode) 87
Nightmare on Elm Street 81–2
Niobe 38
nostalgia 119, 122, 133–4, 166
Novak, Kim 181
Now, Voyager 167, 180–2

The Odyssey 14, 33, 124, 152, 166
Oedipus complex 108, 147, 148–50, 155–57, 193–5, 201
"The Offspring" (*Star Trek: The Next Generation* episode) 113–116
"Once Upon a Time" (*Voyager* episode) 89–90
Orpheus 178
"The Outcast" (*Star Trek: The Next Generation* episode) 39–43, 44, 46
Ovid 78

Paglia, Camille 79
Paradise Lost 141, 152, 188, 202
Paris Is Burning 192
"Parturition" (*Voyager* episode) 84–6, 91–2
"Paul's Case" 201
pedophilia 153, 189
Pellegrini, Ann 154
Penley, Constance 5
Perlman, Ron 189
Petrarch 26
phallic mother 22, 93, 154–5, 178, 181
The Phantom Menace 81
The Phantom of the Opera 106
Pine, Chris 207, 208
Pitch Black 101
Plato 5
"Plato's Stepchildren" (*Star Trek* episode) 21
postmodernity 209

"Projections" (*Voyager* episode) 57
"Prophecy" (*Voyager* episode) 89

queer Freudian aesthetics 7
queer sexuality in relationship to heterosexuality 38–9
queer spectator 15
Quinto, Zachary 204

race: allegory 98, 139; femininity 114; gender 112; Hollywood representation 97, 100; homosexuality 106, 157–60; marking 100; mythification 99; omission 100; racialization 139–40; reading of classic literature 137; sexual desire 213n27; vision 100; visual art 115
radical otherness 37
"Random Thoughts" (*Voyager* episode) 88, 104, 107
rape, male 145
"Rappaccini's Daughter" 25
Ray, Robert B. 1–2
reading 137
"Real Life" (*Voyager* episode) 57
"Rejoined" (*Deep Space Nine* episode) 93
"Renaissance Man" (*Voyager* episode) 62
"Repentance" (*Voyager* episode) 87
"Repression" (*Voyager* episode) 104
reproductive rights of androids 113
"Requiem for Methuselah" (*Star Trek* episode) 25–30, 116
Return of the Jedi 79, 81
"Return to Tomorrow" (*Star Trek* episode) 14, 113
Revenge of the Sith 79–80
revisionism 119, 122
"Revulsion" (*Voyager* episode) 58
Rice, Anne 159
"Riddles" (*Voyager* episode) 88, 90, 91, 92
ritual 162
Roberts, Robin A. 39, 159
Roddenberry, Gene 32, 39, 120, 138
Rubin, Gayle 26
Ryan, Jeri 181, 182
Ryder, Winona 204

Sacher-Masoch, Leopold von 20
sadism 21
Saldana, Zoë 208
The Scarlet Letter 39
Scheerer, Robert 40
"Scientific Method" (*Voyager* episode) 174
"Scorpion" (*Voyager* episode) 170
Scott, Joan Wallach 11, 12
Section 31 123
Section 31: Rogue 160
Sedgwick, Eve Kosofsky 6, 26, 150

September 11 99, 118, 120
Seven of Nine and classical Hollywood femininity 181
The Seven Year Itch 18
Sex and the City 129–30
Shakespeare 24, 25, 143, 146
Shatner, William 31, 145, 208
Shylock (*Merchant of Venice*) 55
Silverman, Kaja 197
Singh, Khan Noonien *see* Khan Noonien Singh
sirens 157
Sirk, Douglas 69
skin 152
slash fiction 5–6, 158
Snow White 114
sodomy 196
The Sopranos 129–30
"Space Seed" (*Star Trek* episode) 26, 33, 139–40
Spartacus (*TNG* novel) 159
Star Trek (2009) 203–9
Star Trek II: The Wrath of Khan 6, 30, 139–51
Star Trek III: The Search for Spock 6
Star Trek V: The Final Frontier 6
Star Trek VI: The Undiscovered Country 45
Star Trek X: Nemesis 147, 157, 187–202, 209
Star Trek: Deep Space Nine 139; race 99; *see also individual episodes*
Star Trek: First Contact 47, 135–8, 151–64, 178, 207
Star Trek: The Motion Picture 118
Star Trek: The Original Series 9–33; race 98; political radicalism 120; *see also individual episodes*
Star Trek: Voyager 35–39, 48–73, 74–97, 123, 165–187; *see also individual episodes*
Stargate 118
"State of Flux" (*Voyager* episode) 86
"Stigma" (*Enterprise* episode) 43–6
Strauss, Leo 120
Studlar, Gaylyn 20
Sullivan, Andrew 95
Summertime 167
Suture 101

Taylor, Jeri 40
Teiresias 78
The Tempest 25
Terminator 142
Terminator 2: Judgment Day 104
Terminator: The Sarah Connor Chronicles 49
third sex 122
"Thirty Days" (*Voyager* episode) 170

"The 37's" (*Voyager* episode) 168–9
"The Tholian Web" (*Star Trek* episode) 108
3 Women 28
Threshold (Braga series) 129
transformation and femininity 166
transgendered identity 114, 148, 190
transporters 108
"Turnabout Intruder" (*Star Trek* episode) 24, 30–33
"Twilight" (*Enterprise* episode) 14

"The Ultimate Computer" (*Star Trek* episode) 102–5
the uncanny 16, 110–111
Uncle Tom's Cabin 106
"Unimatrix Zero, Part II" (*Voyager* episode) 172, 180

vampires 159
Vertigo 19, 181
violence 106, 145; as code for homosexuality 162
"Virtuoso" (*Voyager* episode) 58
La Vita Nuova 56
voyeurism 19–20
Vulcans, new prejudice against 122

"Wagon Train" 119
Wainwright, Rufus 214n8
"Warhead" (*Voyager* episode) 38
Warhol, Andy 147
Warner, Michael 202
westerns 119
"What Are Little Girls Made Of?" (*Star Trek* episode) 116
"Where No Man Has Gone Before" (*Star Trek* episode) 208
white males: body 108–10; heterosexuality 127; rage 144
whiteness, denatured 110, 111, 117, 158; skin 111
Whitman, Walt 10
Winfield, Paul 145
Witchblade 130
woman's film of classical Hollywood 166, 180–2
women: Freud's views 171–3; masculine 169
Woodard, Alfre 136, 138
Wordsworth, William 201
Worf 161

Xena, Warrior Princess 130
X-Men 101

"Year of Hell" (*Voyager* episode) 101, 125, 172, 205

www.ingramcontent.com/pod-product-compliance
Ingram Content Group UK Ltd.
Pitfield, Milton Keynes, MK11 3LW, UK
UKHW041945140426
5217IPUK00014B/661